MANAGING THE INTERNATIONAL BUSINESS ENVIRONMENT

Cases in Political and Country Risk

Charles R. Kennedy, Jr.
Babcock Graduate School of Management
Wake Forest University

Prentice-Hall International, Inc.

0-13-543992-2

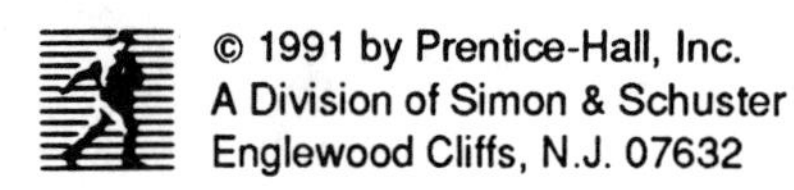

Printed in the United States of America

10 9 8 7 6 5 4 3 2 1

ISBN 0-13-543992-2

Prentice-Hall International (UK) Limited, *London*
Prentice-Hall of Australia Pty. Limited, *Sydney*
Prentice-Hall Canada Inc., *Toronto*
Prentice-Hall Hispanoamericana, S.A., *Mexico*
Prentice-Hall of India Private Limited, *New Delhi*
Prentice-Hall of Japan, Inc., *Tokyo*
Simon & Schuster Asia Pte. Ltd., *Singapore*
Editora Prentice-Hall do Brasil, Ltda., *Rio de Janeiro*
Prentice-Hall, Inc., *Englewood Cliffs, New Jersey*

Contents

Preface

Managing the firm's external environment is an important task for the international business manager. In particular, assessing and forecasting changes in the macroeconomic and sociopolitical environment are key when developing global strategies. Given their importance to international business, the assessment and management of political and country risk will be the focus of this book.

Such focus will address an important need, as perceived by international business managers. A survey of top corporate executives indicates that the macroeconomic and sociopolitical environment is considered a major factor in formulating global strategies.[1] Because of such perceptions, top managers in more and more multinational companies have formalized the political and country risk function, when some person or department at corporate headquarters has been given the explicit responsibility to assess macroeconomic and sociopolitical trends. Most of these assignments, moreover, have been housed in or attached to the corporate planning department.[2]

These perceptions and actions seem to match the reality of what is needed to succeed in the competitive environment of the 1990s and beyond. Interestingly, one study compared *Fortune* magazine's top 500 companies in 1955 with 1985 and concluded the following about most of the 313 firms that fell from the list:

> the failure of most companies can be traced to their *inability to adapt sufficiently to changes in the business environment.* Moreover, since the pace of change is accelerating, it is possible that today's "500" will fare no better than their predecessors of 30 years ago, unless they become better at adapting to a changing business environment.[3]

Amir Mahini, in his study of the government-relations process within 13 major multinationals, had a similar viewpoint; he argued that:

> The consequences of nonmanagement or mismanagement of government relations for MNCs can be serious. Some scholars of international business have warned that competitive success in the 1980s may be determined more by . . . international government-relations management than by traditional performance criteria of the marketplace.[4]

Understanding changes in the macroeconomic and sociopolitical environment is thus a key ingredient in the successful management of the modern, international corporation.

The major reason multinationals started to adopt a more serious and systematic approach to assessing political and country risk was crisis related, namely the bad experiences of greater macroeconomic uncertainty and aggressive host government intervention during the 1970s. In fact, both nonfinancial multinationals and international banks cite the first oil shock as the main reason why political and country risk assessment became a formalized function of management. Relatedly and at about the same time, an upsurge in the expropriation of foreign investment property by host governments occurred.

As we move into the 1990s, these classic environmental threats will remain, although they will probably occur less frequently in the next decade relative to the 1970s and early 1980s. Certainly most host governments have changed their tactics and attitudes toward multinational corporations, but although outright expropriation of foreign investment property is increasingly rare, adverse changes in the regulatory or operating conditions of business have become even more frequent. Over time, many political leaders have become fully aware of the important contributions that international business brings to their economies; therefore, the perceived task of host governments today is to keep multinationals in their countries but in a way that maximizes national benefits and objectives. Such a change in the approach host governments take toward international business poses new challenges and complexities for the management of the external environment. Not only are such interventions against multinationals harder to predict, but those governments which are the most aggressive intervenors are typically found in countries which have the largest, most attractive markets.

The 1990s will pose additional challenges to those trying to better manage the external environment. Increasingly, the distinction between macroeconomic and sociopolitical events on the one hand and industry-competitive developments on the other is becoming blurred as governments around the world attempt to increase their country's international competitiveness through various industrial policies. As national economies become increasingly interdependent through trade, investment and monetary relationships, the probable impact of these industrial policies on any given firm increases and intensifies. How to best manage the threat posed by foreign companies that compete under advantages supplied or engineered by their home governments will be a key question for business managers to address in the 1990s.

This book is designed to help firms improve their skills at assessing and managing the external environment. Chapters and cases in the book will address various forms of political and country risk. The types of risks to be covered include political instability, expropriation, export controls, international negotiations, questionable payments, legal disputes, industrial policies, trade relations, and debt repayment. Chapter 1 will look at basic political risk concepts and tools of analysis. Chapter 2 will then address the issue on how to manage the dual threat of political instability and expropriation, the two political risks most feared by international business managers. Chapter 3 looks at the most common aspect of political risk management today, bargaining power analysis and international negotiations. Chapter 4 explores how one manages international legal disputes, which can often be resolved by out-of-court negotiations. More formal legal remedies will also be discussed. Chapter 5 then turns to a related topic, the threat of political risk emanating from home governments given the enforcement of certain laws and regulations. Chapter 6 looks at another legal issue which has important business and ethical dimensions, the difficult area of questionable payments abroad. Chapter 7 discusses different organizational approaches for the management of the political risk function. Chapter 8 addresses the increasingly important area of industrial policies and international competition. Chapter 9 focuses on the country risk concerns of international banks. Chapter 10 ends the book with a look at future developments or scenarios for both banks and nonfinancial firms.

NOTES

1. Charles R. Kennedy, Jr. "The External Environment-Strategic Planning Interface: U.S. Multinational Practices in the 1980s," *Journal of International Business Studies,* 15 (Fall 1984), pp. 104–105.
2. *Ibid.,* p. 104.
3. W. Brooke Tunstall, "The Mission Statement as a Directive," in *Handbook of Business Strategy: 1987/88 Yearbook,* eds. Haig Babian and Harold Glass, (Boston: Warren, Gorham & Lamont, 1987) p. 1-1.
4. Amir Mahini, *Making Decisions in Multinational Corporations: Managing Relations with Sovereign Governments,* (New York: John Wiley & Sons, 1987), p. 6.

1

POLITICAL AND COUNTRY RISK CONCEPTS

The terms *political risk* and *country risk* are quite similar in that they both refer to the occurrence or likelihood that a firm will suffer losses because of political or macroeconomic developments. Jose de la Torre and David Neckar even argued for a new term, which they called *country political risk.*[1] Regardless of which term is used, political and country risk can be defined as the probability that events in the nonmarket (political, economic, and social) environment of business will cause financial, strategic, or personnel losses to the firm. These nonmarket forces lie within that part of a firm's external environment that is not associated with purely industrial, technological, or competitive dynamics.

This definition encompasses a broad spectrum of events, including terrorism, debt restructurings or nonpayment, demographic changes, expropriation, and the impact of a wide range of government policies (macroeconomic, social, labor, industrial, trade, foreign exchange, and so forth) on a company's financial and competitive position. In many instances, economic and industry trends are fundamentally shaped by the public sector, whether the result of macroeconomic policies or active government intervention in markets to influence global competition. Certainly, Japanese industrial policies have constituted a political and country risk to many non-Japanese firms.

Besides these rather broad notions of political and country risk, these terms have more precise meanings for practitioners. For example, country risk is a term commonly used by international bankers to describe some of the financial risks that are incurred in cross-border lending. Most notably, country risk comes in the form of delayed or nonpayment of debt because of a foreign exchange or balance-of-payments problem in a country. Political risk, on the other hand, is a term often used by nonfinancial, industrial firms to describe adverse developments in the nonmarket environment. Because the average foreign investors are in a country for an indefinite period, they tend to stress politics and long-term societal trends more than bankers. Thus adverse developments in the nonmarket environment are typically called political risks by industrialists. For bankers, on the other hand, problems with debt repayment abroad are often tied to a decision by a country's government to postpone, stop, or cancel external debt payments. As a result, the term country risk arose.

Political risk can be traced to macroeconomic, sociocultural, or political factors. In our definition of political risk, however, these variables are all highly interrelated. This conception is often referred to as political economy. Political risk analysts thus cannot concentrate on purely economic or political factors. Managers should systematically assess the possible and varied types of political risks so that these risks can be better managed. Although many types exist, they can be classified along two dimensions: extralegal versus legal-government risk and macro versus micro risk.

An extralegal risk event is an incident or decision in the nonmarket environment that violates existing laws or regulations and that may cause a firm harm. Examples of extralegal risk events are terrorism, sabotage, military coups, and revolutions. Note, however, that "political instability is neither a necessary nor a sufficient condition for changes in policy relevant to foreign investment."[2] The political events of revolution, military coup, or civil war become political risks only when there is a reasonable prospect that a firm will be negatively affected as a result of this instability.

In contrast, legal-governmental risk refers to an event that may harm a firm and that is a product of, or clearly permissible within, the existing political system. Such events include democratic elections leading to a new government or changes in policies that impact business.

Besides the source or legality of political risk, another useful distinction is the relative impact the event has on multinational firms. For example, Stefan Robock spoke of macro versus micro risks.[3] A macro risk is when nearly all firms are adversely affected by a particular political event; an example of this would be the revolutionary expropriations that occurred in Iran during 1979–80. Micro risk, on the other hand, is when only individual or a select few firms are adversely affected by a certain political event, such as a bureaucratic decision to deny a firm an import license.

One should stress that political risk defined in terms of losses or harm to a firm is perhaps too narrow, in that opportunities as well as risks can arise for firms when managing the nonmarket environment. Even when a firm faces a macro, extralegal risk, such as massive expropriations of foreign investment property after a military coup or social revolution, a few firms may avoid nationalization if they have structured operations in a way that makes the subsidiary an unattractive target. For example, many components in the production process may be sourced from outside the country through intracorporate transfers. Chrysler in Peru avoided expropriation under the Velasco regime in the early 1970s for this reason.[4] Of course, most instances of political risk today are of the micro, legal-governmental type, and the ability of international business executives to manage these risks and turn them into competitive opportunities is greater than normally realized. The key point of whether a political event causes corporate losses or is turned into an opportunity depends on how the situation is managed.

NOTES

1. Jose de la Torre and David Neckar, "Forecasting Country Political Risk," in *The Handbook of Forecasting: A Manager's Guide,* eds. Spyros Makridakis and Steven Wheelwright, (New York: John Wiley & Sons, 1982), pp. 326–327.
2. Stephen J. Kobrin, "Political Risk: A Review and Reconsideration," *Journal of International Business Studies,* 11 (Spring-Summer 1979), p. 74.
3. Stefan H. Robock, "Political Risk: Identification and Assessment," *Columbia Journal of World Business,* 6 (July-August 1971), pp. 68–71.
4. David G. Bradley, "Managing Against Expropriation," *Harvard Business Review,* 55 (July-August 1977), pp. 75–81.

Political Risk In Iran

> Iran under the great leadership of the Shah is an island of stability in one of the more troubled areas of the world. This is a great tribute to you, Your Majesty, and to your leadership, and to the respect, admiration, and love which your people give to you.
>
> *President Jimmy Carter,*
> *December 31, 1977*

These words were part of a formal address to the Shah at Niavaran Palace, Tehran, Iran, during an extravagant New Year's Eve banquet held by the Shah in honor of the U.S. president. Attending the banquet that evening were the representatives of several U.S. firms operating or planning to operate in Iran, including Ray Folsom, country manager for American Telecommunications Company (ATC), Alister Hunt, country manager for Sigma Corporation, and Bruce Anderson, chairman and CEO for Hitech Corporation.

ATC was an old hand in Iran, having operated there since the late 1950s, but its stake in Iran had deepened considerably in the last few years when the company was awarded a large telecommunication contract worth over $100 million. Sigma, like most U.S. corporations, had moved into Iran during the oil boom of the early 1970s. The company provided sophisticated and highly classified military equipment and training to the Iranian armed forces. Hitech, on the other hand, was contemplating its first business contract in Iran or in any other Middle East country for that matter. The Imperial Government of Iran wanted to purchase a highly advanced and specialized reconnaissance system and the training in its use from Hitech. The U.S. government did not place a high priority on the contract, because the system was directed at surveillance along the Iran-Iraq, not Soviet, border, but nevertheless had approved the sale and training program worth some $25 million.

Anderson was concerned about being paid, given his uncertainty about the Shah's regime, and about the $4 million in letters of credit the Iranian government was demanding from Hitech in order to guarantee its performance. The amount of cash Anderson was worried about was small in comparison with total U.S. corporate assets exposed in Iran—over $1 billion—but the deal would constitute more than 75 percent of Hitech's international sales and 15 percent of total sales in 1977. Because of these concerns and the relative importance of the deal to the company, Anderson sought all the advice he could get, including that of Ray Folsom and Alister Hunt:

ANDERSON: What did you think of the President's address tonight? Is he right about the Shah's stability?

FOLSOM: Absolutely. We've operated in this country for nearly 20 years and have seen a lot of change in Iran for the better. The Shah has never been more firmly in control.

ANDERSON: So you wouldn't worry about payment on contracts or how performance letters of credit are handled?

FOLSOM: We certainly haven't had any problems in the past and don't expect any in the future. Look, we have $95 million in letters of credit to Iran guaranteeing our performance, and I haven't lost a wink of sleep over it. The company didn't even think it was necessary to insure any losses on our contract. Every analyst we've talked to in and out of the U.S. government tells us the situation in Iran is very favorable to American business, and our long experience here reinforces that view.

ANDERSON: What about all this terrorist activity in Iran the last few years? I know in 1971 there was an attempt to kidnap the U.S. Ambassador, Douglas MacArthur II. In 1973 an American military advisor was killed in Tehran, and two U.S. Air Force colonels were assassinated two years later. Then in 1976 three American employees of Rockwell International were killed in Tehran. This only includes acts of violence against U.S. citizens. Attacks against Iranian government officials have been numerous as well. Doesn't that kind of activity make you nervous?

FOLSOM: Not really. Remember all countries have their fringe elements, even our own. As the Shah said recently, "I can't waste my time on a few young idiots." Moreover, remember this, today doesn't even compare with the early 1960s, much less the early 1950s. At those times, massive street demonstrations against the Shah were taking place. The Shah even had to leave the country under Musaddiq. What we've seen recently is really a limited number of desperate acts by a few desperate people, and even this kind of terrorism has greatly subsided in the last year.

ANDERSON: What do you think, Mr. Hunt?

HUNT: Well, first of all, remember I've only been Sigma's country manager in Iran for the last four months and don't have the years of experience that Mr. Folsom has, but it would always seem prudent to keep your eyes and ears open in this country.

ANDERSON: Then you don't buy President Carter's assessment?

HUNT: I'm not sure about that, but I do know that the U.S. government has its own interests to protect in this area and that's what President Carter is trying to do. You should do the same.

ANDERSON: How have you protected yourself?

HUNT: We don't have the financial concerns you do. The equipment we provide Iran is sold to DOD [U.S. Department of Defense] first, who then resells the hardware to Iran. All Sigma property in Iran, moreover, is insured by DOD under special contract. Our major concern is the safety of our people in Iran. By summer we'll have 150 employees along with 200 dependents in the country. Certain precautionary and contingency measures have been taken or contemplated to handle any foreseeable development. I think good, prudent business dictates that you do the same.

FOLSOM: I can't disagree with that, but the probability of the Shah falling and this then adversely affecting our business here in a significant way is quite small compared to most countries we've operated in. All you can really do in our business is to grab those big contracts in every place possible, thereby spreading those risks and multiplying those opportunities. Telecommunications is a very competitive business internationally, and competition for such contracts is extremely intense. When we got the contract offer from Iran, we were in no position to bargain or haggle. We took it and ran. Maybe you have other options or a different situation, but don't ever forget that these are tough customers over here. If you get rough, they can get a lot rougher. They're some of the best negotiators I've ever seen.

HITECH

Hitech Corporation, one of the many small high-technology companies that prospered in the Boston, Massachusetts, area, derived most of its business from Graphic Systems and Communications Industries. This business segment constituted about half of total company sales in 1977 and was expected to undergo rapid technological change in the near future. In fact, a major strategic push in the graphic arts and photocomposition industries was planned by Hitech for the next five years, which would boost the segment's percentage of the company total even more. This strategic thrust included major research-and-development expenditures and the acquisition of other companies.

Hitech's next largest business segment was Defense Electronics, which contributed approximately a third of total sales. This area had been Hitech's core business for many years and included such diverse products as airborne threat warning systems and simulation, training, test, and evaluation equipment. The company was, in fact, the world's largest supplier of onboard warning systems that tell pilots when they are being tracked by hostile radar.

The last, and by far the smallest, Hitech business segment was Optical Systems, which contributed approximately 15 percent of total sales. Products within this segment included electro-optical sensors and tactical reconnaissance cameras. All business segments had their separate divisions and officers, and the Iranian contract was directly under the Optical Systems Division. International sales by this division had been practically nil, because Hitech's military sales abroad were concentrated in NATO countries, that did not have a great need for tactical reconnaissance equipment. Iran was viewed, however, as perhaps the first in a string of international contractual opportunities in this product area.

INFORMATION AND THE HITECH DECISION

A few days later and after his return to Boston, Anderson contemplated and balanced the opportunities afforded by the Iranian contract versus the political risks of dealing in Iran. The contract would give the company a big boost in international and general sales. The projected rate of return was well above the company average, whereas current international profitability was below the company average. The opportunities afforded by the contract were obviously attractive and, given the lack of any real competition in this product area, could be fully exploited.

It was the political risk side that bothered Anderson. If the Shah stayed in power, having the contract successfully concluded with full payment was no problem. If the Shah fell from power, however, Hitech could face substantial losses if cancellation of the deal occurred during the production stage, or worse, after production and delivery but before full payment. On top of that, those letters of credit could be cashed because of nonperformance claims. Thus, the stability question was key.

Anderson also noticed on his return that the January-February 1978 issue of the *Harvard Business Review* had an article on political risk by R. J. Rummel and David Heenan, in which the authors described four approaches to political risk analysis: "grand tours," "old hands," Delphi techniques, and quantitative methods. Anderson had just taken the grand tour, and a few others in the company had also. Their collective response was a sense of nervousness about the situation, but they weren't sure this feeling was good intuition or a natural reaction to an alien culture.

In terms of what the old hands or so-called Iranian experts were saying, the clear majority—especially the government officials and businessmen—sided with President Carter's perspective. Academics, on the other hand, were more divided on the issue, as Anderson had quickly observed in his nighttime reading of recently published books on Iran. Donald Wilber's 1976 edition of *Iran's Past and Present* (his first edition was in 1946) was very upbeat:

> In 1976, Muhammad Reza Shah Pahlavi was very much in command of his nation. Ruling, rather than reigning, the Shah continued to initiate proposals in social and economic fields. . . . He stressed that the country was moving toward a great golden civilization. . . . While *The New York Times* chooses to label him the "Shah of Dreams," the infrastructure now building in Iran is not a mirage but an expanding reality.[1]

The judgment of another longtime and highly respected analyst of the Middle East and Iran, George Lenczowski, was in line with Wilber's:

> Although as a son of the reigning monarch, Muhammad Reza was born to a unique position of privilege, his progress has been marked by dangers and obstacles that might easily have broken an individual of lesser willpower, intelligence and determination. Ascending the throne at a time of foreign occupation, the new Shah had to face the onslaught of Soviet imperialism (1945–46). . . . During the next decade (1950s), the Shah had to face a domestic turmoil of unprecedented proportions. He

> emerged victorious from both major trials and in his new position of strength was able to launch a bold program of reforms [White Revolution in the 1960s] designed to put an end once and for all to the social and economic ills that had plagued the Iranian nation for centuries. . . . In the 1970s, a half century after the installation of the Pahlavi dynasty, this ancient legacy [monarchy] was being revived in its full dimensions.[2]

Other respected Iranian academic experts, however, drew a more pessimistic picture. As Robert Looney observed,

> A dilemma now faces the Iranian political elite. First, the elite must enlist the participation and commitment of one of the very classes that threatens them in order to implement and control the Shah's reforms. Second, many of those peasants who benefit from the reforms will move into the already expanding professional middle class, and here they will form another source of threat to the existing status quo. Whether a Marxian type of revolution develops obviously depends on the way the government is able to control the economy for the betterment of the people. . . . By now it has become clear that if the Iranian economy continues to move in its current direction, if the oil revenues fall off and if the structural maladjustments in the economy mount, the system undoubtedly will, as Marx described, collapse.[3]

James Bill expressed essentially the same argument:

> The beginning of the White Revolution in Iran represented a dramatic attempt to preserve the traditional power relationships that infused the web system . . . the White Revolution, however, also carries with it far-reaching unintended consequences. . . . One of the deepest unintended consequences of the White Revolution is the accelerating growth of the professional middle class. Yet this is the same class that threatens the ongoing patterns. And it is the same class that is needed to control and guide the explosive reform program . . . it is highly unlikely that a breakdown in traditional relationships here [in Iran] can be remedied in a way that will preserve ongoing patterns. Much of the reason is that a policy of preservation in the face of a demand for transformation carries numerous unintended consequences. This is especially true in situations where policy is directed around and against those classes that refuse to relate according to the traditional relationships. The politics of system perservation in the midst of a rapidly transforming world is a risky and costly business. The most resilient and persistent of patterns inevitably crumble under the demands of new social forces. In Iran, new groups and classes are in the process of challenging the traditional patterns of politics.[4]

Such conflicting perspectives on Iran reinforced Anderson's sense of apprehension and uncertainty. To some degree, so did the assessments of two leading political risk forecasting services that Hitech subscribed to, Business International (BI) and Business Environmental Risk Index (BERI). Both used Delphi techniques, the third approach to political risk analysis described by Rummel and Heenan, to generate their assessments. The Delphi technique is basically a process in which expert opinions are polled independently through a common format. Experts are then allowed to qualify or further explain their opinions after each analyst is confronted and briefed about major conflicting views voiced by other participants.

BI's political risk service started in 1971 and used hundreds of experts in over 70 countries. The BI political stability index rated each of these countries in one of four ways: a score of 15 for "guaranteed" long-term stability, a 10 for a strong government with a vulnerable constitution, a 5 for active internal factions, or a 2 for strong probability of overthrow, either internal or external. Based on these categorizations, the BI political stability rating for Iran remained a low political risk of 10 throughout the 1971–77 period. The BI view of Iran was best expressed in a 1975 report about business prospects in the Middle East:

> These characteristics (infrastructure development, population size and high absorptive capacity), which favorably distinguish Iran from the Arab Middle East, make the country the prime market in the area for many Western exporters. Political stability, the government's benevolent attitude toward private enterprise, and a well-protected internal market give Iran a similar edge in the eyes of foreign investors. Few international companies will thus want to stand aside as Iran races toward its goal of becoming the Japan of the Middle East.[5]

BERI, the oldest of the political risk services (started in 1966 by F. T. Haner), used 15 variables to "isolate to the degree possible the political process affecting business." These variables included bureaucratic delays, balance of payments, monetary inflation, nationalization, attitudes toward the foreign investor, and political stability. Certain variables were weighted more heavily than others, with the political stability index weighted the most (twice as heavily as nationalization and three times as heavily as bureaucratic delays, for example). The sum total of the weights equaled 25, and each of the 15 factors was then scored at 4 times its weight. Thus the highest possible points and the lowest political risk was a score of 100. A permanent panel of experts, who numbered over one hundred and who resided in the United States and in each target country, subjectively assessed a quantified score for each variable. In terms of the political stability variable, each country was subjectively rated on a 5-point scale, from 0 (unacceptable) to 4 (superior conditions).

In setting these ratings, "a version of the Delphi method is used" by BERI. After initial responses, "a panelist is supplied with his previous reply and the overall average per criterion as input for decisions on current ratings." A consensus score for each country was obtained by throwing out high and low ratings and averaging the rest. Forty to fifty developed and less-developed countries were typically covered (forty-five in 1978), and during the late 1970s, the range of scores averaged in the low 30s to the low 80s. A mean in the 60s was the norm. In fact, scores between 70 and 56 were called moderate risks, which meant that, although "complications" could arise in "day-to-day" operations, the "structure of the political environment is sufficiently stable to permit change without seriously damaging the business environment."[6]

BERI, like BI, rated Iran as being a relatively stable or moderately risky country. BERI rated Iran's "General Business Environment" at 58 in 1975, at 60 in 1976, and at 58 in 1977. Admittedly, these scores were at the low end of the moderate risk category (70–56) but because of legal and governmental events rather than political-stability concerns. As BERI's *Executive Guide to Conducting Business in Iran* stated in 1975:

> The primary problem is the fluid nature of contracts, regulations, government decisions, and so on. Rarely does a written commitment endure long enough to realize expected profits on that commitment.[7]

Iran's political-stability variable, on the other hand, was given a score of 2.9 out of a possible total of 3 points. The 1975 BERI report on Iran in its subsection, "Political Stability," stated:

> The Shahanshah represents long-range progress and increasing power for Iran. He has been responsible for successful land reform and is taking steps to distribute the benefits of economic development to a wider spectrum of the population. Each move away from tradition has carefully given enough to those conceding land, power and/or status to compensate for the loss. A highly efficient intelligence system . . . contributes to decisions on the compensation package. As a result, the Shah and his policies have broad-based support within the country.[8]

BERI's Iranian forecast, however, started to change during 1977 because of a challenge to BERI within Haner's own organization. Beginning in 1976, a new risk assessment approach, called the Political Risk Index (PRI), was being tested and applied to Iran. The 1976 PRI trial test gave Iran 46 out of a possible 100 points, which placed the country in a high-risk category (40–54 points). Although Haner and his associates found the discrepancy between the BERI and PRI scores disturbing, the PRI 1976 rating was viewed with a great deal of uncertainty and skepticism. Eighteen more months of unanticipated PRI trials followed. The composition of the panel of experts was significantly changed as well. The 1977 trial scores, however, indicated a worsening political risk environment, with Iran now rated at 43. These results were verbally communicated to BERI clients, including Hitech, in the fall of 1977 as a for-your-information exercise, not as a definite repudiation of prior BERI forecasts.

The basic reason the PRI results differed from old BERI assessments was that the variables on which expert opinions were focused were dramatically different. Under the old BERI approach, each expert was asked to give his or her conclusion without any standardization as to which underlying causal variables were being used. Under PRI, however, causal variables related to a country's instability potential were identified prior to the experts' judgments. Variables included "fractionalization of the political spectrum," "fractionalization by language, ethnic and/or religious groups," "restrictive coercive measures," "wealth distribution," "strength of forces for a radical left government," "societal conflict," and "instability as perceived by nonconstitutional changes, assassinations and guerrilla wars."

Anderson's uncertainty and perplexity were heightened by these conflicting messages, from both academics and political risk services. Who and which report were correct? Could he reach a definitive answer concerning the probability of political risk in Iran? Perhaps a high degree of uncertainty was impossible to avoid. If it was unavoidable, how did that affect the Iranian contract? Before reaching a final decision, however, Anderson hired a consultant (a highly respected political scientist and former U.S. intelligence analyst) to give him a report (see

Appendix) containing: (1) an economic, social, and political overview of Iran; (2) a quantitative analysis of Iran, and Rummel's and Heenan's fourth approach to political risk studies; (3) an assessment of BI and BERI/PRI; and (4) a three-year political forecast for Iran (the expected length of the export-service contract Hitech was considering). Anderson asked that the report be submitted within a few days because the Iranian government was insisting on a reply and the start of formal contract talks by February 1, 1978.

APPENDIX: CONFIDENTIAL REPORT

TO: Bruce Anderson
FROM: Chester R. Kendrick
DATE: January 15, 1978
RE: Political Prospects in Iran

Before reaching any conclusions about political prospects in Iran under the Shah, a general review of major economic, social, and political trends in the country seems appropriate.

A. ECONOMIC

The Iranian economy in the last four years reminds one of a high-flying roller coaster. As the IMF's *International Financial Statistics* (see Exhibit I) show, GDP growth has been up and down at a high level (see line 99b). The domestic economy grew at a 73 percent clip in 1974, then dipped to 14 percent growth in 1975, followed by a 32 percent surge in 1976. The growth rate in 1977 is estimated to be down again to 17 percent.

The main driver of the Iranian economy has increasingly become the oil industry. The recent cycles in GDP match trends in oil export income (see line 70a), which increased 266 percent in 1974, declined 7 percent in 1975, then rose 22 percent the next year, followed by an estimated 1 percent increase in 1977. This apparent correlation between GDP and oil revenue in part reflects the greater dependency of the Iranian economy on oil revenue since 1974, when oil export revenue equaled 34 percent–35 percent of GDP versus 21 percent–22 percent before 1974.

Another consequence of an economy increasingly dependent on oil was the effect that had on government budgets. During the oil boom years (1973–1974), ambitious development projects had been planned on the assumption of a 16 percent per annum rise in petroleum production, which proved impossible due primarily to weakening global demand for oil, but to infrastruture bottlenecks in Iran as well. Weaker demand caused by world recession and conservation efforts also resulted in declining real prices for oil over the last few years. All of this has had the effect of propelling the Iranian government toward large budget deficits (line 80). After fairly constant deficits in the $700 million range during the early 1970s, the budget jumped to a surplus of $2 billion in 1974. After a small surplus of under $200 million the next year, a deficit about equaling the 1970–73 period returned in 1976. A budget crisis, however, developed last year when the deficit ballooned to an estimated $5.8 billion. Major casualties of the crisis include several postponed development projects and Prime Minister Hovaida, who had been the Shah's right-hand man for the past twelve years.

The basic balance of payments deteriorated at the same time (subtract line 77bd from 77ad). After a basic balance surplus of over $7 billion in 1974, it declined to less than $1.5 billion the next year, followed by a virtual balance in 1976. A balance deficit was projected for 1977. These crises in the budget and basic balance, however, seem manageable given Iran's large international reserves (line 1d), which surpassed $12 billion by the end of last year.

The major economic problem instead relates to inflation. It is not clear that this problem is manageable. Over the 1974–76 time period, the CPI (line 64) has climbed 13 percent per annum. Some analysts insist that the real rate is double these official figures. On top of that possibility, the published figure will jump to nearly 30 percent in 1977. Even though wages have increased faster than the inflation rate (30 percent–40 percent per annum in 1974–77, line 65), this masks the fact that most urban and rural incomes are not measured by this figure. Real wages for most urban and rural workers have decreased over the last two to three years.

B. SOCIAL

In discussing the social dimensions of Iran, two major topics will be addressed: culture and demographics. In terms of culture, two dominant characteristics in Iran are the Shi'a religion and tribal-ethnic-linguistic diversity. Since about 85 percent of the population are Moslems of the Shi'a sect of Islam, the values of this religion have a great impact on Iranian society. An important Shi'a value is the belief that the state (the Shah) has legitimate authority only if it (he) rules as a viceregent of the Hidden Imam. Rebellion or martyrdom against an illegitimate regime is a religious duty and honor. This fact must be kept in mind when assessing the stability of the Shah.

Iran's small Sunni population, the other and larger Islamic sect worldwide, is concentrated within certain ethnic-tribal minorities. The most important are the Kurds (two million), Baloch (600 thousand), Turkomans (500 thousand), and Hawalah Arabs (600 thousand). These Sunni groups also speak non-Persian major languages. In fact, only about one-half of Iranians are primarily Persian or Farsi speakers. The largest linguistic-ethnic minority is the 4.5 million Azarbaijanis. Geographic locations for these various groups can be found in Exhibit II.

Demographically, there is a rapid rate of urbanization. In the 1966–76 period, the growth rate for the urban population was nearly double that of the general population, 4.8 percent versus 2.7 percent. The increase for the latest urban centers (cities over 50,000) was even higher, 5.3 percent. Tehran alone contained 13 percent of Iran's total population by 1976 and had grown from 2.9 million people in 1966 to 4.5 million ten years later. The major factor behind this rapid urbanization was the large migration rates from rural areas, which followed the 1972 land reform program in particular, the so-called third phase of the White Revolution. By the middle 1970s, a 10 percent reduction in the rural population per annum was estimated. By 1976, however, still a little less than half of Iran's population was considered urban, meaning that the pressure on urban and government resources had only begun and would mount considerably and quickly if past trends continued.

C. POLITICAL

Four major political trends deserve discussion: the Shah's recent liberalization program, the nature and pattern of urban terrorist activity, land reform politics, and last week's religious disturbances in Qum. During 1977, the Shah took several steps to liberalize his regime, which had been quite repressive throughout the 1970s. The election of President Jimmy Carter and his subsequent human rights campaign was certainly a factor in this decision but so was the Shah's past record of balancing lion-like suppression with manipulative and cooptive foxlike politics. One aspect of this change in tactical emphasis was the reining in of SAVAK, the Shah's secret police force, which had systematically used arbitrary arrests and torture for the first time in Iran's history during the last few years. Such practices decreased dramatically in 1977.

The Shah also relaxed press censorship to a significant degree. In July, an "open letters" campaign was encouraged, when Iranians were asked by a leading newspaper, "What is wrong in Iran?" In response, 40,000 letters were received. High government officials, moreover, became publicly self-critical. Late last year, for example, a powerful advisor to the Shah, Hushang Ansari, said that "expecting political liberties is the logical prolongation of developments achieved by the [White] revolution. It is only through these liberties that the will and interests of both the individual and the society as a whole could be safeguarded." Then in the past few days, another close confidant of the Shah stated in *Kayhan International* that "far more political imagination will be required to ensure the continuous consent of the new urban middle class. The nation's political life cannot lag behind its economic and social achievements." Such talk by the Shah's top echelon is unprecedented. Clearly this new emphasis on *mosharekat* (or "participation") is a conscious shift in tactics by the Shah himself.

The liberalization offensive has taken other forms as well. A well-publicized judicial reform study is proceeding. Iran's judicial system has been a sore point among the Western-educated middle class, who resent the intrusion of military tribunals into areas traditionally reserved for the civil courts and the appointment of legally unqualified judges. The replacement of Prime Minister Hovaida by Jamshid Amuzegar in August was also a move directed at the professional class, the fastest growing group in Iran, constituting nearly 15 percent of the population. Hovaida was not only associated with the earlier emphasis on police state suppression but with failures in development policy as well, particularly those affecting the middle class. The most dramatic of these failures was the electrical power shortages and blackouts that occurred in Tehran during the spring and summer of last year. This was a humiliating incident for a regime that was proud of its technical and administrative prowess. Amuzegar was given the responsibility of correcting these kinds of development problems, including the nagging problem of inflation; moreover, he was to make the political party system more effective. The Rastakhiz or National Resurgance Party, created in 1975 as Iran's only legal political organization, had tried to force participation by making membership virtually mandatory; the Shah had publicly stated that nonmembership meant the individual was a traitor or non-Iranian. The party, however, has never received broad popular support, and rumor has it that Amuzegar may allow it to vanish. What alternative channels for political participation will be presented are unclear.

Another key and related political trend in Iran is the nature and pattern of urban terrorism. Thousands of terrorist incidents have occurred in Iran during the 1970s, and this activity has intensified as state repressive tactics increased. The Shah has publicly blamed this violence on "Islamic Marxists" or on the unholy alliance between the "red and black" forces of communism and religious reactionarism. An analysis, however, of the several hundred Iranians arrested for terrorist activity between 1972 and 1976 pinpoints their origin more precisely; over 90 percent of them are the young men and women of the professional middle class. The liberalization program thus is directed at this problem as well as demands by mainstream, nonviolent members of the middle class for more political liberties and participation. Apparently, the Shah's shift in tactics is meeting with some success because last year the number of terrorist incidents declined markedly.

The Shah's recent land reform program has had a significant impact on the social structure of Iran. After 1,750,000 peasants became land owners under the reforms of the 1963 White Revolution, it was decided that most of the resulting small farms were economically inefficient. A process of consolidating them into large farm corporations run by the government was begun in 1972. A heightened rural-to-urban migration rate was anticipated as a consequence. From all indications, this policy has been a disaster both politically and economically. Agricultural production has lagged behind the needs of the economy, growing under 3 percent per annum in recent years. The rural-to-urban income gap has widened considerably as well, from a 1 to 1.5 ratio in the 1960s to a gap two to three times that wide today. Besides these economic problems, potential political drawbacks loom even larger. Many bewildered and alienated former small farmers are crowding the streets of major Iranian cities. At the very least, these new and poor urban dwellers will significantly increase the state's welfare burden. At the very worst, they could become a major source of social tension and instability. Given their traditional religious orientation and values, they could be mobilized in an anti-Shah direction by Shi'a leaders who have also lost land in past and recent reforms.

An anti-Shah, religious movement was manifested last week in the holy city of Qum, the Shi'a religious center near Tehran. A government article attacking an exiled Shi'a leader (or *mujtahid*), the Ayatollah Ruhollah Khomeini, sparked a demonstration by 4,000 religious students and varied supporters, who demanded a return to genuine constitutional government among other things. The demonstration was ruthlessly suppressed by Iranian troops, resulting in dozens killed and hundreds wounded. This incident underscores a long-running feud between the Shah and the *mujtahids,* who represent the last or twelfth *Imam,* the direct descendants of the Prophet Muhammad and Ali, the Prophet's cousin and son-in-law. According to the 1911 Constitution, the Shah is required in his oath as king "to be the guardian of the Constitutional law of Iran, to reign in conformity with established laws and to promote and protect Twelver Imam Shi'ism." The *mujtahids* with some justification claim the Shah has violated this pledge. If they can mobilize the new urban poor to their cause, who are already beholden to the Shi'a leadership for material benefits distributed through a religious welfare system, then the professional middle class stands to benefit the most.

D. OTHER POLITICAL FORECASTS

The BI political stability categories are not really relevant to the Iranian context. Although the Shah's regime is basically stable, a categorical rating of Iran being "a strong government with a vulnerable constitution" makes little sense. The BI rating system seems to suffer from Western ethnocentrism and liberal-democratic bias. Such a perspective could blind one to the real political realities and possibilities in Iran. The old BERI system probably suffers from the same deficiency, although that is unclear from the formal system itself. However, the value biases of their experts could have the same effect. It is interesting to note that the worldwide forecasts of BI and BERI the last few years are highly correlated, with an *r* coefficient of 0.894.

The PRI approach is a much more interesting system. It seems to be based on a theory of political development and change, unlike BI and BERI, which minimizes the effect of preconceived value biases of experts. Although PRI's instability rating for Iran may be a little too harsh, any disagreement with it concerns latent versus manifest conditions in Iran. The same can be said about a certain statistical approach to political forecasting, which also saw Iran as potentially unstable.

Douglas Hibbs developed a statistical, causal model of mass violence in 1973. By employing factor and regression analysis, Hibbs generated a model of instability that had a multiblock recursive structure. Many variables were used to determine the relative probability of collective protest (operationalized as the number of riots, general strikes, and antigovernment demonstrations) and/or internal war (operationalized as the number of armed attack events, assassinations, and deaths from political violence) in 108 countries. All variables incorporated into the causal model were derived from major qualitative theories about political change and statistically were found to have coefficients at least twice their respective standard errors. Such variables included the extent of negative sanctions used by the state against the domestic population; the extent of discrimination against distinct ethnolinguistic groups; the interaction between the degree of ethnolinguistic factionalism, the degree of social mobilization, and whether or not the country had received independence since 1945; the size of communist party membership in noncommunist countries; and the extent of negative sanctions and internal war in the previous decade.

The Hibbs model predicted a high probability of revolutionary change in Iran under the Shah. In 1973, quantitative scores were given for 108 countries, including Iran and two other Persian Gulf states, Iraq and Saudi Arabia. Their scores regarding collective protest and internal war are presented below, along with the 108 country mean, standard deviation, and *z* scores for Iran.

In terms of both collective protest and internal war, Iran was rated more potentially unstable than either Iraq or Saudi Arabia, particularly the latter. Iran, in fact, was one of the most politically unstable countries in the world, as indicated by statistical *z* scores; they show that Iran's potential for collective protest and internal war was within the top 17 percent and 15 percent of all countries, respectively.

Interestingly, the PRI approach contains ten variables of analysis, many of which are incorporated within the Hibbs model. Similar variables include the "fractionalization of the political spectrum" (group discrimination, political separatism), "fractionalization by language, ethnic and/or religious groups" (ethnolinguistic fractionalism), "restrictive coercive measures" (internal security forces, negative sanctions), "wealth distribution" (group discrimination), "strength of forces for a radical left government" (communist party membership), "societal conflict" (collective protest), and "instability as perceived by nonconstitutional changes, assassinations and guerrilla wars" (internal war). It is perhaps not a coincidence that two political risk approaches utilizing many of the same variables reached or produced similar forecasts about Iranian stability under the Shah.

E. THREE-YEAR POLITICAL FORECAST

No matter how attractive the PRI/Hibbs forecasts are, they do not address the critical issue of timing, or when those latent conditions or variables manifest themselves in an instability crisis. The Shah's ability to forestall a serious challenge to his regime by tactical policy moves is largely ignored by these models. This omission is critical, given the Shah's past record in this respect. Recent signs of successfully placating his most serious

Hibbs' Instability Ratings for Persian Gulf States

Country	Collective Protest	Internal War
Iran	4.548	7.421
Iraq	3.894	7.075
Saudi Arabia	2.082	0.983
108-country mean	3.234	4.734
Standard deviation	1.389	2.671
Iran *z* score	.949	1.01

Source: *Mass Political Violence: A Cross-National Causal Analysis* (New York: John Wiley and Sons, 1973), pp. 293–294.

opponents, the professional middle class, during the 1977 liberalization initiative makes such considerations even more important.

Over the next three years, therefore, the most likely regime to be in power is the one now headed by the Shah. The probability of the political system staying the same is about 70 percent. Mounting economic problems are not yet severe and seem manageable, given ample financial and natural resources at the Shah's disposal. Politically, the intensity and scope of overt opposition to the Shah in no way compares with the early 1960s or 1950s, and even if opposition to the Shah becomes serious, the Shah still has sufficient coercive means to suppress challenges to his rule. SAVAK and the military have never been stronger or more loyal and disciplined. There are no visible cracks within the Iranian security-military forces for the opposition to take advantage of. Of course, behind the Shah also stands the enormous power of the United States.

An unexpected event, however, such as failing health for the Shah or an assassin's bullet (the Shah has narrowly escaped two previous assassination attempts), could occur. Even so, the probability is good that the Shah would simply be replaced by another family member, probably the Shah's wife, Empress Farah, as regent until the Shah's son is old enough to reign in five or six years. Essentially the political system would remain the same under such a scenario, albeit more vulnerable. The probability of such an eventuality is no more than 10 percent.

The increased vulnerability of the Shah's system in his absence could propel Iran toward a genuine constitutional monarchy. Under such a system, the crown's power would no longer be absolute, with most policy-making authority residing instead within the *Majlis* or Iranian parliament, as the 1911 Constitution originally dictated. In effect, this scenario describes the return of the 1951–53 Musaddiq era, where the Western-educated and politically liberal professional middle class leads a broad-coalition of antiroyalist forces. There is a small chance that the Shah himself would reluctantly allow this to happen as an extreme consequence of his liberalization program. One could envision this only if overt opposition to the Shah became so massive as virtually to destroy the economy. The only foreseeable way this could happen is for the recent religious disturbances to spread and get out of hand. If they did, the professional middle class-*mujtahid* alliance that propelled Musaddiq and his National Front-Party to power would reemerge. Policy changes that would follow such a newgovernment include an end to press censorship, the dismantling of SAVAK, amnesty for all political prisoners, unrestricted political party activity, slower economic growth targets, significant reductions in defense spending, which now constitutes over 30 percent of the budget, and a more independently nationalistic foreign policy that distances Iran from the U.S. Certainly the U.S. would lose its special surveillance bases along the Soviet border. The probability of such a government and set of policies emerging within the next three years, however, is fairly low, around 20 percent.

Exhibit 1 Selected Macroeconomic and Balance-of-Payment Trends

	1974	1975	1976	1977
International Reserves (line 1d, millions of $)	8,383	8,897	8,833	12,266
Consumer Prices (line 64, 1970 = 100)	139.2	157.0	174.8	222.4
Wages (line 65, 1970 = 100)	243.3	342.7	465.5	N.A.
Total Exports (line 70, billions of rials)	1,459	1,367	1,651	N.A.
Oil Exports (line 70a, billions of rials)	1,414	1,328	1,609	N.A.
Current Account (line 77ad, millions of $)	12,267	4,707	5,064	N.A.
Long-Term Capital (line 77bd, millions of $)	(5,110)	(3,281)	(4,645)	N.A.
Government Budget (line 80, billions of rials)	140	12.7	(48.1)	N.A.
Current GDP (line 99b, billions of rials)	3,160	3,589	4,689	N.A.
Constant GDP (line 99bp, 1970 prices)	1,691	2,027	N.A.	N.A.

Exhibit 2 Ethnographic Map of Iran. (Adapted from *Central Asian Review,* IV, 1956, p. 418.)

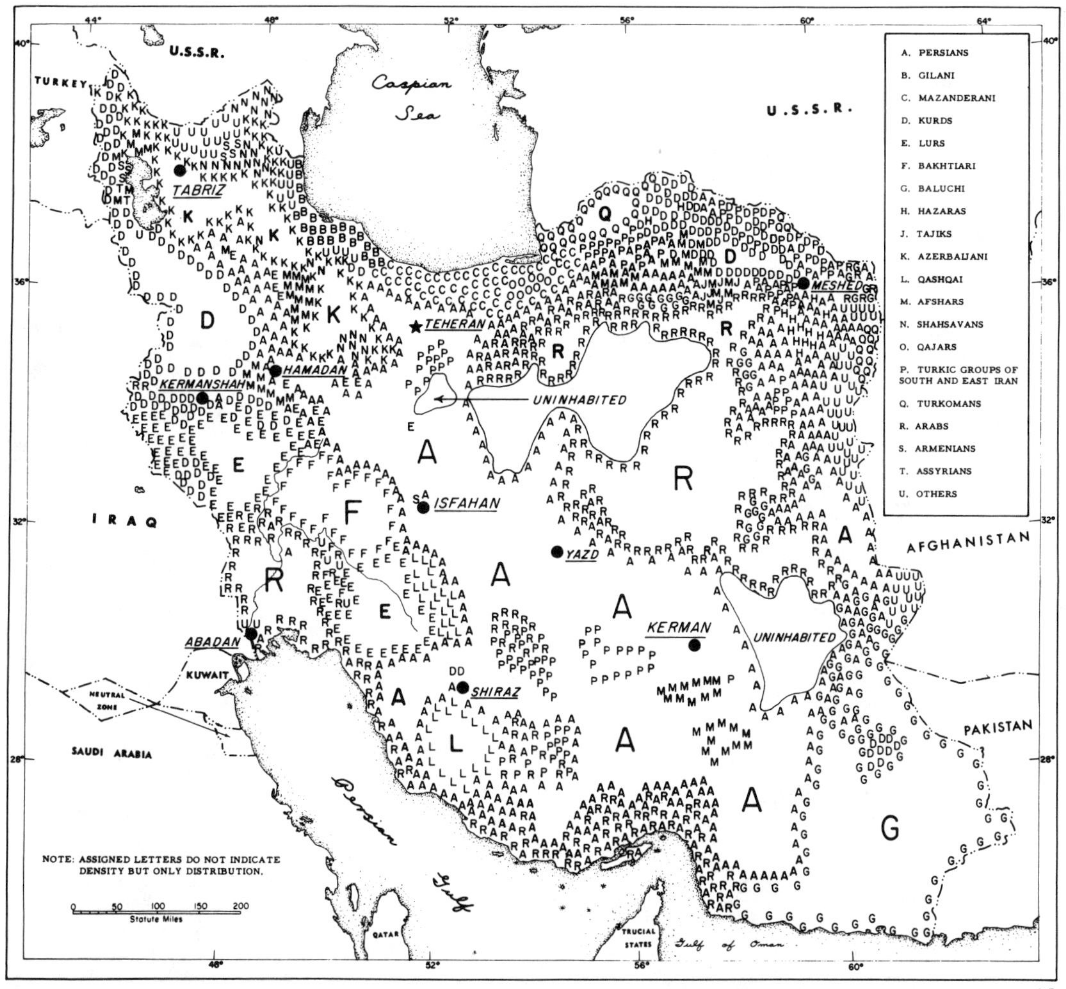

NOTES

1. *Iran's Past and Present,* Eighth Edition (Princeton, N.J.: Princeton University Press, 1976), p. 332.
2. *Iran Under the Pahlavis* (Stanford, Calif.: Hoover Institution Press, 1973), p. 478.
3. *Iran at the End of the Century: A Hegelian Forecast* (Lexington, Mass.: Lexington Books, 1977), pp. 119–120.
4. *The Politics of Iran* (Columbus, Ohio: Charles E. Merrill, 1972), pp. 153–156.
5. "Business Prospects in the Middle East," *Business International,* April 1975, p. 127.
6. F. T. Haner, "Business Environment Risk Index, Appendix B," *BERI, Ltd. System for Selected Countries* (Newark, Del., April 1981), p. 9.
7. BERI, *Executive Guide to Conducting Business in Iran* (Newark, Del.: September 1, 1975), p. 2.
8. *Ibid.,* p. 8.

2

MANAGING INSTABILITY AND EXPROPRIATION RISK

Surveys of international business executives have indicated that their greatest concerns when addressing the risks of doing business abroad are political instability and expropriation.[1] At the same time, academics have argued that political instability is neither a necessary nor sufficient condition for political risk. As Stefan Robock observed, "With such a high sensitivity to 'political instability,' it is quite possible that inexperienced international enterprises have missed business opportunities because they have perceived more political risk than actually existed."[2] Stephen Kobrin concurred; he stated: "Given the survey results that indicate judgments about political risk are likely to be subjective and based upon generalized notions of instability, we suggest that those risk assessments are often overstated."[3] Kobrin went on to suggest the following:

> While the assessment and evaluation of political risk are admittedly difficult, more rigorous and objective procedures could alleviate some of the problems. This does not necessarily mean the use of formal mathematical models. Rather it requires a better understanding of the variations in the political process and an attempt to identify explicitly the effects (if any exist) that political events are likely to have upon the firm's operations.[4]

One effect that political instability can have on multinational firms, particularly when it takes the form of military coups or revolutions, is that it appears to be related to expropriation activity. As David Jodice observed, 40 percent of all expropriations which occurred during the 1960–79 period followed revolutionary transformations of socioeconomic and political systems.[5] In addition, a recent study found a statistically significant correlation between "outright government takeover by coup or revolution" and expropriation.[6]

The above two studies saw a significant relationship between extralegal changes in political regimes and single acts of expropriation. The relationship is even stronger if one associates such events of political instability with the extensiveness of expropriation policy. For example, of 276 political regimes that governed 79 less developed countries in the 1960–80 period, 25 had expropriated foreign firms in all major sectors of the economy—banking, natural resources, services and manufacturing. Acts of expropriation by these regimes totaled 355, versus 584 acts of expropriation for all regimes in the 1960–80 period. Thus 25 political regimes were responsible for 61 percent of all expropriations.

Interestingly, 18 of these regimes (72 percent) had gained power as a result of a violent colonial struggle, military coup or social revolution. By contrast, of the 251 regimes that had not extensively expropriated foreign direct investment, only 97 governments (39 percent) had gained power by force or violent means. Thus, there seems to be a clear and strong relationship between violent, extralegal changes in political regimes and the intensity of expropriation policy.

However, even in the midst of extensive, cross-sectoral expropriations, some firms avoid nationalization. In Peru during 1968–75, for example, the Velasco government expropriated 52 foreign firms in 22 separate industrial sectors (3-digit SIC code), but Chrysler was not nationalized because the company sourced major production components from abroad through intracorporate transfers. Likewise in Chile under the Allende regime, which nationalized 47 foreign companies in 27 sectors during 1970–73, Revlon avoided expropriation because the subsidiary's production of pharmaceutical products was dependent on technological secrets known only by personnel at the New York headquarters. Perhaps even more noteworthy, the largest foreign copper company in Peru, the Southern Peru Copper Corporation (SPCC is principally owned by Asarco, a U.S. firm), was not nationalized by Velasco, even though other copper firms were seized, because SPCC agreed to expand operations in Peru by developing a huge, new mine through enormous capital investments.

These three cases highlight some generalizations about bargaining power which tend to reduce or increase the likelihood of expropriation, but these generalizations must be applied with caution. Typically, firms with technological advantages and proprietary knowledge have a greater chance to avoid adverse intervention by host governments.[7] The Revlon case demonstrates this tendency. Of course, the Chrysler situation reflects the following generalization: Subsidiaries which are highly integrated with global operations have a better chance to escape expropriation.[8] In addition, larger firms are generally attractive targets for adverse intervention,[9] but the SPCC case suggests there are exceptions to this tendency, particularly if the firm has certain technical skills and is willing to commit tens of millions of dollars into new investments. Perhaps an even more important message is that managers can be rewarded if they proactively seek mutually acceptable arrangements with even the most radical governments.

NOTES

1. Stephen J. Kobrin, John Basek, Stephen Blank and Joseph La Palombara, "The Assessment and Evaluation of Noneconomic Environments by American Firms: A Preliminary Report," *Journal of International Business Studies,* 11 (Spring/Summer 1980), p. 41; and Charles R. Kennedy, Jr., "Political Risk Assessment Practices in U.S. Corporations," in *Political Risk in International Business: New Directions for Research, Management, and Public Policy,* ed. Thomas Brewer (New York: Praeger Publishers, 1985), p. 229.
2. Stefan H. Robock, "Political Risk: Identification and Assessment," *Columbia Journal of World Business,* 6 (July-August 1971), p. 15.
3. Stephen J. Kobrin, "When Does Political Instability Result in Increased Investment Risk," *Columbia Journal of World Business,* 13 (Fall 1978), p. 120.
4. *Ibid.,* pp. 120–121.
5. David A. Jodice, "Trends in Political Risk Assessment: Prospects for the Future," in *International Political Risk Management: New Dimensions,* eds. Fariborz Ghadar and Theodore Moran (Washington D.C.: Ghadar and Associates, 1984), p. 16.
6. F. N. Burton and Hisashi Inoue, "A Country Risk Appraisal Model of Foreign Asset Expropriation in Developing Countries," *Applied Economics,* 19 (1987), pp. 1018–1023.
7. David G. Bradley, "Managing Against Expropriation," *Harvard Business Review,* 55 (July-August 1977), p. 81.
8. *Ibid.,* pp. 81–82.
9. Thomas A. Poynter, "Government Intervention in Less Developed Countries: The Experience of Multinational Companies," *Journal of International Business Studies,* 13 (Spring/Summer 1982), pp. 17–18.

Sigma Corporation In Iran (A)

On the night of December 5, 1978, Alister Hunt, the country manager for Sigma Corporation in Iran, was staring out his front window toward the main street that ran by his house. It was still a sight that was new and bizarre. He was looking at a Sherman tank that had moved in during the day to protect the Shah's sister, who lived next door. The Shah himself often stayed at the Summer Palace within eyesight of Hunt's home. Hunt now knew the situation in Iran had become a very serious threat to Sigma personnel, who numbered 175 employees and 215 dependents. Seventy of those personnel were scattered where the rest of Sigma's operations were based, in three locations remote from Tehran, the capital. Should Hunt be concerned enough to begin pulling out his people? If he felt a major reduction in personnel was needed, how could they be sent home with little publicity and without bruising a very profitable relationship with both the U.S. and Iranian governments? According to prior agreements, only tripartite decisions could lead to such a move, and such a consensus among Iran, the U.S. government, and Sigma was unlikely at this time. Short of that, Hunt wondered what other measures could be taken to protect his people better. In other words, had his contingency planning been adequate? The lives of several hundred people, including women and children, depended on it.

SIGMA CORPORATION

Founded in Cambridge, Massachusetts, in 1922 as the American Radio Corporation, a producer of radio tubes, the company adopted the Sigma name in 1925. Given the tremendous growth of the radio industry in the 1920s, Sigma was able to gain a foothold in the market in spite of the presence of larger, dominant competitors such as General Electric, Westinghouse, and its subsidiary, RCA. Sigma, however, remained a small company (total sales of $3.2 million in 1939) until the outbreak of World War II, when the company began production of military electronics, radar, and communications equipment. By 1945 total sales equaled $148 million, with all but $6 million the result of U.S. government contracts. After the war, Sigma became a leader in missile guidance systems, credited with the first midair interception and destruction of both aircraft and missiles. Although U.S. government contracts remained strong, the company made a conscious effort to diversify into civilian lines of business such as industrial electronics, components, and tubes. By 1962 civilian sales exceeded $100 million and constituted 17 percent of total Sigma revenues. Sigma continued this diversification policy in the 1960s by acquiring kitchen appliance, publishing, seisomographic, and construction companies. By 1974 U.S. government contracts had fallen to 41 percent ($800 million) of total sales ($1.929 billion).

International business operations at this time were focused in three areas: Western Europe, where Sigma had been heavily involved since the late 1940s; Saudi Arabia, where a small operation had been in place since 1964; and Iran, where the first contract had been recently signed. In 1974 international sales were $530 million or 27 percent of total sales. The lion's share of that activity was derived from NATO military contracts. Between 1974 and 1978, however, Iran came to equal Western Europe as Sigma's biggest export market; each contributed over $600 million in sales during those years. As a consequence, international revenue climbed to 34 percent of $3.24 billion in total sales by 1978.

THE IRANIAN OPERATION

Sigma's involvement in Iran started at a low level in 1972, with educational systems provided to the University at Shiraz. In late 1973, however, Sigma's business in Iran expanded dramatically with the signing of a military service contract. Sigma was to provide Iran with a highly sophisticated missile-defense system called the Eagle. The equipment would be built in top-security plants in the United States, sold to the U.S. Department of Defense (DOD), and then resold to the Imperial Government of Iran. Profit margins were standard for U.S. government contracts, plus an extra 4 percent markup for the higher risks and expenses of operating in Iran. Such operations related to training programs conducted by Sigma personnel within Iran.

Over the next three years, Sigma trained 3,000 Iranian Air Force personnel at bases in the Tehran area. By 1976 Sigma had 120 employees and nearly 200 dependents in the country. Although many employees and their families suffered from culture shock, that was a common and expected reaction to a strange country. In 1976, however, the situation in Iran became especially tense and unsettling as political terrorist activity mounted dramatically; it took a decidedly anti-American business tone when two Rockwell International employees were murdered. Nevertheless, Sigma's "attrition rate," or the number of employees who quit the firm and left the country, was much lower than most other U.S. companies. During 1976, only 20 Sigma employees and their families left Iran in such a manner (17 percent of the total), half the rate in other U.S. firms such as Bell Helicopter. Sigma's loyalty to its employees, which resulted in a very low turnover rate for the company as a whole, helped explain this record. Sigma's decision to take organized measures to protect itself during the upsurge in terrorism (defensive-driving courses, increased intelligence gathering, and contingency planning toward a pyramid communications system) also served to heighten employee morale.

During 1976 Sigma began to negotiate a new contract with Iran to provide on-the-job training in equipment maintenance. Essentially, company instructors would take the Iranian military technicians through a series of U.S. Army maintenance programs related to the Eagle missile system. The major change the new contract brought to Sigma's Iran operation was that much of the training would take place in "down-country" locations, far from the Tehran base. After several months of negotiations, the new contract was signed in July 1977. Two months later Alister Hunt moved to Iran as Sigma's new country manager, his first such assignment overseas after many years as an engineer and administrator in Sigma's U.S. missile and antisubmarine warfare divisions.

SIGMA AND THE 1978 IRANIAN REVOLUTION

In February 1978 Sigma operations on the new contract began in earnest with the first arrival of additional personnel to man the remote training sites. There would eventually be five such sites manned by 30 to 35 Sigma personnel each. The sites were located at Bebahan, Vahdati (near Ahwaz), Bushire, Isfahan, and Char Bhabar. The Vahdati and Bushire sites were to be staffed first, followed by Isfahan and then the others (see Exhibit 1).

Recruiting and staffing these positions proved to be a big problem. Every attempt was made to find bachelors, because no dependents were allowed at the remote training sites, but not enough single males were found. Married men hired for the job had their families permanently based in Tehran. All personnel at the down-country locations rotated with others at thirty-day intervals.

For general management, the arrangements caused a "baby-sit the families" problem. Sigma handled the situation by increasing the sense of community among its employees by starting a company newsletter in February and by building full recreational and (limited) housing facilities for employees—the Sigma compound, if you will. Funds for the project were fully provided by the Iranian government, which technically owned the property. All in all, Sigma visibility in the country was getting appreciably higher because of the compound and because of a rising number of cars (35) and buses (8) in the Sigma fleet. Nevertheless, life for the Sigma community carried on in a pretty normal American way, as the June 1978 Sigma Newsletter attests (see Exhibit 2).

Events in Iran outside the Sigma community, however, were becoming more and more turbulent. Following the January 1978 Qum incident, when fighting between the religious community and Iranian troops resulted in dozens killed, including two mullahs (religious leaders), a cycle of religious-based violence set in. According to Shi'ite custom, ceremonies mourning the martyrs of Qum were scheduled for the fortieth day after the killings. The traditional mourning procession on February 18 took place peacefully in 15 of 16 cities. The lone but important exception was Tabriz, where rioting erupted when the provincial government closed three mosques on the day of the demonstration. Army intervention was required to squelch the rioting, which was the first sustained clash between the army and civilians since 1963. The fighting resulted in at least 26 dead and 260 wounded (opposition leaders claimed 300 killed and 700 injured). The forty-day cycle continued on March 30, but the violence really escalated in April, when there was at least one serious incident per day. In May, violence and death returned to Qum, and armored cars were deployed in Tehran for the first time. A particularly tense atmosphere existed in all major Iranian cities, especially Tehran, on June 5, the fifteenth anniversary of Khomeini's exile. A major clash was avoided, however, in part because of the intimidating presence of Iranian tanks in the streets for the first time.

Sigma top management reacted to these incidents with a great deal of concern. As Hunt remarked, "Religious dissent had now risen above the noise-level." As a result, Sigma began implementing many of its tentative contingency plans in regard to a pyramid communications system and concrete evacuation procedures. A 200-page document was written in June and July to organize the system formally and to detail those procedures. The so-called *warden system* was the core of the system and evacuation plan. In the system, the Sigma community was grouped into twelve teams, based mainly on the geographic location of residences. Each team was headed by a warden or leader, who was the only member of the team with full knowledge of emergency and evacuation details. This kind of activity and planning seemed to help reduce tension and anxiety within the Sigma community, but so did a lull in the fighting and demonstrations that developed between early June and late July. As a result, the Sigma contract operations continued at an escalating pace, with the number of new personnel arriving each month increasing to approximately ten during July. Hunt also felt comfortable enough to allow his wife and kids to take an Iranian vacation to some down-country areas the same month. He then returned with his family to the United States in early August for a well-deserved vacation.

On August 19, however, a major turning point in the Iranian political crisis took place in Abadan. At the Rex Cinema, a fire broke out that killed over 400 people. The laxness and slow reaction of local police and firemen convinced many that SAVAK, the Shah's secret police, was responsible. Suspicions were further heightened by the fact that the Abadan police chief, General Reza Razmi, had been the Qum police chief during the January rioting. The Shah tried to counter the resulting countrywide protests by replacing Prime Minister Jamshid Amouzegar with Ja'far Sharif-Emami, who was a member of the royal family's inner circle but was also the son and grandson of prestigious clerics.

The new appointment and cabinet reshuffle failed to appease the opposition. The intensity of the anti-Shah movement reached a new high, and the clergy announced a mass march for September 4 and 5 to celebrate the end of Ramadan, the Moslem month of fasting. The government refused parade permits but decided to ignore the demonstrations anyway. In Tehran demonstrators numbered over one hundred thousand each day. The clergy then called a countrywide general strike for September 7. The Shah reacted by declaring martial law in thirteen cities with a 10:00 p.m. to 5:00 a.m. curfew. Public gatherings of over three people were forbidden as well. The clerics then called for antimartial-law demonstrations for September 8, a Friday and the Moslem day of worship. A bloody confrontation ensued that day, initially at Jaleh Square in south Tehran, where army units opened fire and killed at least 100 people when the crowd refused to disperse. Major riots and fire-fights then erupted in most parts of the city. By the end of the day, approximately 400 people had died and 4,000 were wounded. After "Black Friday," what had been an anti-Shah protest movement appeared to have become a full-scale revolution.

The reaction within the Sigma community was mounting panic. Hunt rushed back to Tehran from vacation and on September 11, 1978, issued a memo to help clarify the situation and, he hoped, reduce the panic level among his people.

MEMORANDUM

TO: All Sigma Employees and Dependents
FROM: Alister Hunt
DATE: September 11, 1978
RE: Operations Under Martial Law in Iran

The following guidelines are issued to help you with the present state of martial law in Tehran and other cities in Iran. As new operational procedures are developed, we will keep you informed; in the meanwhile I urge you to monitor your radio and TV and one of the English-language newspapers for day-by-day changes in regulations.

I. TRAVEL

Local Tehran travel via automobiles and other ground vehicles is not restricted. Common sense should be used in selecting times of travel so as not to interfere with curfew limits, presently 10:00 p.m. through 5:00 a.m. A safety factor of 30 to 45 minutes should always be allowed. Main routes should be used to the greatest extent possible. In the event you become stuck and believe that you have violated the curfew, proceed as follows:

a. If telephone communications are possible, notify by phone Bill Glade, head of Sigma security, at home or in the office and request assistance.
b. If neither time nor communications permit, present yourself to the first available policeman or soldier and request assistance. Communication may be difficult due to language problems, but don't give up; they will try to help you. You will be escorted to a precinct station or central point and communications provided. It is most important to do this *before* the curfew begins; after that, you will be arrested. Sigma does not recommend travel by train at this time for security reasons. Airline travel is unrestricted although again somewhat flaky because of extensive rescheduling delays. Obtaining reservations for out-of-country travel is about normal, i.e., a few days. Restrictions on travel to the airport have been lifted; however, no one is allowed in the terminal without a ticket. Departure or arrival assistance can be provided to a limited extent by travel-agency personnel upon request by the company during noncurfew hours. During curfew hours Iran Air will transport via bus from the airport to in-town hotels. Taxis with special passes are permitted similar privileges. The company will escort all new arrivals in the country for the time being to minimize confusion at arrival.
c. Company buses/vehicles will continue to operate in support of travel to/from work locations, the recreational center, and the Zafar offices. Schedules have been revised and are attached to this memo. Personnel waiting to be picked up should not congregate in groups larger than two persons. Shopping transportation will continue as before, as will school buses. Mothers accompanying children to bus stops should avoid the appearance of congregating; if questioned (not likely), display the previously issued Farsi notice explaining your presence on the street.

II. CURFEW

Adherence to curfew is *mandatory.* The government of Iran takes it quite seriously. Violators *will* be arrested by the authorities and expect to be inconvenienced and/or discomforted until released. If stopped or challenged, do not resist or argue; comply with all instructions (try to smile a lot). Again, if for any unforeseen reason you are unable to reach your destination before evening curfew, go to the nearest Sigma home, police station, or government agency and communicate. Carry telephone numbers with you at all times (and a two-Rial coin).

III. EMERGENCY ASSISTANCE

Assistance in communicating in Farsi with your local police station for emergency support (ambulance, fire, other) may be obtained from the U.S. Embassy as follows:

a. Call the U.S. Embassy: 820-091 through 099.
b. Ask for the Marine duty officer.
c. State your problem and type of assistance you require.
d. Hang up and wait for a Farsi-speaking embassy employee to call you back. He/she will assist you and communicate your needs to the police precinct.
e. Call Bill Glade and advise him of the problem.

IV. SECURITY

Martial law is imposed upon Tehran to end threats to public safety and destruction of private and public property. We expect it to be quite effective for the foreseeable future. Prudence is still required, however, and the company recommends observance of the following guidelines:

a. Stay out of southern and eastern Tehran unless absolutely necessary. This includes the bazaar and the railroad station.
b. Avoid public facilities (restaurants, theaters, movies).
c. Don't linger in stores, banks, gas stations.
d. Stay off the streets if a public demonstration or celebration is announced.
e. September 15 is the seventh day after the recent fighting occurred. It might occasion another challenge to government authority. Be aware.
f. Don't be surprised if sporadic incidents continue, particularly involving attacks on police or military personnel.

V. GENERAL

The company understands the restrictions and limits imposed on us all by the new martial law and continuing security alerts. We will attempt to deal with the problem in as many ways as we can to make the situation more pleasant. Constructive suggestions will be most welcome. In the meanwhile stick together and help each other as you can.

Alister Hunt, Vice President, Program Manager

Throughout the remainder of September, Hunt initiated a number of crisis-management moves. Practices of the first dry runs of the emergency plan caused some updating of evacuation procedures. Flights of incoming personnel, who were numbering approximately ten a month in September and October, were changed to go via Athens instead of Paris to have them land in Tehran during the day, not night. A rumor-control bulletin was also developed to counter undue concern or panic. Contacts and information exchanges between Sigma, other companies, and the U.S. Embassy increased as well. An example of such activity is provided by this memo from the head of Sigma security to Hunt.

MEMORANDUM

TO: Alister Hunt
FROM: B. Glade
DATE: September 16, 1978
RE: Security Status from U.S. Embassy

Status regarding security in Tehran and other Iranian locations is as follows: Tehran—no known incidents occurred during the weekend. Expectancy is that the situation will continue to be calm and stable during the next few days. Isfahan—four significant incidents occurred in Isfahan over the weekend. All were tied to the Molatov-cocktail incidents. Against: (1) the Ministry of Tourism, (2) two banks, (3) Grumman motorpool. Molatovs and pipebombs were used against the Grumman motorpool on Friday. No one was injured, but a Paykan car was destroyed. Minor damage was done to other vehicles in the installation. U.S. Embassy is concerned that the American community reaction may be overly excitable under the present circumstances. They also feel that the Grumman motorpool was poorly enclosed and/or secured. Note: Suggest that we discuss this with our managers so that they can, with perspective, counter any undue Sigma reaction. Other cities—no significant disturbances in other Iranian cities over the weekend. Travel—surface travel is still discouraged. Air travel is preferred. Response to specific questions regarding Sigma personnel traveling to Hashenabad is to travel by air to Isfahan. Hence surface to Hashenabad base is OK as long as we comply with martial law regulations and use good judgment about leaving the base unnecessarily. Surface movement of Sigma vehicles from Tehran to Hashenabad is OK if done by an Iranian driver without passengers and if the driver complies with martial-law regulations. Outlook for stability in Iran under martial law still remains good. The embassy is conducting briefings as follows: Bomb threat management: Monday, September 18, 1400 hours, Carvansarai lounge. General security briefing: Tuesday, September 19, 1330 hours, Carvansarai lounge. Driving training: September 25, 0800 hours, American Embassy.

In general, Sigma's U.S. government contacts remained optimistic about the situation in Iran. Another source of information for Sigma had a dramatically different viewpoint, however. In late 1977 Hunt had sought and hired a local Iranian analyst, who came highly recommended as "well-connected" by government sources back in the United States. Hunt only knew him as "Colonel G." and as a former Iranian police colonel. The two men arranged telephone contact numbers, and Colonel G. visited Hunt at fairly regular intervals. In one such meeting on October 24, Colonel G. assessed the situation as being very bad. He described how junior and senior high school students were joining the guerrillas, and all labor strikes were totally political now. He listed the three main opposition elements: the religious leaders; the National Front led by liberal, Western-educated professionals; and the angry and poor urban mob. Colonel G. stressed that all three elements had a strong communist presence and predicted Iran would go communist if the Shah left Iran. He also predicted that Americans would increasingly become the targets of revolutionary violence. The opposition had become particularly incensed over President Carter's telephone call of support to the Shah on "Black Friday."

Another meeting with Colonel G. took place on October 31. Colonel G. was extremely agitated, saying the situation had reached a "bursting point." He described the Shah as alone and despondent, and indicated that even the military might not back him completely. He said anything could happen in the next two months.

Colonel G.'s prediction proved accurate in a very short time. On November 5, the worst riots to date occurred in Tehran. Seventeen police stations in Tehran were attacked in a coordinated action, with two of the stations captured. At the same time, over eighty banks and hundreds of "Westernized" shops were set afire and looted, and the Ministry of Information was totally destroyed, as were all airline offices except Air France. (Khomeini lived in France.) Perhaps most frightening to some in the Sigma community, a bus of foreign-born children on their way home from school was attacked with verbal abuse and small missiles. The Shah reacted to these events by replacing Prime Minister Emami with a new military government, led by the Iranian Army Chief of Staff.

Sigma reacted to these events by halting the arrival of any new personnel into Iran. Hunt also issued the following situation report, the first general release to the Sigma community since the September 11 memo. The report was issued because the panic level had reached an all-time high and guidance was needed for the difficult weeks ahead, especially for December, the religious month of Moharram.

MEMORANDUM

TO: All Sigma U.S. Personnel and Dependents
FROM: Alister Hunt, Program Manager
DATE: November 12, 1978
RE: Situation Report

Now that the turmoil of the past week has quieted, I thought it would be useful to try to put it all in perspective for you and to attempt to forecast where we go from here. Along the way I will answer some of the questions that have been put to me in the past few weeks. I realize that any prediction I make is bound to be wrong in some or many ways; however, it represents a best estimate at this time and you should know that at least. First, the past: About 18 months ago it became obvious that the Iranian economy was not healthy. This was obvious in different ways at different levels. At the people level, inflation in rent and food prices has stripped away any gains made by the people in the last decade. It seemed to be the cause of most of the dissatisfaction. In response to this pressure, the government of Mr. Hoveyda was changed for that of Mr. Amouzegar. He was reported to be a good manager, and his goal was to get a handle on the economy and the development program. About nine months ago, the decision was announced to liberalize the political process. This decision, coming without a guide, rapidly created chaos within the government. New parties sprang up by the dozen, and the press and other media were not able to provide any balanced coverage. The government also did not offer a transition plan. The religious leaders then became more aggressive, and the prime minister, Amouzegar, finally lost control. The pressure from the clergy led to demonstrations; the demonstrations led to bloodshed; a crisis rapidly developed late this summer. July was characterized by growing trouble in the provinces and almost total silence by the government. In August large-scale violence broke out. The government changed to one headed by Sharif-Emami, and large concessions were made to the Moslem clergy in hope of quieting things down. This was patently unsuccessful, and on 8 September, martial law was declared in most large cities throughout the country. This action was immediately effective in restoring order in the cities. But as the opposition sensed an opportunity to gain control of the government, violence flared up in those areas not under martial law.

The new government then made several attempts to defuse the situation. Among these were televised debates of the Majlis, removal of press censorship, release of prisoners, arrests of some officials believed to be corrupt, and large wage settlements for dissatisfied government employees.

None of these actions appeared to be effective, and still the pressure grew. The students appeared on the streets late in September, and demonstrations and violence returned to Iran and other large cities. While this was happening, the military showed great restraint and allowed the government to try to control the situation. It was clear that another government change was required, however, and the process of forming coalitions began. The National Front, the outlawed party of old, showed the most strength and was the best organized. Several other former leaders threw their hats in the ring. Success, however, required the coalition of a strong political force with the clergy. The Shah for his part required a *constitutional* government (this had the effect of perpetuating the monarchy). Late in October it appeared that the National Front behind Mr. Sanjabi and the clergy behind Ayatollah Khomeini would join forces. The situation in the country continued to worsen. The strikes became political, the oil fields nearly shut down, and the government revenue dropped to a trickle. Iran was close to a state of anarchy. Khomeini at that point must have sensed victory and stated that a revised constitution would be necessary. This meant the elimination of the monarchy and its replacement by the Shi'ite clergy at the head of the country. This was unacceptable to the Shah, and at this point, he had no option left other than to install his military commanders in key government positions.

This brings us to the present—wondering where we go from here. As I see it, there are three critical periods before us.

We are in the first of these periods now, and it will last for only a week or two. During this time, the economy must restart. There will be challenges to the new government by the students, National Front, and the clergy. But the real test will be whether everyone returns to work. If they do not, many foreigners and foreign companies will have to leave because they cannot be paid. Goods and services will become scarce, and routine operations will become difficult. This will be the economic test of the new government.

The second period, or test, will begin early in December and could last up to a month. I think of this as a force test. At this time the clergy will have to make its move if it wishes to fight or resist the new government with force. The logical time for this to begin will be at Ashura. The government will be well prepared then, and so I expect a challenge to be made later, say in early January. If the clergy is unsuccessful in this, I foresee an increase in acts of urban sabotage against government installations. In any event, government success is necessary here if law and order are to prevail.

The third period will be the most difficult. It is the political test and it will occur between the New Year and July. At this time we will find out whether a new government can be chosen through a political process or whether a military regime must remain. I have no predictions for this, but I will point out the obvious conclusion that, until we are through this period, normal conditions will not return to Iran.

While all of this is going on, the various interest groups will be jockeying for position: clergy, students, political aspirants, and so forth. I expect a continuing campaign to harass foreigners (us). This will take the form of warnings, threats, no service, rocks, and so forth. We can only hope that it does not become more vicious. I would like to think that these groups will lose interest in us as they become absorbed in their own future. Now for the questions:

I. WHERE DOES THIS LEAVE SIGMA?

We have a job to do here. We think that it is a worthwhile one and necessary to global U.S. interests, and we intend to do it. *We are not leaving nor do we intend to send our dependents home.* The seriousness of the situation and the risks to which we are exposed here are real. They are different from those which we are used to in living and working at home. However, they are not higher in any demonstrable way. Each of us made his own decision in coming here. Each of us will have to make his own decision about staying. I sincerely hope you all see your way clear to finishing the job we have started.

II. WHAT IS SIGMA DOING ABOUT THE SITUATION?

We have taken several actions and have several more to take. The company in the United States monitors the political situation on a daily basis through the State Department. The company here monitors the political and security situation daily through the U.S. Embassy and the U.S. Air Force security office. In addition, we employ an analyst to interpret the meaning of our data in local terms. This does not enable us to foretell the future, but it does provide us with some lead time. We were able, for instance, on November 5th to return all of our employees to their homes several hours before the major rioting and looting occurred.

In recent weeks I have met with either the U.S. Ambassador, the U.S. Military Chief, or both, at least once a week. This provides them with information as to what we are doing and us with the same information about their reactions.

The U.S. Embassy, incidentally, has received a lot of bad press lately concerning the credibility of its announcements. This is undeserved. The U.S. Embassy's job is not to protect the American community here or to provide it with advice on how to protect itself. Its job is to promote and implement an American policy regarding Iran, coordinate military assistance to Iran, and to establish government-to-government communication.

III. DO WE HAVE AN EVACUATION PLAN?

We have developed a plan for dealing with different emergencies. This plan, among other things, provides for evacuation of employees and/or dependents should either we or the U.S. government think the situation warrants such an action. The U.S. government also has such a plan. Neither of us believes the evacuation is warranted at this time.

Many of you have asked to have the plan. I don't believe, nor does the company nor does the U.S. government, that releasing the plans is appropriate. The reason for this is that the plan contains many data which are private and which would compromise the plan if they were to fall into the wrong hands. For example, the names, addresses, phone numbers, and location maps on each of you, your families, and your residences, are contained in the plan. Pickup points, communication methods, and travel plans are also contained.

I can tell you how the plan will be implemented, should it become necessary. (A) I will convene the emergency management team and announce the decision. (B) The warden system will be activated and used to deliver a packet of data to each employee or family. This packet will tell you what is being done, what you can take, when you will be picked up, where you are going, and when you are going. (C) The wardens will arrange to move you to the pickup point at the arranged time. (D) Either the U.S. government or the company will provide transportation from the pickup points to the airport. The organization calling the action will provide transportation. In the case of a company, this transportation will be by bus or automobile. (E) After reaching the airport, you will be flown out of the country to one of three European cities. From there you will be flown to the United States. If the U.S. government signals the evacuation, it will provide the aircraft from Iran to Europe. If Sigma signals the action, we will provide the aircraft. (F) Teams will accompany you on each leg of the journey to provide money, food, housing, and direction.

There are several other things you might like to know about the plan as it presently stands. (A) We have a military communication channel available to us if the civil system goes out between Iran and the United States. (B) We have a contract with an American fleet carrier to provide charter aircraft to us within 72 hours should we request it. (C) Personnel residing down-country will be evacuated with U.S. military personnel and reunited with their families in Europe. (D) Personal belongings which you have to leave behind are insured under the provisions of our contracts. You should of course maintain an inventory of your personal effects, their costs, and other descriptive material (photographs, for example) in a safe place. The personnel jacket or a family member in the United States should be considered a safe place. (E) Animals will not be evacuated by the U.S. Embassy.

The emergency plan has been under continuous review since early this summer. The key element of it, in my opinion, is communications. The warden system is the way we implement communications. We have continually exercised this system in recent months and will continue to do so. I am proud of how effective it is and can assure you from my contacts with other companies here that there is none better. There are several aspects of the plan which we are not satisfied with as yet: (A) Our dependency on the telephone system for communication within Iran and between Tehran and down-country. We have requested of the government of Iran, and I believe will shortly receive, licenses to operate our own radio communication system throughout the country. In anticipation of this, we have already ordered the necessary equipment in the United States. (B) The transportation between Tehran and down-country is dependent upon the Iranian Air Force in the event commercial facilities are not available. So far it has taken good care of us, but in an emergency its mission will take precedence over our needs.

We have sought permission to operate charter aircrafts in and out of our training sites. Should this permission be granted, we will have much better control of personnel movement within the country (we may, for example, be able to reunite families in Tehran prior to evacuation). (C) Transportation within Tehran is dependent upon our being able to operate vehicles, which in turn is dependent upon fuel being available. The recent strike with fuel suppliers shows us how vulnerable we are to this situation.

To counter this we are investigating means to establish our own fuel reserves. Other actions which the company is taking or investigating include protection of work buses from flying rocks and other missiles and alternative means of transporting children to and from school. These actions are in response to concerns voiced by many of you. We have no firm answers to these items as yet.

IV. WHAT IS A LOW PROFILE?

We have from time to time advised you to maintain a low profile. Some of you interpret this to mean: Stay at home. This is not the case. When we think you should stay at home we will say so in plain language. Low profile means: (A) Avoid areas of the city such as bazaars, mosques, universities, movie theatres, and restaurants. (B) Minimize time spent in supermarkets and banks. (C) Avoid large parties, public group activities, and tours.

V. WHAT IS ASHURA?

The month of Moharram which begins this year on December 2nd is the period of deep mourning by Shi'ite Moslems. It commemorates the martyrdom of Hassan and Hussein, grandsons of Mohammad and second and third Imams of the Shi'ites. Passion plays are given depicting the death of Hussein and mourning processions are held for the dead heroes. Two religious days occur during the Moharram: the eve of martyrdom of Imam Hussein (Tassua) and the day of his martyrdom. Both of these days are marked by increased observations of mourning. The procession of self-flagellation, where the faithful beat themselves with chains, occurs on the second day, Ashura. This period has always posed a danger to non-Moslems who happen to be in the way of the faithful. The faithful can be in a highly emotional state and have been known to attack others who cross their paths. It is also the time when Mullahs enjoy maximum authority.

Sigma will be advising you to remain at home for three evenings prior to Ashura, the entire day and evening of Ashura, and the evening after Ashura. This advisory is traditional and has nothing to do with current events.

This has been a long and perhaps arduous message. I hope, however, it has served its purpose of imparting information. I will be happy to attempt answers to other questions of general interest as I receive them.

We are in for difficult times, times which will require innovation, imagination, and cooperation among us all if we are to accomplish our job. I, for one, enjoy the stimulation of a challenge, and am confident that together we can all come out of it proud of ourselves and proud of what we have accomplished.

Alister Hunt, Vice President

In the last two weeks of November, the situation continued to intensify. Between November 20 and December 1, at least 600 demonstrators were killed. Tanks reentered Tehran for the first time since June on November 22. And from November 26 to 28, the Iranian economy came to a virtual standstill in the wake of a general strike called by Khomeini.

Besides the importance of Sigma's mission in Iran to U.S. foreign-policy interests, the tripartite decision-making arrangement and the fact that 40 percent of Sigma's business was with the U.S. government dictated that the company try to find a way to cope with the situation. This task meant at least addressing deficiencies in the evacuation plan mentioned by Hunt in his November 12 memo. To correct the transportation problem within Tehran, a secret fuel dump was built in the Sigma compound and filled or topped-out during night deliveries. Additionally, since approval from the Iranian government for a Sigma communication system had not been given, Hunt and U.S.-based management decided on their own course of action: Paul McGrath, U.S. Program Manager for the Iran operation, and two assistants left for Tehran on December 1 to assess the situation and to smuggle 12 walkie-talkies into the country. The entire evacuation plan depended on communications with and between each warden, and frequent telephone and power outages in Tehran had made that difficult to impossible.

While Hunt was contemplating his future options that memorable day of December 5, when the crisis really came home to him and his wife with that tank outside their front door, he learned of a disturbing incident that had occurred in Bushire the same day. Paul McGrath, while visiting the down-country site, had found his car on fire in the parking lot. The message he received was quite clear: Iran was now a very dangerous place for Sigma personnel. A U.S. government source, moreover, told Hunt that of 52,000 Americans in Iran at the beginning of the year, now only an estimated 28,000 were still in the country. Hunt somehow had to find a way to balance Sigma's business interests and obligations with the need to protect Sigma people. Corporate headquarters was obviously concerned with the situation. Paul McGrath's presence proved that. So did their weekly phone calls. Hunt's only orders were to keep the business going if at all possible. Decisions about whether business operations were untenable or too risky were basically Hunt's alone.

Exhibit 1 Iran.

Exhibit 2 *Sigma Newsletter*, June 1978, Tehran/Iran, Volume 4, Issue 6.

SIGMA'S SPECIAL GUESTS

On May 10th Sigma employees and their wives met at the recreation center for a reception to greet Paul McGrath, Sigma's Program Manager, and Mr. G. Burns, Vice President for Marketing at Huntsville, Alabama. Guests were also honored by the attendance of Major General Reisler, Commanding Officer of the U.S. Military Mission in Iran. He spoke to Sigma families and complimented them on their successful work in Iran.

Following the guest speakers, everyone adjourned to the buffet while Kent Griff, a member of the Bushire team, entertained them with a selection of country/western music. Inside there was dancing to lively taped music and congenial conversation among the guests.

SIGMA GRADUATES

The month of May is the end of another school year and, for some, a time to celebrate graduation. Sigma proudly extends its warm congratulations to the following children who graduated from kindergarten: Peg Dill and Berry McGill, Jr. from Golestan School, and Alex Jones from Piruzi School. Congratulations are also extended to our Tehran American High School graduates: Bill Mix, Steve Smith, Pat Best, and Charles Burt. We wish them the best of luck in their future endeavors.

NEW ARRIVALS

Congratulations are in order for the parents of the two youngest members of the Sigma family. Beth and Steve O'Grady are the parents of a 7 pound, 7 ounce baby boy born on the 17th of May. The baby has been named David O'Grady. Donald Martin Greene, Jr. is the 6-pound son of Dan and Bobby Greene. He was born on the 23rd of May.

SOCIALIZE

Manzarieh Scout Camp was the setting for the ladies' picnic, held on May 9th. The cool, clean mountain air was quite a contrast to the usual smog found in lower Tehran. Ladies were joined this month by three brave gentlemen, Steve Ducas, Bill McKnight, and Jeff Simms. Those men who are in Tehran on R & R are welcome to join these meetings. Linda Mitchell contributed a cake for the enjoyment of all. Next month, plans will be for cool drinks served at the recreation center. All ladies are encouraged to come.

TEHRAN SOFTBALL SEASON BEGINS

The softball season begins in Tehran and the Sigma men in red had really been putting their all into the games. The win-loss record looks a bit one-sided at this point in the season (0-5), although improvement can be seen in every game played. The players can be proud of their batting average which is around 500. What the players need now is a crowd of Sigma fans to root for them. Everyone interested should get in touch with Bill Mix to find out when the next game is being played. Sigma will provide transportation to the game if six or more people request it. So add your voice to the crowd and be at the next Sigma softball game!

SIGMA TEENS TO ISFAHAN

Approximately 150 local students journeyed to Isfahan to entertain students of Isfahan American School. Some of the students making the trip on May 8th were four Sigma dependents. Both Susan Mix and Charles Burt made the trip as members of the jazz band, which was a real crowd pleaser drawing a standing ovation in performing an encore. It was a tired but happy group that returned to Tehran at 4:30 p.m. on May 12th.

BUSHIRE BEACH PARTY

April 28 was such a beautiful day at Bushire that everyone on the Bushire crew was in a good mood (even Charlie)! A barbecue party has been planned at the nearby beach and Ray Walden, Kent Griff, and Dan Pool made up the advance crew to get the site ready for picnicing. The men left Bushire with two trash barrels full of supplies: one trenching tool, two Frisbees and a football early in the morning. Later they were joined by Billy Smith, Fred Dean, Jerry Malory, Jim Martinez, and Felix Santiago. The food was good, the sun was hot and lively entertainment was provided by Jim Martinez, who played the guitar while Felix Santiago did the Mexican hat dance.

That's all for now. We will be talking to you next month.

Occidental and Belco Petroleum in Peru (A)

It was a mild mid-October afternoon in 1985 when William West, country manager for Occidental, and Jose Timbre, country manager for Belco, sat in their respective offices pondering a recent government proclamation. Alan Garcia, the recently elected president of Peru, had reiterated his demand that Occidental and Belco renegotiate their oil contracts by November 30, 1985. The demands of the Garcia government were quite severe, requiring the companies to make substantial investments in exploration, while reducing profits and limiting their repatriation through tax increases and tighter regulatory controls. In fact, Garcia had recently banned all profit remittances by foreign oil companies, retroactive to August 28th, when Occidental's and Belco's old contracts were unilaterally rescinded. Since that time, moreover, all oil produced by the two companies had been retained by Petroperu, the state oil company, for a flat fee, and this arrangement would remain until a new contract was signed. Additionally, Garcia mandated that compensation be remitted to Peru for "past imperialist exploitation." The proposed changes would drastically impact future returns from Peruvian petroleum operations. Confronted by this hostile environment, West and Timbre faced similar alternatives:

1. Withdraw from Peru, securing the most favorable settlement possible.
2. Capitulate to Garcia's demands, and continue operating in Peru.
3. Negotiate a compromise agreement.
4. "Wait-out" Garcia's threats, risking expropriation.

Unfortunately, time was running out for the two managers. The decisions before them would not only have an effect on the companies they served, but also determine the future direction of their careers.

PERU: OIL IN HISTORICAL CONTEXT

Slightly less than twice the size of Texas, Peru is situated on the western horn of South America, just below the equator. Peru, straddling the Andes Mountains, was the historic center of the Incan Empire, whose influence is still evident in Peruvian society today. The mineral wealth of the Incas attracted the Spanish conquistadors in the early 1500s. Following Pizzaro's conquest, Peru was dominated, either politically or economically, by foreign concerns for more than four centuries. Even in the

This case was prepared by Bret Holden, Darden MBA '88, Roger Buehner, Darden MBA '89 and Associate Professor Charles R. Kennedy, Jr.

mid-1960s, U.S. firms accounted for over 10 percent of Peru's GNP and 55 percent of commodity exports (minerals, petroleum, and agricultural products), which were its primary source of foreign exchange. For years, however, the focus of development in Peru was targeted at mining and agricultural products instead of petroleum.

Although oil production lagged behind other sectors in growth, it was often a leader in controversy. In 1890, the International Petroleum Company (IPC), originally a British firm, first contracted to search for oil in Peru. IPC had purchased the La Brea and Parinas oil fields. In 1913, Standard Oil of New Jersey bought IPC, and with it, ownership rights to the Peruvian oil fields. Standard Oil was attracted to the purchase of IPC because of the extremely favorable tax concessions IPC had secured from Peru. Shortly after the acquisition was consummated, a dispute arose over these tax rates. The Peruvian government contended that the tax arrangement had been made under false pretenses and was therefore void. Peru demanded taxes be determined by current law, but after eight years of litigation and arbitration (and possibly unethical coercion), Standard Oil was granted a favorable agreement which nationalistic sentiment in Peru never fully accepted.

Standard Oil went on to enjoy 40 years of lucrative profitability with IPC in Peru. The majority of earnings was repatriated, which left, according to Peruvian officials, inadequate amounts for reinvestment in exploration. Thus, the agreement with IPC became an issue in nearly every presidential campaign that followed. Tensions came to a head in 1959 when IPC demanded and received an increase in the previously controlled gasoline price. At that time, IPC accounted for 57 percent of Peru's crude-oil production, 70 percent of refinery capacity (at Talara), and a virtual monopoly on retail gasoline sales.

Fernando Belaunde Terry, president from 1963 to 1968 and again from 1980 to 1985, had promised during his 1963 campaign to solve the IPC controversy within ninety days of taking office. Five years later, in August of 1968, the so-called "Act of Talara," an agreement between the Peruvian government and IPC, was signed. The negotiations had dragged on for so long because Belaunde had vacillated between the pressures of the U.S. government and the demands of Peru's Congress. The act had been written in response to the Peruvian Congress' declaration that IPC owed 45 years in back taxes and that the IPC fields were national reserves.

If the "Act of Talara" had been implemented, IPC would have turned over title to the Parinas and La Brea oil fields to the Empressa Petrolea Fiscal (EPF—the Peruvian state oil agency). In exchange, the government would have dropped a tax claim of US$144 million. In addition, the government had granted IPC a concession to operate the refinery at Talara as long as IPC bought EPF crude oil at specified prices.

The "Act of Talara" was never implemented due to an accusation made by the president of the EPF. The accusation claimed that Belaunde had concealed the last page of the agreement, which allegedly specified important currency concessions to IPC in purchasing EPF's crude oil. Although no proof was found to substantiate either side, the resulting scandal was enough to undermine Belaunde's presidency. Belaunde was arrested and exiled on October 3, 1968, by a small group of military leaders. The new military government quickly nationalized IPC and created Petroperu, which continues to manage IPC's former holdings as a state-owned company.

Throughout the 1970s, Petroperu assumed a more active role in the industry. At the same time foreign oil companies were invited to explore new fields in jungle areas of interior Peru. By 1971, in fact, 16 international firms had signed risk contracts but, of these, only Occidental found commercially viable fields. The other 15 companies allowed their exploration rights to revert back to Petroperu. By 1985 Petroperu accounted for 36 percent of all crude-oil production in Peru, with Occidental accounting for 49 percent. Occidental operated a wholly owned subsidiary in the northeast jungle and a joint venture with an Argentine firm, Bridas Exploraciones y Production SA, in a secondary recovery program in the old IPC fields along the northern coast. The only other foreign oil company in Peru, Belco, operated offshore fields near Talara and produced the remaining 15 percent of Peru's oil. Petroperu, on the other hand, operated in several locations around the country (see Appendix A and Exhibit 1). Despite its growing presence, Petroperu lacked both the capital and expertise in exploration to expand Peru's oil sector significantly; so it was forced to rely on foreign companies. This reliance had enabled Occidental and Belco to build profitable operations in Peru.

BELCO PETROLEUM

Belco Petroleum Corporation, now a wholly owned subsidiary of Houston Natural Gas (HNG)/Internorth, began exploring operations in Peru in 1959. Internorth Corporation, headquartered in Omaha, Nebraska, was concentrated in natural gas, but acquired Belco in August 1983 for diversification purposes. Internorth, in fact, had just acquired HNG in June 1985, after their acquisition of Belco two years earlier. While Belco was primarily an oil producer, HNG, like Internorth, focused on natural gas. Financial highlights for HNG/Internorth can be seen in Exhibit 2.

Belco was currently Peru's only offshore producer, sharing all oil produced with Peru on a 50–50 basis. Jose Timbre described Belco's past relationship with Peru as amiable. Prior to the IPC scandal, Belco was only the fifth largest foreign producer in Peru; however, when IPC's Talara refinery was nationalized, Belco was contracted to operate it in return for lucrative offshore exploration concessions. (The capacity of the Talara refinery in 1985 was 61,000 barrels per day (b/d); the country's other refinery was in Lima (La Pampillo) and had a capacity of 94,000 b/d, after an expansion by Technip of France in the mid-1970s. Both refineries were owned by Petroperu.)

Since Petroperu was unfamiliar with and technologically deficient in offshore exploration, Belco often negotiated from a position of strength. Mr. Timbre, however, was not sure if this remained a Belco advantage since many offshore platforms were already built, and new offshore oil finds were more uncertain relative to the jungle fields of the interior. Nevertheless, Belco had been actively exploring for new offshore fields in recent years and had spent considerable funds in the process (see Exhibit 3). But how President Garcia valued Belco's expertise and technology was uncertain, even though Belco's recovery techniques had allowed the offshore fields to remain highly productive over many years. For example, relative to an all-time-high production rate of 29,000 b/d, Belco's offshore fields were still yielding over 27,000 b/d in 1985.

Aside from its Peruvian operations, HNG/Internorth had mainly focused on North American operations, with very little international exposure. Exhibit 4 gives a geographic breakdown of HNG/Internorth's oil reserves and production. Recently, Belco had signed exploration agreements with Ecuador, Australia, and Indonesia, but Peru still constituted the overwhelming majority of its international operations. The operations in Peru contributed nearly $12 million to corporate profits in 1983, over $34 million in 1984, and over $24 million in 1985 (excluding corporate overhead and interest charges). Belco's assets in Peru also carried a book value of $400 million.

OCCIDENTAL PETROLEUM

Starting in 1957, Occidental's legendary chairman, Armand Hammer, had built the company from a small natural-gas producer into a major firm that had vigorously and successfully challenged the dominance of the so-called "Seven Sisters" of the petroleum industry (BP, Exxon, Gulf, Mobil, Royal Dutch/Shell, Socal and Texaco). Exhibit 5 provides some recent financial highlights. Occidental was well diversified, with interests in chemicals, agribusiness, meat packing, and an integrated oil business. Exhibit 6 shows Occidental's performance by industry.

William West, and the other managers of Occidental's foreign operations, were encouraged to continuously reassess political and economic risks in their countries. They were evaluated on performance—how they managed systematic and unsystematic risk. In essence, Hammer felt that uncertainties could be significantly reduced by active information gathering and analysis. Occidental's organizational structure also emphasized the importance of the international businesses, with foreign oil operations incorporated separately, reporting directly to the Chief Executive Officer. By 1985, Occidental managed large exploration and production operations in over 12 countries, including the politically volatile Libya, Pakistan, and China. Occidental's strategy involved acquiring profitable, well-managed companies which provided diversification, either within or outside the oil industry, while divesting itself of relatively unattractive operations. It had recently sold 50 percent of its Colombian operation to Shell to raise $1 billion in cash. Exhibit 7 illustrates the composition of Occidental's international oil operations (reserves, production, and contribution to earnings).

Occidental began exploring for oil in Peru in 1970 and did so in a very innovative way. As one author observed:

> The placidity of the international petroleum industry was jostled by the contract signed between Occidental Petroleum Corporation and Petroperu. Occidental received a service contract—in contrast with a concession, which implies that the private party obtains control over the operations—that included a 35-year exploration and production right on a 3-million-acre parcel and a commitment for a $50-

> million, 7-year development program. What was particularly innovative in the agreement was that Occidental would incur all of the exploration and production expenses and would pay no taxes; Petroperu would receive 50 percent of Occidental's production and would pay all taxes due from the operation. . . . Other foreign petroleum companies followed Occidental's lead, with the number of such contracts reaching 7 within a half year and 14 within 18 months.[1]

By investing aggressively in exploration during the 1970s, it had emerged as the largest producer in Peru; the company's jungle operations, however, had experienced constant declines in production, from over 100,000 b/d in 1981 to around 80,000 b/d in 1985. Occidental was very interested in exploring new jungle tracts in both the northeast and central regions. Indeed, the company had recently borrowed large sums from U.S. banks for investment in Peru, and these expansion plans were in part motivated by the fact that their Peruvian operations had recently been the company's most profitable oil venture worldwide. Peru was also viewed as having potentially rich fields in unexplored areas, which was the same conclusion reached by other major oil firms, particularly Royal Dutch/Shell, which had aggressively moved into Peru since 1981.

RECENT DEVELOPMENTS IN THE PERUVIAN OIL INDUSTRY

Peru gained oil self-sufficiency in early 1978 when a feeder pipeline connected Occidental's jungle fields with the Transandean pipeline that ran to the port of Bayovar near Talara. As a result, oil production in Peru increased 48 percent in one year, and oil exports soared from nil to 58,000 b/d in 1978. Nevertheless, with domestic consumption at 125,000 b/d in 1979 and expected to grow at an annual rate of 4 percent in the 1980s, Petroperu estimated that exploration investment between 1980 and 1985 would have to amount to $1 billion if oil self-sufficiency was to be maintained.

In spite of the need to attract foreign capital in these exploration efforts, the military government in late 1979 revised Peruvian oil laws to the detriment of foreign companies and justified these changes because of developments in international oil markets, particularly rapidly rising prices. At that time, new regulations replaced the "Peru Model Contract," which, for example, Occidental had signed in 1971 and which had twenty-seven years remaining. The law was changed to shift tax payments from Petroperu, which previously had paid the foreign company's bill after and out of the 50-percent split in production, to Occidental and Belco. The new tax rate would be 55 percent on income and 30 percent on remittances, meaning an overall tax rate of 68.5 percent.

By mid-1980, both Occidental and Belco had signed new contracts. After hard negotiating, the two companies convinced the new Belaunde government to make an exception to the tax rate by reducing it to 41 percent. In return Occidental

[1]George M. Ingram, *Expropriation of U.S. Property in South America,* (New York: Praeger Publishers, 1974), p. 80.

and Belco promised to increase exploration efforts. Nevertheless, the new contract still caused a reduction in the amount of oil each company received after all costs and tax obligations were met. Beforehand, the two companies had a net return of 30 percent of production; now Occidental's net return had been reduced to 9 percent, versus Belco's 12 percent.

Peru, moreover, failed to attract needed investment in oil exploration from other foreign companies. As a result, the government passed a new petroleum law in late 1980, which provided for a 40-percent tax credit for foreign oil income that was reinvested in Peru. This provision had an immediate impact. By the end of the year, Royal Dutch/Shell and Superior Oil had signed new risk contracts, followed by Belco and Hamilton International Oil in 1982 and a consortium led by Union Texas in 1984. All but Belco's offshore concession were for exploration in jungle areas. The Shell contract was particularly significant given A) the psychological impact of a "Seven Sister" reentering Peru, B) its large exploratory expenditures (estimated at $100 million from 1981 to 1984), and C) the announced discovery of a significant natural-gas and condensate field in 1984. The field was located in the south-central jungle between the departments of Ucayali and Cuzco, with reserves and production estimated at 10 trillion cubic feet and 100 million cubic feet per day, respectively. Shell was so encouraged by opportunities in Peru that the company signed a second risk contract in late 1984 for exploration rights in the southeast jungle near Bolivia. Occidental was reportedly negotiating with Peru to gain access to new tracts in the central jungle as well.

The tax credit provision seemed to have encouraged these new exploratory efforts. Favorable regulations, in fact, were particularly important in Peru because of the many obstacles to oil exploration in the country. These obstacles were geographic, historical, and political. Namely, Peru's rugged terrain in the most prospective areas were far from consuming and exporting regions. As a result, the costs of production in Peru were relatively high. At the same time, the exploratory failures of the early 1970s reminded companies that these high costs could go unrewarded. Superior Oil, in fact, spent $18 million on its first well, which proved to be dry in 1982. Lastly, the expropriations of Esso (IPC) in 1968 and Gulf in 1975 frightened many companies as well. Thus, Peru appeared to need significant tax and investment incentives if it wished to attract foreign oil companies into the country.

Even companies already in Peru, namely Occidental and Belco, insisted on favorable tax treatment if new exploratory efforts were to proceed with the greatest vigor. During 1984 and early 1985, for example, tax disputes between the companies and Peru were affecting the conclusion of new risk contracts and the continuation of exploratory programs in areas already under contract. These disputes centered on tax overpayments that flowed from the 1979 regulations, which required the prepayment of income taxes each month based on estimated sales. The system worked well enough in 1980 and 1981 when production and prices were rising, but problems of overpayment arose afterward when prices started to fall and when companies began to apply tax credits for reinvestment. These problems were compounded by the fact that reimbursement at the end of the year was calculated in Peruvian soles at the average exchange rate during the previous year, without taking into account subsequent depreciation. As a result, Occidental's claim for overpayment was around 2.7 million barrels of oil by the end of 1984, worth about $65 million, while Belco's claim was around 600,000 barrels.

In this legal environment, Petroperu convened an oil conference in March 1985 to convince Peruvian citizens and politicians that present laws were insufficient in attracting needed foreign capital. Petroperu noted that the country's proven reserves had declined steadily from 833 million barrels in 1981 to 696 million barrels in 1984. Relatedly, Peru's reserves-to-production ratio had dropped from twenty-eight years in 1975 to 9.6 years in 1984. At current levels of investment, Petroperu estimated that domestic demand would exceed production by 1989. To reverse these trends, oil investments would have to average $1 billion a year for the next ten years, with most of this money coming from foreign investors.

Petroperu noted that only changes in Peruvian law could attract these needed investment funds. They recommended the following:

1. Full cost recovery (cost of exploration and development will be recovered before taxes).
2. As a corollary, the tax credit program will be eliminated or modified.
3. Accelerated depreciation for a four-year period.
4. Accounting in U.S. dollars rather than soles.

Foreign oil companies that attended the conference—BP, Occidental, Pecten International, Royal Dutch/Shell, Sohio, Tenneco and Union Oil of California—generally applauded these proposals. Alan Garcia, APRA's candidate for president, also spoke at the conference and outlined an oil policy that was ambiguous but not totally opposed to Petroperu's; he proposed:

1. Laws that would recognize Peru's need for foreign capital and technology.
2. Elimination of the tax credit program, which he said was impossible to monitor in order to assure full compliance with actual investment.
3. The "possibility" of accelerated depreciation.
4. The need for a "common oil policy" between all Latin American countries.

A leader of APRA in the Peruvian Senate and a former finance minister, Dr. Javier Silva Ruete, however, was extremely hostile toward Petroperu's proposals at the conference. He opposed full cost recovery and tax credits because oil companies could not be trusted to provide factual information. He also rejected Petroperu's estimates for needed investment, saying that $500 million per year would be adequate. Such views would certainly have a great deal of influence on the future APRA government.

After being elected in June, Garcia subsequently moved against Occidental and Belco. On August 28th, the company's contracts were rescinded, and all their oil production was retained by Petroperu. Garcia, moreover, demanded that new contracts be signed within ninety days. For West and Timbre, deciding how to respond required not only an assessment of the oil industry, but of socioeconomic and political developments in Peru as well.

SOCIOECONOMIC AND POLITICAL DEVELOPMENTS IN PERU

Peru is comprised of three distinct geographic areas: the coastal plain, the mountains, and the jungle. Each area has its own "people," with separate customs, languages, and ways of life. Peru has been described as more heterogeneous than the United States. This cultural diversity has resulted in heightened social tensions. A number of factors magnify this problem. First, power and wealth are concentrated in the coastal plain, which enjoys the majority of governmental development assistance. Second, the Indians of the mountain and jungle regions are discriminated against, both politically and economically, by the Spanish-speaking occupants of the coastal plain. In fact, an estimated 46 percent of the population suffers from systematic and institutionalized discrimination by the state. Until recent changes in legislation, voters had to pass a literacy test in Spanish, alienating a majority of the Indian population. Lastly, the focus on the coastal plain, especially the capital city of Lima, has lead to rapid urbanization. In 1960, the urban population was estimated at 46 percent of the total population. By 1985, an estimated 67.7 percent of the 19.7 million total population was living in urban areas. As a result, the percentage of the workforce in agriculture dropped to 17 percent (1984) from 20 percent (1977). Even though the rate of urbanization has fallen from 5.3 percent during the 1960-to-1970 period to 3.9 percent per year since, Lima's population has swelled to over 5 million. This growth has overburdened the available infrastructure, resulting in expansive, primitive "shanty towns." The growing "shanty towns" have added to the unemployment problem and caused difficulties for the country in providing education, medical care, and basic social services.

Peru is a classic example of mismanaged Third World development. With its wealth of natural resources (minerals, oil, and coastal waters abundant with fish), Peru should have aggressively used its earnings from exported raw materials to finance the development of local industries, both for satisfying domestic demand and for exporting value-added goods. Unfortunately, manufacturing comprises only 20 percent of national production in 1983 (from a high of 27 percent in 1976), and as Table 1 illustrates, an even smaller percentage of exports.

Peru's failure to expand the manufacturing sector increased its dependence on the world economy, specifically commodity prices. Aside from this structural shortcoming, Peruvian growth was quite impressive during the 1960s and up to the mid-1970s. GDP grew at an average annual rate of 5.5 percent in real terms

Table 1 Export Composition (Percent)

	1965	1983
Fuels, Minerals, and Metals	45	69
Agricultural Products (Sugar, Coffee, Fishmeal)	54	17
Textiles	0	8
OTHER MANUFACTURING	1	5

through the period. This success should be tempered, however, by the high commodity prices and the strength of the economy in the United States, Peru's major trading partner.

Because of strong economic performance during the 1960s and early 1970s, and the discovery of additional oil fields, banks stood in line to lend money to Peru. Instead of expanding its industrial base with these funds, Peru, under military rule for much of this period, chose to improve its infrastructure as well as its armed forces. Dams, roads, hydro-electric plants, and municipal buildings were constructed. Even though these projects provided jobs initially, in the long term they produced no new jobs or products (other than electricity, which most homes cannot use anyway). The massive defense expenditures (Peru has the best-equipped Air Force and Navy—per capita—in Latin America) were also debilitating because they added no economic value.

Since the late 1970s, the Peruvian economy has deteriorated. Between 1980 and 1985, Peru's GDP fell in real terms at an annual average rate of 0.5 percent. In 1984, per-capita annual income was the equivalent of $882, the lowest in Latin America. After inflation had averaged 51 percent per year between 1975 and 1980, the average annual rate has increased to 102 percent during the 1980s. One result of the increase in inflation was that real wages in Lima dropped 25 percent during the period. In addition to shrinking real wages, approximately 400,000 jobs were lost. Exhibit 8 gives data on several macroeconomic indicators for Peru.

President Garcia has taken the following steps in an effort to solve the economic difficulties he inherited. The inti (In), Peru's new currency, was devalued and fixed at a new rate.[2] Similarly, prices and wages were raised and then frozen. Interest rates were reduced and foreign deposits frozen. Garcia hoped that these measures, and many other similar tactics, would dampen inflationary expectations and break the devaluation-inflation-higher-interest rates-devaluation cycle.

A problem that has Garcia's utmost concern is the country's plunging per-capita income. In 1985, the per-capita income had fallen near 1965 levels. A mere 2 percent of the country's population generates 60 percent of the wealth. At the opposite end of the scale, 38 percent of Peruvians struggle to survive on just 2 percent of the GDP. To remedy this inequity in income distribution, Garcia set out to curb speculation, so that investment funds would be channeled to more productive ventures. Limited fiscal austerity was also important to Garcia's plan, so that the gains made from declining inflation would not be lost. He also has attempted to nationalize all financial institutions in order to remove the powerbase of the wealthy. The owners of banks and other financial institutions have received a court order which has delayed their nationalization, but a slightly modified nationalization proposal is expected to be passed by the Congress shortly.

The goal of Garcia's economic program is to reactivate the economy through agriculture in order to promote a domestic market. In support of his program to build through agriculture, Garcia recently said, "We have no use for a

[2]The inti (In) had replaced the sol as the unit of exchange in February of 1985, at a rate of 1 inti for every 1000 soles. The In was pegged to the U.S. dollar at a rate of 13.945 In per dollar. In late 1985 the rate had not changed significantly; $1 was worth 13.943 In.

socks factory if millions of people don't wear shoes." He has instituted comprehensive price controls and increased wages. Over 200 products have been restricted from import availability. Garcia has also forced the renegotiation of many foreign contracts besides those of Occidental and Belco. It was too early to tell if Garcia's programs would pull Peru from the economic disaster of the 1980s; however, Garcia had support of the public and the Congress.

Politically, Peru is governed under a three-branch, bicameral system. The government operates under a constitution written in 1933. In spite of the constitution, the military has often wielded considerable influence in Peruvian politics. Exhibit 9 chronicles the volatility associated with the Peruvian political system in recent history. The most notable shift was the previously mentioned ousting of Belaunde in 1968. Belaunde was removed from office by General Juan Velasco. When Velasco's health failed in the midst of economic difficulties and rumored corruption, General Francisco Morales Bermudez replaced Velasco in 1975. Morales returned the government to civilian rule in 1980. In the elections of 1980, Belaunde, the man who had been deposed twelve years earlier, was elected president. In the next election, in June of 1985, Alan Garcia won the presidency.

Peru's political party organization is highly fragmented, with the exception of the American Popular Revolutionary Alliance (APRA), which has been in continuous existence since 1924. The military has traditionally been extremely conservative (with the exception of the left-leaning, Velasco-lead section of the officers' corps), while the APRA has anchored the political left-of-center (Social Democrats) position. Because of the diametrically opposed ideologies of the military and APRA, the military has worked to constrain, and occasionally dismantle, APRA's powerbase. More recently, Belaunde's Popular Action Party (AP) has successfully assumed the right-of-center (Conservative) position, with the backing of the military. The far left is comprised of a number of smaller groups, ranging from Leninists to Maoists to Castro-inspired Marxists espousing the violent doctrine of the guerrilla Che Guevara. Most recently, far-left activities crystallized in the "Shining Path" movement, whose stronghold was in the Indian-dominated province of Ayacucho in south-central Peru. The Shining Path advocated the overthrow of the "imperialist-backed puppet government." Its methods were extremely violent, attacking villages, police, public officials, and power stations. As Table 2 indicates, the number of political deaths in Peru has dramatically soared as a result of its activities.

The military was obviously concerned with this upsurge in leftist violence. Although there had not been a coup attempt since 1980, when the current political system was put in place, the military might intervene and cast the deciding vote if a coalition government could not be reached or national security was threatened.

President Garcia, as head of APRA, was inaugurated on July 28, 1985. He thus inherited a foundering economy, an ongoing guerrilla revolt, and a public

Table 2 Deaths from Political Violence

1981	1982	1983	1984
50	150	976	984

displeased with the ineffective former president, Fernando Belaunde Terry. Before this date, APRA had never been able to gain control of the government. The military had successfully opposed the APRA movement in the past. In fact, a military coup occurred in 1963 in order to prevent APRA's leader, Victor Raul Haya de la Torre, from gaining the presidency.

Garcia's election was not a complete surprise since APRA had been gathering strength and electoral support during the Belaunde presidency. In 1983, for example, APRA had made significant gains in the municipal elections, receiving 34 percent of the total vote. In the national elections of 1985, the 36-year-old Garcia received 53 percent of the vote in an election that involved five parties. This overwhelming victory for APRA forced the military to accept and support Garcia's presidency, at least initially.

In his inaugural speech, Garcia made several pronouncements: debt repayments would be limited to the equivalent of 10 percent of Peru's exports; he offered to hold peace talks with the Shining Path guerrillas; and, in the presence of six Latin American presidents, he made a bid for regional leadership. U.S. bankers are not overly disturbed by Garcia's tactics for debt repayment. Peru's economy is small and the $14 billion debt is insignificant when compared to the $103 billion and $96 billion owed by Brazil and Mexico, respectively. The only fear the bankers would have concerning Garcia's policy is its influence on the other debtor nations of Latin America.

The peace talks with the Shining Path were intended to put an end to the violence and counter the unpopular measures taken by the military to check the movement. Garcia immediately replaced the chief of the military's joint command to show he was serious about the peace talks. Garcia felt that if the talks were not effective, there would be more public support for the government if stronger action against the Shining Path were required in the future.

Garcia's bid for regional leadership upset many of the older and more seasoned leaders of Latin America, but at the same time he gained respect due to his stand against the U.S. banks. As one Chilean official said, it would be fantastic to do what Garcia is attempting—dictate the rules of the debt game. Garcia's move against international banks struck a responsive, nationalistic chord among most Peruvians.

President Garcia also took extreme measures to remove corruption from the government and to remedy what he felt was foreign exploitation. In addition to releasing the chief of his joint military command, Garcia fired 37 police generals, some of whom were allegedly connected to Peru's $800 million drug trade. He then began a campaign against drug trafficking. To remedy foreign exploitation, the oil-production contracts with Occidental and Belco were withdrawn and threats of expropriation were made. Nevertheless, Garcia claims to encourage foreign investment in general. He argues that the Occidental and Belco cases are unique, due to the tax concessions the oil companies had been given. The problem with the tax concessions, according to Garcia, was that they were difficult to monitor, and even if reinvestment took place, 95 percent of the benefits, amounting to hundreds of millions of dollars, was used to extract oil faster. So Peru had lost oil reserves, as well as tax revenues.

Garcia is well received by the working population. He is considered a qualified, hard-working leader by most politicians and the press. He is perceived as one who is truly committed to doing everything possible to remedy the problems which plague Peru. Garcia has tremendous popular appeal. The people enjoy his frequent appearances on the balcony of the palace and his unannounced appearances in the marketplaces of Lima. Housewives, moreover, are mesmerized by his wife and her high-fashion wardrobe. In addition, his four young daughters have stolen the hearts of all who see them as they accompany their father or play in the presidential palace.

Garcia's aggressive style has also won him a great deal of popularity; however, aside from increased wages, Garcia's political and economic plans were disquieting to the military. For instance, the removal of the head of the joint chiefs of the military was considered an extremely unpopular move by most military leaders. The military had been a beneficiary of the Belaunde regime. Now, Garcia is opposed to an arms buildup, and his anti-American rhetoric may threaten the military aid that the United States had given in the past.

THE CURRENT SITUATION FOR OCCIDENTAL AND BELCO

In late August 1985, Garcia suspended Occidental's and Belco's operating agreements. The previous contract had stipulated that the oil companies pay a "royalty" of 50 percent of their production, which went to Petroperu, and then pay taxes on profits generated from the remaining 50 percent. Garcia had given the companies 90 days to sign new contracts with the following conditions:

- The tax rate of 68 percent would be restored.
- Tax credits would be eliminated.
- Peru was to be compensated for the past improprieties resulting from earlier, illegal contracts.
- Exploration expenses would not be deductible.
- Foreign firms would be paid a per-barrel fee instead of sharing in production.
- Occidental and Belco must spend several hundred million dollars on exploration over the next four years.
- Royalties and service fees would be suspended indefinitely.

Many observers felt that the primary target of these demands was Occidental, although Belco was certainly at danger as well. As the *Oil and Gas Journal* noted in early September, Garcia's demand for a new contract

> apparently holds true for Belco, although to a lesser extent, because the company's tax overpayment and resulting use of tax credits was less than Oxy's. In addition, Belco has a fairly extensive exploration program in Peru.[3]

Nevertheless, both managers feared the prospect of expropriation, even though Petroperu's new president assured them privately that the government had no

[3]*Oil and Gas Journal,* September 9, 1985, p. 70.

plans to seize their assets in spite of their contracts being rescinded. Moreover, West and Timbre were very concerned about the severity of Garcia's contractual demands. If they decided to remain in Peru, operations would be less lucrative and more tightly controlled by the government; however, if they chose to withdraw, worldwide sales and profits would suffer. It was each manager's job to assess the tradeoffs between the various alternatives and make a detailed recommendation to his corporate operating committee. Whatever recommendation was made had to address the following political risk issues. How stable was the Garcia government? If Occidental and Belco did strike a deal with Garcia, how politically viable would the agreement be? Also, what was the probability of expropriation regardless of whether an agreement with Garcia was negotiated?

Appendix A Occidental and Belco in Peru

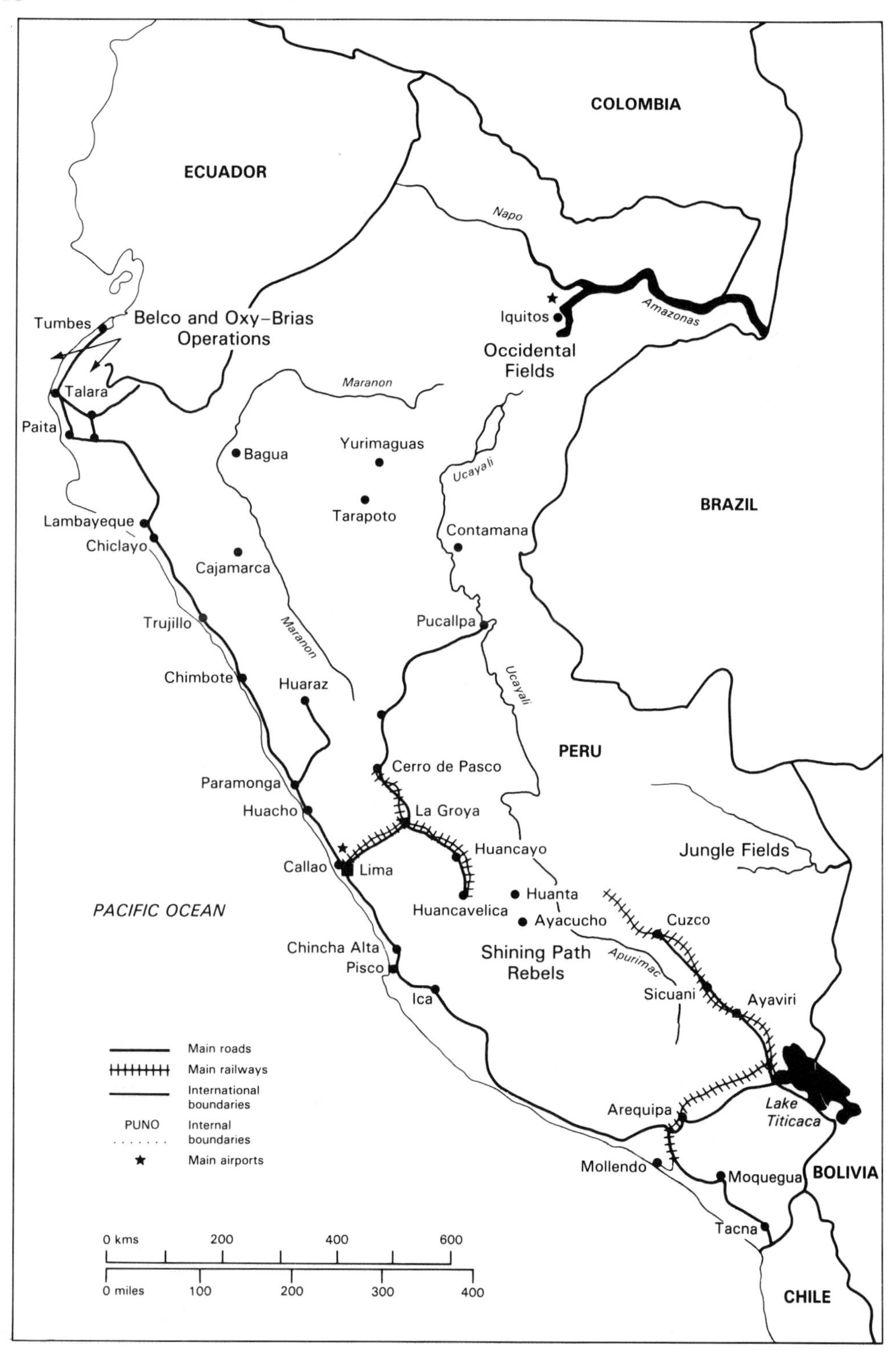

Exhibit 1 Oil Production in Peru (barrels daily)

Company	1982	1983	1984	1985
Petroperu				
North Coast	24,465	15,634	21,510	26,537
North jungle	27,965	30,961	30,790	40,538
Central jungle	862	845	800	734
Sub-total	53,292	47,440	63,100	67,809
Contractors				
Oxy-Bridas (North coast)	18,712	13,222	10,895	10,889
Occidental (North jungle)	95,914	86,032	84,105	82,210
Belco (offshore)	27,643	24,413	25,900	27,553
Sub-total	123,557	110,445	120,900	120,652
Total production	195,561	171,107	184,000	188,461

Exhibit 2 HNG/Internorth Financial Highlights

(000,000s)	1982	1983	1984	1985
Sales	3,980	4,580	7,300	10,253
Net Income	135	233	297	(14.1)
Total current assets	1,186	1,554	2,371	2,256
Total Assets	3,955	5,010	6,120	9,893
L/T Assets	952	1,056	1,116	2,294
Total current liabilities	1,064	1,368	2,253	4,764

Exhibit 3 Peru: Investment in Oil Exploration and Development (millions of U.S. $)

Foreign Contractors	1980	1981	1982	1983	1984
Belco	22.7	77.9	74.1	70.4	66.4
Occidental	80.3	159.7	178.5	122.1	68.5
Oxy-Bridas	150.9	141.4	62.6	5.0	6.6
Others	—	12.7	35.0	60.0	40.0
Sub-total	253.9	391.7	350.2	257.5	181.5
Petroperu	45.1	116.8	170.8	156.3	214.3
Total	299.0	508.5	521.0	413.8	395.8

Source: Petroperu

Exhibit 4 Belco's Proven Reserves and Production by Country

	U.S.	Peru	Canada	Total
Reserves:				
Natural Gas (mmcf)*				
1983	906	94.4	57.3	1057.7
1984	940	90.3	62.5	1092.8
Crude Oil (million bbls)				
1983	17.5	61.3	5.3	84.1
1984	20.1	61.1	5.1	86.3
Production:				
Natural Gas (mmcf/day)*				
1983	88.5	3.8	4.4	96.7
1984	133.7	11.8	10.6	156.1
1985	235.2	10.8	11.1	257.1
Crude Oil (000 bbls)				
1983**	1390.0	1870.0	240.0	3500.0
1984	2580.0	4870.0	650.0	8100.0
1985	2500.0	3450.0***	735.0	7635.0

*(mmcf = million cubic feet)

**Production only since Belco acquisition in August.

***Production only before Peruvian contract rescinded in August.

Exhibit 5 Occidental's Financial Highlights

(000,000s)	1982	1983	1984	1985
Sales	17,717	19,686	16,009	15,479
Net Income	156	869	962	975
Total current assets	5,362	2,645	3,352	2,973
Total Assets	15,773	11,775	12,273	11,586
L/T Debt	4,128	2,684	3,775	3,750
Total current liabilities	4,813	2,569	2,367	2,469

Exhibit 6 Occidental's Performance by Sector

	Oil and Gas				
1983 (000,000s)	**Expl & Prod.**	**Mktg & Trans.**	**Chem.**	**Agi Bs.**	**Coal**
Revenues	5,166	6,111	1,704	6,186	509
Net Income	563	283	(38)	78	(17)
Cap. Expend.	687	10	74	54	19
1984 (000,000s)					
Revenues	4,967	2,241	1,645	6,616	540
Net Income	898	(6)	76	34	(40)
Cap. Expend.	625	0	116	48	35
1985 (000,000s)					
Revenues	4,862	1,943	1,621	6,510	543
Net Income	821	8	91	52	3
Cap. Expend.	715	0	124	51	36

Exhibit 7 Occidental Reserves and Production

Oil Reserves (000,000s of bbls) **Region**	**1982**	**1983**	**1984**	**1985**
United States	275	242	263	261
Latin America*	190	167	285	318
Canada	17	0	0	0
North Sea	155	164	137	126
Libya	367	342	312	222
TOTAL	1,004	915	997	927
Production (000,000s of bbls) *Region*				
United States	31	30	29	n/a
Latin America*	28	26	24	n/a
Canada	2	0	0	n/a
North Sea	35	32	30	n/a
Libya	23	23	18	n/a
TOTAL	119	112	101	—

Oil and Gas Sales (000,000s of $)	1983		1984	
	Lat. Am.*	Total	Lat. Am.	Total
Revenues	641	3,856	575	3,540
Net Income	59	435	80	534

*Peru accounted for 45 percent of Reserves, 65 percent of Production, and 80 percent of Net Income from Latin American Operations

Exhibit 8 Peru's Macroeconomic Indicators

Trend of GDP

Total:	1981	1982	1983	1984	1985
(mm In)*					
Nominal GDP	8,520	14,183	26,315	58,710	159,259
Real GDP**	348	351	309	324	339
Percent Real Growth	3.0	0.9	−12.0	4.8	8.5
Per Capita:					
Nominal GDP	479	779	1,407	3,057	8,084
Real GDP**	19.6	19.3	16.5	16.8	16.8
Percent Real Growth	0.4	−1.8	−14.5	1.8	—

*Millions of Intis (Peru's unit of exchange)

**Based on 1970 prices.

Expenditure on GDP at 1970 Prices

(mm In)

	1980	1981	1982	1983	1984	1985
Private Consumption	233	240	236	213	219	224
Gov't Consumption	43	42	45	41	37	39
Gov't Capital Formation	25	31	33	29	29	22
Gross fixed Private Capital Formation	30	36	34	21	20	19
Change in Stock	2	6	3	−4	−1	0.1
Exports	59	57	63	55	58	61
Imports	−54	−64	−62	−48	−37	−34

Total may not equal above GDP total due to rounding

Index of Prices and Wages

(1979 = 100)

	1980	1981	1982	1983	1984	1985
Annual Percent Change in Consumer Prices	60.8	72.7	72.9	125.1	111.5	158.3
Salaries[a]	111.9	116.0	117.0	98.4	92.6	85.5
Wages[b]	112.5	106.8	106.8	84.0	73.9	60.2

[a]Taken in November of each year, for Lima only.

[b]Taken in October.

Exhibit 9 Leaders of Peru (1963–85)

President	Years	Party	Political Fate
Belaunde	63–68	AP	Deposed by military due to alleged scandal.
Velasco	68–75	Military (Nationalist)	Illness and economic problems led to a bloodless coup.
Morales	75–80	Military	Returned Peru to civilian control.
Belaunde	80–85	AP	Economic downturn and political violence resulted in electoral defeat.
Garcia	85–	APRA (leftist)	Current president.

3

MANAGING INTERNATIONAL NEGOTIATIONS

Incidents of classic expropriation have dramatically decreased during the 1980s, but at the same time, adverse intervention by host governments against specific multinational corporations has increased and taken many different forms, such as localization measures, demands for technology transfers, local content regulations, foreign exchange controls, adverse trade policies, and expatriate employment restrictions. These forms of intervention, moreover, are usually associated with a negotiation process, in terms of both the adoption and implementation of these various measures and regulations.

In this changing environment, two of the traditional approaches to political risk management have become less useful. For example, avoidance as a political risk strategy can be counterproductive when applied to the new set of intervention risks, since the countries most likely to implement adverse regulations and controls are also the biggest, most attractive markets. In addition, political risk insurance, an effective hedge against expropriation, is less effective in protecting the firm against the newer, more subtle forms of intervention. Disputes, for instance, can arise between the insurer and the firm over claims since present-day intervention risks are harder to define and measure. Because of these difficulties and the pervasiveness of such interventions, the cost of political risk insurance has risen as well.

Multinational corporations, therefore, must find better ways to manage micro, legal-governmental risks. In the late 1960s and 1970s, extralegal risks predominated, particularly in the form of extensive expropriations that were associated with political instability. This earlier era of confrontation has now been replaced by an era of negotiations, which means that the new forms of intervention risk can be better managed through a give-and-take bargaining process. As a result, bargaining power analysis and concepts are key ingredients in current approaches to political risk management. For Yves Doz and C. K. Prahalad, this describes the political risk strategy of "counteractive" response, when the firm stresses the management of "its bargaining power vis-a-vis the host government in order to gain some competitive advantages against other multinationals."[1]

Bargaining power analysis has long been recognized as important for the management of government relations.[2] Only recently, however, has empirical research of a large number of companies confirmed and clarified its importance. Interestingly, Nathan Fagre's and Louis Wells' quantitative study of 178 companies in Latin America reached conclusions that mirrored those of Thomas Poynter, who qualitatively examined 104 firms in three African and one Asian country.[3] Certain factors were seen to increase a multinational's bargaining power in both studies. These factors were the operational and managerial complexity of the subsidiary, the extent of technological innovation in the firm as a whole, the presence of significant export sales by the subsidiary, and the degree to which the subsidiary's operations are globally integrated with the rest of the corporation. Poynter also saw more politically proactive firms as being able to negotiate less adverse government intervention.

Other factors, however, decreased a firm's bargaining power, such as the presence of corporate competitors in the same industry and firm size. The larger the subsidiary, the more politically sensitive and visible it was to host government intervention. Relatedly, Poynter also found strategic industries (natural resources, infrastructure, petrochemical and steel) to be more vulnerable to adverse government policies because of their political sensitivity. Many of these conclusions, moreover, were recently supported by research undertaken by Donald Lecraw in Asia.[4]

A major limitation of these studies is that they are overly focused on the characteristics and behavior of the firm. Government and country considerations should also be included in a bargaining power analysis. Obviously, the more attractive a country is, due to natural resources, market size and growth, infrastructure supports or export potential, the more bargaining power a host government has. One should consider the character of government negotiators as well. If there is disunity within the government concerning how multinationals in an industry should be regulated, then the firm's bargaining position may be enhanced. The same is true for the stability of the government, for if the prospects for a military coup or electoral change is high, the bargaining power of current government negotiators may be reduced. Conversely, if the firm perceives those conditions as leading to aggressive behavior against multinationals, the reverse could be true; that is, an unstable and divided government could erode a firm's bargaining power if certain perceptions about their consequences take hold and are known to the other side. Certainly, the importance of perceptions and how they are managed cannot be overly stressed when conducting negotiations. Lastly, the competence of government leaders and negotiators should be considered. Since the competence and technical skills of most governments have dramatically increased over time, political leaders worldwide have turned more to the new forms of intervention, which places a premium on good negotiation skills.

In approaching negotiations, five general principles should be followed.

As already mentioned, one should make an objective assessment of bargaining power; it might also be useful to make a separate calculation of the stakes each side has in the negotiations. In other words, what do the negotiating parties stand to lose if a mutually acceptable agreement is not reached? Second, negotiations should be rarely approached with the attitude of "beating" or "dominating" the other side. Negotiations, of course, imply a certain degree of conflict between the two parties, but for an agreement to be reached, a good deal of cooperation and conciliation is usually required. Third and relatedly, one must try to empathize with the other side. This is important not only to maximize one's chances of reaching win-win solutions, but for tactical reasons as well. Particularly in international business negotiations, cultural and language misunderstandings often arise, and those causes of failed negotiations can best be avoided by knowing how the other side typically thinks and acts. Fourth, a better understanding of one's negotiating adversary will also allow one to plan negotiation tactics on a contingency basis. Interdependent decision making is crucial. Lastly, public confrontations should be avoided in most cases. Informal, behind-the-scenes bargaining is the more effective approach, for it reduces the impact of politically motivated opinions and allows negotiators more room for face-saving compromises.

Being an effective international negotiator is increasingly important. It requires timely responses, strategic thinking, adaptability, perseverance and cultural sensitivity. Many of these qualities are instinctive, but awareness of them and practice can improve one's negotiating skills. Certainly, such skills are crucial in the successful management of the modern, international corporation.

NOTES

1. Yves L. Doz and C. K. Prahalad, "How MNCs Cope with Host Government Intervention," *Harvard Business Review,* 48 (March-April 1980), pp. 152–153.
2. Raymond Vernon, *Sovereignty at Bay,* (New York: Basic Books, 1971), pp. 26–59.
3. Nathan Fagre and Louis T. Wells, Jr. "Bargaining Power of Multinationals and Host Governments," *Journal of International Business Studies,* 12 (Fall 1982), pp. 9–23; and Thomas A. Poynter, "Government Intervention in Less Developed Countries: The Experience of Multinational Companies," *Journal of International Business Studies,* 13 (Spring/Summer 1982), pp. 9–25.
4. Donald J. Lecraw, "Bargaining Power, Ownership, and Profitability of Transnational Corporations in Developing Countries," *Journal of International Business Studies,* 15 (Spring/Summer 1984), pp. 35–41.

Honeywell in France (A)

In November 1981, Edson Spencer, chairman and chief executive officer of Honeywell, Inc., was contemplating the start of negotiations between Honeywell and St. Gobain, the two principal joint-venture partners in CII-Honeywell Bull (CII-HB). Spencer had become increasingly pessimistic about the general business climate in France since the election of Socialist Party leader Francois Mitterrand to the presidency in May 1981; however, he had also been recently informed by high French government officials that Honeywell's role in the Bull joint venture could yet be rewarding. This was possible in spite of the fact that St. Gobain was being nationalized and that the role of Honeywell in the joint venture would have to change as a result. Given these recent conversations, Spencer decided to explore the possibility of a mutually beneficial relationship through negotiations.

In this context, a number of questions were weighing on Spencer's mind: What should Honeywell's negotiating strategy be? What were the relative bargaining strengths between Honeywell and the French side? What were the intentions and options of French government officials, who were always in the background behind St. Gobain? How should Honeywell's negotiation effort be organized and what should its negotiating tactics be? Answers to these questions required analysis of Bull's importance to and position within Honeywell, the history of the computer industry in France, and the backgrounds of the individuals involved in the actual negotiations.

HONEYWELL, INC.

Honeywell was formed as the Minneapolis Honeywell Regular Co., after a 1927 merger between Minneapolis Heat Regular Co. and Honeywell Heating Specialties Co. (Its present name was adopted in 1964.) Originally, therefore, Honeywell was a specialist in thermostatic controls. Over time and through subsequent acquisitions, Honeywell broadened its activities into measuring instrumentation, pneumatic controls and avionics. Control systems, however, remained its core business, comprising 46 percent of total sales and 59 percent of total profits as the company moved into the 1980s. Edson Spencer and past Honeywell chairmen, in fact, had all been the previous heads or executive vice presidents of Honeywell Control Systems.

Diversification into the computer business started in 1955 and was furthered by the 1965 acquisition of Computer Control Company. International activity followed immediately afterward with the formation of Honeywell Europe in 1966. Computers or information processing systems remained a minor part of Honeywell, however, until the 1970 purchase of General Electric's Information Systems Equipment Division. Nevertheless, Honeywell Information Systems (HIS) never surpassed control systems in relative sales or profits. As the company entered the 1980s, computers and information systems comprised 34 percent and 32 percent of sales and profits, respectively. Increasingly, however, Honeywell saw a major area of future competitive strength as being based in the synergy between control and computer systems, with one of the main battlefields focused on the rapidly growing office automation market.

BACKGROUND OF THE COMPUTER INDUSTRY IN FRANCE: PRE-CII-HB

CII-HB had its roots in a French computer company called Compagnie des Machines Bull (CMB), which started as a small punch-card machine producer in the 1930s. By the late 1950s, CMB had become a relatively large and prosperous computer firm, with an average annual increase in sales of 25 percent between 1953 and 1960. In fact, by 1960 CMB employed 11,000 workers, making it one of the top 30 employers in France, and held about one-third of the French computer market, which was the largest share of any domestic firm. CMB also held about 10 percent of the computer market in Western Europe. CMB was such a success and stimulus to French national pride that it was often called "the Brigitte Bardot of French industry."

During the early 1960s, however, serious problems for CMB began to emerge, most notably the challenge posed by International Business Machines (IBM), who, along with other U.S.-based computer firms, expanded very rapidly in Europe during the post-World War II period. IBM in particular offered European computer customers new, technologically advanced mainframes that CMB lacked. In response, CMB had no choice but to develop a "state of the art" mainframe in order to compete with the Americans. Such product development, however, was difficult to achieve technologically and was enormously expensive.

These obstacles to product development were greatly aggravated by CMB's relationship with the French "Gaullist" government. CMB was largely a family-owned-and-managed corporation that had had strong ties to the Vichy government during World War II. As a result, the French government under the leadership of Charles de Gaulle refused to give CMB any financial support or special development contracts. In fact, several large loans to CMB that required Ministry of Finance approval were turned down during the early 1960s, a time in which research-and-development capital was critical. In order to survive in an increasingly competitive world, CMB was forced to look for other sources of capital.

General Electric had decided to enter the computer market in 1959 and began selling computers in France via limited export sales in 1962. Given GE's general lack of experience internationally, particularly in the computer business, the company preferred to expand its operations in Europe through acquisitions or joint ventures with established firms. GE had offered to buy a 20-percent equity position in CMB in 1962 at the prevailing market price, along with promises of massive financial and technical support. CMB initially refused, but by the end of 1963, CMB's competitive position relative to IBM had deteriorated to such an extent that negotiations with GE were renewed. An agreement that largely duplicated the 1962 offer was then reached.

Before the deal could be consummated, however, Ministry of Finance approval, which in actuality meant President Charles de Gaulle's approval, was needed. The French president's decision, which came in early 1964, was an emphatic rejection of an "American solution" to CMB's problems, primarily because computers were perceived to be a vitally important strategic industry. Of course, de Gaulle was also generally concerned with the growing American business presence in Europe, which he felt was aided by the U.S. government's international monetary policies, but he was particularly angered by the U.S. government's recent embargo of computer sales to the French military-nuclear industry. In other words, U.S. business dominance of the computer industry had political-military implications that de Gaulle was unwilling to accept.

CMB was then forced to try a "French solution" by increasing its ties to domestic banking and electronic firms. This attempt proved futile, however, since French banks refused to back CMB with the funds it needed because of the company's weak financial and technological position. As a GE negotiator observed:

> They [CMB] felt that even if necessary financing were forthcoming from French sources, this still wouldn't have been enough to make the company safe in the face of the onslaught of IBM competition. They had to have some stronger backing than that.[1]

CMB still needed the capital and technical support that only a major firm like GE could offer.

By April 1964 the French government had apparently come to the same conclusion; it completely reversed the earlier decision, which it had termed "irrevocable" and now accepted "in principle" a GE-CMB joint venture. During the summer of 1964, a final agreement was struck and approved by the French government on terms much more favorable to GE than before. Instead of a 20-percent minority equity share, GE purchased 51 percent of the marketing and 49 percent of the manufacturing arms of GE-Bull (two separate corporate entities were created) for a price that was 25 percent less per share than had been offered six months earlier. Such a corporate structure and equity share were very much to the advantage of GE, for the company was mainly interested in CMB's extensive European marketing network (as was Honeywell six years later). Most of GE's computer manufacturing and product development would be centered in Phoenix, Arizona. As one GE executive stated about the 1964 merger:

> The main point is that we are acquiring a first-class distribution system. We will integrate production and distribution to make the best use of the strengths of both companies.[2]

In spite of favorable entry terms, GE's computer business in France, and worldwide, did not prove very successful. Between mid-1964 and early 1967, for example, GE invested around $200 million in Bull's operations. Each and every quarter in that time period showed negative operating profits. GE's reaction was retrenchment: Headquarters recommended a 25-percent reduction in Bull's labor force, or the layoff of 2,500 workers, and the dropping of the Gamma 140 computer line, which had been designed by CMB before the GE merger. French protests over "foreign domination" ensued and were aggravated by a renewed U.S. computer embargo to the French nuclear industry. The French government reacted to these developments by announcing that it no longer considered GE-Bull even a quasi-French computer firm (in fact, GE now held 66 percent of Bull equity as a result of capital contributions in the 1964–1967 period) and thus GE-Bull would no longer receive preferential treatment in government purchases or research-and-development assistance. Labor and product cuts were also implemented by the fall of 1967, and it was in this atmosphere that William R. Hart became managing director of Bull's operations.

GE-Bull's retrenchment policy proved financially successful under Hart's management. By 1969, Bull reported its first net profit, $650,000. Nevertheless, GE finally decided in February 1970 that the company should withdraw from the computer business worldwide and focus its resources on nuclear, jet engine, and other "core" electrical products instead. Although GE's chairman denied it, IBM simply proved to be too strong a competitor to warrant the risks and massive capital infusions required in the computer industry.

By May 1970, GE and Honeywell announced what many analysts regard as a "textbook" merger. It combined GE's mainframe technology and European marketing network with Honeywell's compatible computer line and management experience. Together, GE's and Honeywell's computer businesses held a 10-percent worldwide market share, making it the "undisputed No. 2" behind IBM. In France, Honeywell Bull had around 20 percent of the market versus IBM's 52 percent. Of course, French government approval was needed for the Honeywell arrangement. Such approval was quickly given after Honeywell agreed to merge much of its other European operations into Bull's orbit. In fact, such a merger was gladly accepted by Honeywell because Bull's marketing and manufacturing network dwarfed what Honeywell already had in place within the Common Market.

In October 1970 the GE and Honeywell merger was finalized with the creation of Honeywell Information Systems (HIS), 81.5 percent owned by Honeywell and 18.5 percent by GE. (GE's 18.5 percent was to be sold to Honeywell by 1980, which in fact occurred.) HIS represented the entire computer operations of both Honeywell and GE and included HIS's 66-percent ownership of Honeywell Bull.

HIS quickly proved a financial success. As Honeywell's *1971 Annual Report* stated:

> Earnings of the company were up 12 percent on a sales increase of 1 percent. . . Improved earnings in our worldwide computer business contributed significantly to this performance. This was due in part to the fact that we have begun to realize the benefits we foresaw in merging GE's computer operations with ours.

HIS revenue in 1971 had climbed to $950 million or 47 percent of total Honeywell revenue, versus a premerger (1969) level of $763 million in computer-related sales and revenue, which was only 24 percent of the corporate total. Over half of 1971 HIS revenues, moreover, came from foreign computer operations, primarily those of Honeywell Bull. The French joint venture, in fact, marketed over half of its production in 38 countries outside France. Clearly Honeywell had taken a huge step toward establishing a major multinational presence. As Honeywell's *1970 Annual Report* stated:

> We stepped up our evolution as an international company through the merger. We now employ 42,000 people outside of the United States (versus under 20,000 before 1970) and our volume there was $662 million or 34 percent of total sales (versus under 20 percent in premerger years). About two-thirds of the computer operations that we acquired from GE are (in fact) overseas.

The internationalization of Honeywell continued to bear fruit in subsequent years, although the recession years of 1974 and 1975 crimped sales and earnings for HIS and Honeywell in general, as revealed in Tables I and II. It was within this financial backdrop that intensive negotiations concerning the future status of Honeywell Bull took place in France during 1975.

During the 1960s, in conjunction with the falling out between the French government and GE-Bull, another "national champion" in the computer industry had been created, Compagnie Internationale pour l'Informatique (CII). The French government had merged three small computer firms and provided CII massive infusions of capital and preferential purchases in the hope of challenging the American multinationals. By 1973 the effort was clearly faltering, as CII had not gained above 10 percent of the French market. There was some discussion within the Gaullist government of President Pompidou to merge CII with Honeywell Bull, but an "all-European solution" was attempted instead. Consequently, with government prodding, CII in mid-1973 formed a French-German-Dutch combine called Unidata, with Siemens of Germany and Philips of Holland as partners.

Unidata did not meet French expectations or interests. CII sold virtually no machines in its partners' home countries, while Siemens and Philips made substantial inroads into the French market. As a result, the French government withdrew from Unidata and negotiated a merger of CII and Honeywell Bull by mid-1975, thus effectively ending the attempt for an all-European solution.

Table 1 Total Revenue (millions of $)

	1972	1973	1974	1975
HIS	1061	1177	1233	1324
Percent Increase over Previous Year	12	11	5	7
Honeywell, Inc.	2125	2391	2626	2760
Percent Increase over Previous Year	9	13	10	5
HIS Percent of Total	50	49	47	48

Table 2 Earnings Before Taxes (millions of $)

	1972	1973	1974	1975
HIS	54	75	53	57
Honeywell, Inc.	169	209	188	173
HIS Percent of Total	32	36	28	33

(Sources: Honeywell, Inc., *10-K Annual Report,* 1973, p. 8; *10-K,* 1974, 1975, pp. 9–11.)

Honeywell's *1975 Annual Report* listed the benefits of this agreement: (1) a substantial increase in its share of the French computer market from around 20 to 25 percent; (2) French government subsidies of $270 million over four years; (3) French government promises of preferential purchases totaling $1 billion; and (4) a $58 million payment to Honeywell for decreasing its equity share from 66 to 47 percent in the newly merged company, which represented a net gain of $14.8 million.

Other benefits, which the *1975 Annual Report* did not mention, were significant as well. Honeywell retained certain specific management rights, including a veto power over capital increases, mergers, acquisitions, and other significant investments. Honeywell also had the right to appoint the chief executive officer, although the managing director would, by subsequent practice, always be a French national. In addition, Honeywell obtained a comprehensive set of security guarantees designed to protect the value of its equity share, namely a French legal commitment to buy Honeywell's 47 percent in CII-HB at book value in the event of nationalization. This provision was particularly important because in the 1974 presidential elections, Francois Mitterrand had campaigned for the nationalization of the French computer industry and lost by only 400 thousand votes. The concept of a common product line was also agreed to and would be implemented by a Technical Committee, the chairmanship and majority of which were assigned to Honeywell. Common product line development was augmented by a royalty-free, cross-licensing agreement and by a "mirror-image" distribution system arrangement in which each party agreed to market each other's products based on the present status quo. From the view of Honeywell and the French government, the result of this merger was a big plus for both parties.

THE PRE-1981 HISTORY OF CII-HB: FINANCES, PRODUCT DEVELOPMENT, AND POLITICS

As the 1975 negotiations were under way, Bill Hart, the old managing director of the GE-Bull joint venture in the late-1960s, was lured away from GE to become HIS's senior vice president. One of his principal responsibilities was to oversee CII-HB relations.

Financially, CII-HB's performance and importance to HIS are reflected in Tables III and IV.

Table 3 Selected Financial Records of CII-HB (millions of $)

	1976	1977	1978	1979	1980
Net Assets	230	250	293	354	450
Total Revenue	655	765	1486	1215	990
Net Income	8.5	5.6	21.1	29.9	32.4

(Sources: Honeywell, Inc. *Annual Reports,* 1977–80.)

Moreover, Honeywell's earnings per share rose $1.60 in 1980. As Edson Spencer, Honeywell's chairman and CEO noted, "In 1980 our equity share in the French company's operating profit increased Honeywell earnings by $1.45 per share."

In the area of product development, a major dissimilarity between HIS and Bull was found in the large-scale mainframe business (memory capacity of over one million bytes or at least one megabyte). Bull's large mainframes were based on the old CII's Iris 80 line, which was a product development undertaken during Unidata days. As a replacement for the Iris 80, Bull was developing two new large mainframes, the so-called Y4 and Y5. These two large-scale systems, however, were viewed as a halfway state in the project to develop a completely common product line between HIS and Bull by the mid-1980s. Of course, politically and commercially, this temporary dissimilarity was seen as necessary. In the interim, however, potential product competition existed between Bull's large mainframes and HIS's.

At the medium-scale mainframe level, similar differences between HIS and Bull were present. Bull was the sole manufacturer of the Level 64 line, which had a memory size of between 192K bytes and 768K bytes, depending on the particular model. HIS produced instead a Level 66 line of machines that had a memory size that started at the upper end of the Level 64 but reached a top capacity of four megabytes. (The Level 66 thus included large-scale and medium-size mainframes.) Potential competition, therefore, existed at the upper end of the 64s with the lower end of the 66s.

Attempts to avoid such competition leading to HIS-Bull conflicts were based on two policies or actions. First, Bull by 1980 was producing and marketing Level 66s as well as Level 64s within its own sales territory. Second, marketing guidelines were established to sell Bull 64s in the United States and other HIS markets. If a customer had a current memory-capacity need in the 700K to 800K byte range, a Level 64 would be sold if that customer did not need greater expansion capacity in the future. If such expansion was highly probable, then Level 66s were sold instead.

Table 4 CII-HB Percentage of HIS and Honeywell, Inc., Net Income

	1976	1977	1978	1979	1980
CII-HB Percent HIS	40.7	15.1	38.6	36.0	31.2
CII-HJB Percent Honeywell, Inc.	7.5	3.9	10.5	11.5	11.0

(Sources: Computed from Honeywell, *Annual Reports,* 1977–80.)

The minicomputer business also experienced close cooperation. In 1975 the Level 6 system was introduced by HIS, with manufacturing extended to France in 1978. Although Bull called these the "mini-6s," they were the same machines as produced by HIS. These minicomputer systems were becoming increasingly critical to HIS and Bull as add-ons to medium-scale and large-scale mainframes.

This high degree of product development and marketing cooperation can be seen in the relative research-and-development expenditures and product flows between HIS and Bull, which are demonstrated in Tables 5 and 6. All of these financial and product/market factors were critical ingredients of negotiating strategy between Honeywell and the French government in 1981–1982.

Political pressures on Honeywell's role in Bull had been mounting well before the 1981 presidential election. Protests had been heard since the inception of the 1975–1976 merger between CII and Honeywell Bull. The French Communist Party termed the deal "sabotage," while the Gaullist party (UDR) called it a deception. In large part, these criticisms were political posturing against President Valery Giscard d'Estaing and his UDF coalition, a French conservative but internationally liberal party. In another sense, however, these criticisms reflected a genuine debate over who, the French nation or Honeywell, had benefited most from the deal. Giscard and Honeywell naturally argued that both parties had benefited to a substantial degree—after all, IBM was the common threat to the aspirations of each side.

IBM certainly saw the Honeywell-French government relationship as a coalition formed against its interests. Since the CII merger with Honeywell, "IBM's share of government computer orders [in France] had dropped steadily, from 37 to 26 percent, according to IBM officials. They attribute the decline to French government support of CII-Honeywell Bull." In addition to government controls, IBM asserted that they had lost some private contracts "because of government pressure." IBM decided not to protest this alleged favoritism formally because as an IBM spokesman remarked, "as they say in the French Foreign Legion, things could always get worse."[3]

In spite of possible Honeywell-French government collusion against IBM, the French political challenge to CII-HB increased substantially during the parliamentary elections of 1978, when Giscard's moderate-conservative coalition narrowly defeated the leftist alliance. As the Honeywell president stated afterwards, he "was very relieved" by the election results because "we would have lost our business" if Mitterrand and the leftists had won. The 1978 elections, however, did not end or

Table 5 R&D Expenditures, CII-HB and HIS (millions of $)

	1976	1977	1978	1979	1980
CII-HB	69.4	91	108	127.9	129.6
Total HIS	331.5	397.7	431.7	551.4	720.6
Percent CII-HB to HIS Total	20.9	22.9	25.0	23.2	18.0

(Source: Honeywell, *1980 Annual Reports*, p. 7.)

Table 6 Intercompany Sales Between CII-HB and HIS (millions of $)

	1976	1977	1978	1979	1980
HIS Sales to CII-HB	74.1	89.9	93.6	113.5	131.1
CII-HB Sales to HIS	66.6	69.6	51.3	48.2	48.8

(Source: Honeywell, *Annual Reports*, 1977–80)

reduce the threat to Honeywell's French operation. During 1979, for example, St. Gobain (with tacit government approval) bought out Compagnie General d'Electricite's 20-percent share in the French majority side of the computer group and began to negotiate the full or partial purchase of the government's 20-percent share as well. The threat to Honeywell was that St. Gobain would begin to "dominate the otherwise fragmented French side, achieving effective control of CII-HB".[4] These efforts continued into 1980 because "now the French want to squeeze out American Honeywell's remaining minority stake."[5]

In short, the potential threat to Honeywell's position in CII-Bull had a long history that predated the socialist election victory in May 1981 and was rooted in French national pride, which transcended the political ideologies of the right and left and had been hurt by the fact that 75 percent of the roughly $8 billion worth of computers installed in France were sold by American companies. Many Gaullists, out of the nationalistic tradition of their founder, General Charles de Gaulle, had pressed for the nationalization of the French computer industry, and this conservative-nationalistic policy goal dovetailed quite nicely with the Socialist Party's objective of "recapturing the domestic market."

THE POST-MAY 1981 ENVIRONMENT

On May 10, 1981, Edson Spencer received a phonecall from Roger Fauroux, head of St. Gobain, informing him that Mitterrand's election was imminent and that the nationalization of St. Gobain (now the majority French partner in CII-HB) was a near certainty. Its exact impact on Honeywell, however, was far less certain.

The Socialist government moved quickly on its election platform in all respects. Minimum wage and social security benefits were increased 10 percent and 20 percent respectively. In addition, paid-vacation benefits were extended, and the work week was reduced from 40 to 39 hours. Presidential decrees also added 210,000 new jobs to the public sector. More fundamentally, a nationalization plan affecting 11 major industrial groups, including St. Gobain, was approved by the National Assembly in July 1981 by a 302 to 107 vote margin. Three firms with large foreign ownership (CII-HB, ITT-France, and Roussel-Uclaf) were targeted for intensive negotiations on their future status. The compensation bill flowing from the government to private stockholders of the 11 industrial groups was initially $5.5 billion, but it increased to $7 billion after French court pressure and rulings.

These policies had been implemented within an economic climate that had been deteriorating during the last year or two of Giscard's presidency, as Exhibit I reveals. The primary cause of these economic reversals was not domestic policies but the consequences of the second oil shock, which followed the Iranian revolution. Many analysts were wondering if Mitterrand's domestic policies would help or aggravate the situation.

Spencer and other Honeywell executives visited Paris frequently to assess the situation. Commercially, CII-HB was suffering and on its way to a 1981 operating loss that would reduce Honeywell's corporate earnings by $14 million or 61 cents per share, which represented 5 percent of Honeywell's total earnings per share in that year. Politically, Spencer found the overall business climate less than desirable. Thus, as Spencer commented, "Every indication was negative. We had only one viable option—to take our assets and get out."[6] Spencer's pessimism, however, obviously did not extend to all Honeywell business interests in France, because in July 1981 Honeywell expanded its French control systems subsidiary with an infusion of $6 million in cash. The sellout option for Honeywell's stake in Bull was made possible by the 1976 agreement, which gave Honeywell the right to sell those assets at book value and be paid in dollars from an escrow account in a London bank if nationalization occurred. Based on the 1981 CII-HB balance sheet, Honeywell would be entitled to around $200 million, slightly more than the amount it had invested in 1970. With the nationalization of St. Gobain, CII-HB was also technically nationalized, which gave Honeywell the legal option to pursue or demand the implementation of the 1976 agreement.

Before taking this course of action, however, Spencer, during an early November visit to Paris, "began to hear from high Ministry of Industry officials that France was determined to become a world-class computer power and that Honeywell's role could be interesting and rewarding."[7] Shortly thereafter, Spencer was invited to the Elysee Palace for a discussion with Jacques Attali, Mitterrand's special counselor. Spencer reported that "Attali made it clear that he was speaking for the president and that *le President* wanted Honeywell to stay in France."[8] Spencer then decided to explore what possibilities existed between Honeywell and the French government.

Within days of the Attali-Spencer meeting, negotiations between Honeywell and the French were scheduled to begin. The French side was to be represented by executives of St. Gobain. The Honeywell negotiating team was to be composed of three individuals: William R. Hart, the senior vice president (second in charge behind the president) of HIS; David Louis, Honeywell's chief financial officer; and John Karis, Honeywell's assistant general counsel. Of the three, Bill Hart, of course, had the greatest experience with Bull and the French government. He had been involved with Bull since the late 1960s, was a Bull board member during the present negotiations, and had known many of the St. Gobain negotiators in that capacity for several years. The other two individuals had never been intimately involved in Honeywell-French relations.

The central question for the negotiators remained: Given Bull's importance to Honeywell and the history of the computer industry in France, what should Honeywell's negotiating strategy be? And how should Honeywell's negotiating effort be organized?

NOTES

1. *Fortune,* "Business Around the Globe," 9/64, p. 59.
2. *Ibid.*
3. *Wall Street Journal,* 4/7/80, p. 24.
4. *Economist,* 11/17/79, p. 81.
5. *Economist,* 4/5/80, p. 63.
6. *Fortune,* 6/28/82, p. 97.
7. *Ibid.*
8. *Ibid.*

Exhibit 1 Macroeconomic and Balance-of-Payment Trends in France

	1976	1977	1978	1979	1980
Francs per US Dollar (end of year)	4.78	4.91	4.51	4.26	4.23
Consumer Prices (1975 = 100)	109.6	119.9	130.8	144.8	164.1
Labor Costs (1975 = 100)	116.5	133.0	151.9	175.1	203.2
Nominal GDP (billions of francs)	1,678	1,885	2,141	2,439	2,755
Merchandise Trade Balance (millions of $)	(4,592)	(2,709)	716	(2,003)	(12,038)
Foreign Direct Investment (millions of $)	(586)	908	898	503	327
Portfolio Investment (millions of $)	1,259	900	(125)	(1,630)	91
Short-term Capital (millions of $)	2,448	(641)	(513)	3,785	17,418
Change in Reserves (millions of $)	2,834	(240)	(3,438)	(3,972)	(11,609)

Source: *International Financial Statistics,* Vol. 34, November 7, 1981, pp. 152–155.

4

MANAGING INTERNATIONAL LEGAL DISPUTES

International business law is primarily the collection of the many laws and regulations that are observed in individual countries. The closest thing to an international legal framework is the patchwork of treaties, codes and agreements between certain countries that deal with limited aspects of international business activity. The most important of such agreements for settling international legal disputes are foreign investment guaranty agreements, the International Center for Settlement of Investment Disputes (ICSID), the Convention of Paris, and the UN Convention on the Recognition and Enforcement of Arbitral Awards.

Nearly all major investor countries have foreign investment guaranty programs, which are made possible by agreements between the corporation's home government and the host government. These investment guaranty agreements do not usually forbid expropriation, but the host government does agree to provide prompt and fair compensation in most cases. With the more than 100 such agreements negotiated by the United States, procedural matters in the event of expropriation are stressed.[1] U.S. firms with investments in those countries can buy political risk insurance from the Overseas Private Investment Corporation, an autonomous government corporation. Such a program and set of agreements reduce the likelihood of international legal disputes arising over expropriation.

Relatedly, ICSID was established to provide a procedural framework through which international investment disputes could be resolved. Sponsored by the World Bank, ICSID contains guidelines for how disputes will be arbitrated if both parties agree to the Center's jurisdiction. Arbitrators are selected by the parties to the dispute, and decisions are final and binding on the more than 80 governments associated with the ICSID Convention. Interestingly, the region least represented in the ICSID is Latin America, where the so-called Calvo Doctrine dominates legal thinking. The doctrine states that a foreign company, once it enters a country, implicitly agrees to be treated as a national firm; therefore, multinational corporations have no right to receive protection from their home governments in investment disputes. Despite the potential for international legal disputes because of these different legal traditions, the importance of the Calvo Doctrine has been diminished by the growing presence of bilaterally negotiated investment guarantee agreements.[2]

A growingly contentious area of international legal conflict is that of industrial property rights and patent protection. Patents are granted and trademarks registered by individual governments; their protection is only assured within those countries. Multinationals thus need to initiate protection procedures in every country a patented or trademarked product enters. However, the requirements for patent protection and trademark registration differ significantly across countries, leading to potential legal and international disputes.[3] The recent controversy between the United States and Brazil on computer software protection is one notorious example. As an attempt to avoid such conflicts, a group of more than 50 countries formed the Convention of Paris to provide national treatment to industrial property rights. In other words, each country in the Convention agrees to give nationals of other member countries the same rights it gives to its own nationals. Broadening such an agreement to include more countries would certainly reduce international legal disputes in this area.

If and when international legal disputes involving a company arise, there are several possible forums through which their resolution can proceed.[4] Besides out-of-court negotiations, multinational corporations can have the dispute heard at the International Court of Justice at The Hague if their home government presents the case. If such disputes involving a private party reach the court, which is rare, there is still no method of enforcement unless both governments agree to the court's jurisdiction. Of course, a firm can also initiate litigation within a national court system. This has the following advantages: If the firm wins the case, monetary rewards are usually large relative to what could be expected through other legal options; payment is more assured if that court system was specified in the contract; and there is abundant precedent in case law to draw on. There are also numerous disadvantages: Adverse publicity could emerge from a public trial; litigation can be very expensive and time-consuming; and the firm could face biases in a national court system because of cultural, language and political factors.

For these reasons, the option of international arbitration has become increasingly popular.[5] Arbitration has the advantage of being relatively inexpensive, largely because it is less formal and quicker than litigation. Arbitration is also a less antagonistic method of addressing legal disputes, and since it is a private deliberation, adverse publicity is avoided. Lastly, the potential prejudices of national court systems are minimized. Nevertheless, arbitration can result in smaller monetary awards relative to litigation, and since there is an absence of case law and legal precedent, rulings of arbitrators can be varied and more uncertain.

If arbitration clauses are negotiated in the initial contract, several points need to be stressed. First, the results of arbitration should be binding. Second, the location where arbitration takes place should be in a country that has ratified the UN Convention on the Recognition and Enforcement of Arbitral Awards. Over 50 countries are signatories, and under the convention, member countries agree to enforce arbitration clauses and awards. The governing law of the arbitration should also be specified. In the absence of such agreement, the law of the place of arbitration will apply, which could cause unexpected problems. In general, arbitration in the United States will be governed by the rules of the American Arbitration Association, whereas in Europe the procedures of the International Chamber of Commerce will be followed. Lastly, the contract should specify how arbitrators are selected and the language in which the proceedings will be conducted.

The main message here is that when international contracts are negotiated, one should plan for the possibility of dispute. The contract should be very specific in how disputes will be resolved. The form, location, governing law, and language of the procedures should be explicit. Of course, expert legal advice should be consulted before making detailed decisions, but the international manager needs a general understanding of the potential legal problems that might arise and how they might be resolved. Only through such understanding can legal disputes be properly managed, before they occur and during their resolution.

NOTES

1. Organization for Economic Cooperation and Development, *Investing in Developing Countries*, 3rd ed. (Paris, 1975), p. 16.
2. Henry Steiner and Detleo F. Vagts, *Transnational Legal Problems*, 2nd ed. (Mineola, N.Y.: Foundation Press, 1976), pp. 522–530.
3. Philip R. Cateora and John M. Hess, *International Marketing*, 4th ed. (Homewood, Illinois: Richard D. Irwin, 1979), p. 197.
4. For a detailed account of these options, see Noyes E. Leech, Covey T. Oliver and Joseph M. Sweeney, *The International Legal System* (Mineola, N.Y.: Foundation Press, 1973).
5. Business International Corporation, "International Arbitration: A Popular Option with Some Pitfalls," *Business International*, April 27, 1984, pp. 130–131.

Amco and Finnco: Contract Termination (A)

It is exactly one week before Christmas 1980. Frank Carbone, 39 years old and president of Amco's Marine Systems Division (MSD), sits staring out his window looking across the Seattle harbor, barely noticing the ever-present rain this December evening. His eyes transfixed, Carbone is not thinking of all the holiday shopping he's yet to do but rather he's attempting to reconstruct all of the events which had led to the meeting he's about to chair. The topic for discussion this evening is how Amco can recoup its losses against Finnco as a result of the latter's abrupt termination the previous February of Amco's contract to provide automated oil drilling systems for use on Soviet oil drilling rigs by Finnco's Soviet customer, Sovietco.

Approximately six (6) months after entering into a contract in which Amco was to supply certain diagrams, data and prototypes on a preestablished installment basis, Finnco terminated the contract. The termination was precipitated by Finnco's perception that Amco would be unable to supply goods and services pursuant to the agreed-upon contract schedule. The Finnish party based this conclusion primarily upon President Carter's decision in January 1980 to suspend temporarily U.S. export licenses for high-technology goods and services bound for the Soviet Union or other East bloc countries and Amco's inability to offer absolute assurances that the necessary licenses would be granted within a specific timetable. President Carter had invoked his authority under the foreign policy provisions of the Export Administration Act of 1979 in reaction to and as leverage against the Soviet Union because of its December 1979 invasion of Afghanistan.

Carbone has requested that the following individuals attend the meeting:

- Bill Sullivan, 58, Project Manager for the Finnco project, and an employee of Amco's MSD for 32 years.
- "Red" McWhinney, the recently appointed 35-year-old comptroller of MSD and the individual most knowledgeable about the costs associated with the Finnco project, and
- Michel "Mike" Pichet, 37, Amco's European counsel, a French-born but American-educated attorney, currently working in Amco's Paris headquarters but who is in Seattle on home leave for the holidays.

Carbone is aware that each of these men has different and strongly held views of the Finnco contract termination. Indeed, for each of these men the course

This case was prepared by T. Mitchell Willey, Darden MBA/JD '76 and Charles R. Kennedy, Jr., Associate Professor of Business Administration, The Darden Graduate School of Business.

of action which Amco decides to pursue may have a very significant impact on their respective careers. Carbone himself realizes that a misstep in the Finnco matter could prove to be a major career setback in what has, to date, been a very rapid rise through the engineering and marketing ranks, resulting in his selection two years ago as president of the Marine Systems Division. MSD has for the past five years averaged $150 million in annual sales and, thus, comprises a significant department within Amco's Engineering Services Division area which itself makes up $600 million of Amco's $1.4 billion in annual sales.

Carbone had enthusiastically endorsed MSD's entry into subcontracting for Soviet oil drilling projects because he believed it represented substantial growth potential for MSD—a division often plagued by few new business opportunities as a result of its competitors' more sophisticated products, which in turn resulted from competitors' larger financial commitments to research and development. Therefore, he was not only disappointed in the Finnco termination because of its adverse impact on MSD's profitability, but it could be interpreted as a fundamental error in judgment for entering into this particular subcontracting area. In addition, Carbone knew that he was being considered for a very substantial promotion to become president of all of Amco's European operations and, thus, a successful resolution of the Finnco matter could tip the scale in his favor with top management.

Bill Sullivan was extremely anxious about this evening's meeting and had, characteristically, been popping Tums all day. He had to admit to himself that he had made some rather fundamental errors on the Finnco contract. Fortunately, though, since Finnco had terminated the contract last February, management had focused almost exclusively on the circumstances surrounding what was perceived to be Finnco's premature and unjustified cancellation of the contract and Amco's resulting lost profits. Although Carbone was an extraordinarily fair and sympathetic manager, Sullivan was certain that he would not hesitate to demand answers to tough questions about this contract, including an assessment of the lost profits to Amco on the basis of the five (5) months of Amco's operating history with Finnco.

Red McWhinney viewed the meeting with a mixture of anxiety and relish. This was his first opportunity to impress Carbone with his mastery of the quantitative aspects of this contract. In addition, he might be about to use this as an opportunity to demonstrate to Carbone his own analytical skills as he had some pretty strong opinions about the type of financial exposure Amco had accrued as a result of the Finnco contract.

Amco's European legal counsel, Mike Pichet, viewed the Amco/Finnco contractual dispute as the perfect opportunity to gain some important and much-desired visibility of top management. Pichet was coming to the evening's meeting to aggressively push the arbitration option available to Amco under its contract with Finnco. Such an arbitration would undoubtedly take place in Pichet's professional backyard (the contract specified The Hague) and since it involved termination in the European context, he was confident that he could assert control of the legal function managing such an arbitration. Amco had never in its 85-year history engaged in a major arbitration, and Pichet was anxious to demonstrate to management that it was a relatively rapid and inexpensive way to resolve disputes in the international commercial sector. In addition, Pichet was of the opinion that in the international commercial environment Amco had to demonstrate to present and future companies doing business with it that it would hold them to their financial and contractual obligations.

Pichet was also anxious to use this opportunity to impress Carbone. Pichet prided himself on having the inside track on the corporate rumor mill and had heard from trustworthy sources that Carbone was very likely to be the next president of Amco-Europe which would then make him Pichet's boss.

Carbone asked Pichet to start the meeting by summarizing, in chronological order, the events which had led up to Finnco's cancellation of the contract and any major relevant events thereafter. An abbreviated and somewhat sanitized version of Pichet's wandering and rather emotional description of the facts follows. Exhibit 1 lists, in chronological order, a summary of the important written exchanges which took place between Amco and Finnco.

PICHET'S FACTUAL OVERVIEW

In late March, 1979, Amco contacted Finnco's project manager of the Soviet oil drillship program, Mr. Veroken, about the Finnish company's participation in the project, hoping this tender offer would be favorably received (Exhibit 2). Two weeks later, Amco followed this up with another telex inviting Finnco to a meeting at a trade show in May (Exhibit 3). Amco was obviously intent on securing the contract. The May meeting went well, and Amco started proposing specific contractual arrangements as a result; it commenced by proposing a specific plan of action to Mr. Lattisla, Finnco's vice president for oil-drilling operations who, along with his assistant, Mr. Satosaki, were the primary executives at Finnco responsible for the program. Indeed, Mr. Lesslo, Amco's Finnish country manager, had met with Finnco's management team on several occasions by June 1979 and was impressed with its operation (Exhibit 4). By early August 1979, an installment performance contract was signed between Amco and Finnco, pursuant to which Amco was to provide state-of-the-art offshore oil drilling equipment and technology to Finnco who would, in turn, integrate this technology into a Soviet oil drilling project. The contract was contingent on Finnco gaining approval of the Soviet customer, Sovietco, to use Amco as a subcontractor. Finnco had 30 days to obtain said approval. Amco commenced its performance immediately after the contract signing (on September 1, 1979) notwithstanding the fact that Finnco had not yet received formal approval from Sovietco to engage the American subcontractor. Although it proceeded with its performance, Amco was sufficiently concerned about this lack of formal approval that it repeatedly asked Finnco for written assurances that the work it was undertaking in the context of its installment performance contract with Finnco would be paid notwithstanding this lack of formal approval. The communication between Amco and Finnco with respect to Sovietco's approval, or lack thereof, has been summarized in Exhibit I. Unfortunately, as the communication exchange indicates, Amco did not receive such assurances as the contract proceeded into the fall of 1979.

Performance by Amco during the first year of the contract was due as follows:

December 31, 1979	Submission of project plan to Finnco for review and approval, and initial purchasing of materials by Amco.
February 5, 1980	Amco's submission of taut wire drawings.
October 1, 1980	Amco to provide prototype of the oil drilling system for testing by Finnco.

As already noted, a pattern of communication developed between the parties, culminating in a December 27, 1979 telex in which Amco specifically advised Finnco that its anticipated costs through the end of 1979 would be $1.6 million (see Exhibit 5). Once again, Finnco did not respond directly to the cost issue but underscored the necessity to moving ahead on the project, notwithstanding the lack of formal approval by Sovietco.

Later in December 1979 the parties agreed to meet on January 3, 1980 to discuss "contractual problems." At the conclusion of this meeting Finnco revealed that notwithstanding Amco's continued questions and the anxiety it had repeatedly expressed that Finnco obtain the necessary approval of Sovietco the fact remained that Sovietco had not yet approved the contract and thus Amco should stop work; Finnco issued a stop-work order to Amco the following day. Amco's response can be seen in Exhibit 6. Finnco's independent recollection of the January 3rd meeting is shown in Exhibit 7.

On January 9, 1980, the U.S. government announced the temporary suspension of outstanding export licenses for commodities and technology destined for the USSR in the context of the imposition of a temporary license review period, which also effectively placed a temporary prohibition upon pending export license applications. Amco advised Finnco that while the U.S. government had imposed this temporary review period it had also assured exporters that it would complete its review of export licenses for products or technology bound for the Soviet Union within 4 to 6 weeks from the date the suspension was imposed (see Exhibit 8).

On January 11, 1980, Finnco suggested to Amco that the parties discuss a prolongation of the delivery time for both the taut wire drawings and prototypes to be developed by Amco. Finnco also advised Amco that the Finnish side was not responsible for the costs incurred because of the work stoppage (see Exhibit 9). Furthermore, on January 28th, Finnco asked Amco to advise it of the status of its export license application and to provide it with a "guarantee" with respect to its ability to obtain a validated export license in a timely manner (see Exhibit 10). Amco responded on February 1st to Matti Kerkola, Finnco's in-house counsel, and Mr. Lattisla by advising Finnco that the export license was still being reviewed by the Commerce Department; Amco also advised Finnco that it would keep it advised of the status of the license. Amco stated that it could not, of course, provide a "guarantee" as to the status of the license while the review was ongoing. However, Amco did indicate that it would undertake all reasonable efforts to achieve immediate authorization. Amco once again reminded Finnco that delivery of the prototype was not due for another eight (8) months (see Exhibit 11). Amco had delivered the taut wire drawings to Finnco on February 1, 1980.

On February 8th Finnco responded by stating, in essence, that Amco's vague assurances concerning the export license were insufficient. Finnco stated that in light of the need for certain and complete performance it was forced to cancel the contract and by implication to find another supplier who could guarantee that the product and technology would be provided in a timely manner (see Exhibit 12). Therefore, as of February 8, 1980, the agreement between Finnco and Amco was terminated by Finnco.

In early April 1980 Finnco approached Amco about the possibility of reviving the contract, but Amco was reluctant to do so and negotiations never really progressed further.

In late November 1980 Amco learned that Sovietco had, in fact, approved Amco as the contract supplier as of January 18, 1980. Immediately after learning of this Amco applied for a validated export license to export its oil drilling system to the Soviet Union. The license request was approved within six (6) days by the Commerce Department. The presidential-imposed ban on export licenses and concomitant "review period" had been lifted as of March 1980.

Following Pichet's chronological review of the facts surrounding the Finnco contract, Carbone asked everyone in the group to consider and present the various options which might be available to Amco. Top management of Amco's Engineering Services Division had asked Carbone to submit a recommendation and a detailed plan of a course of action no later than year end. Inasmuch as Carbone and his family were leaving on Christmas Eve for Utah for their annual holiday ski vacation, he was anxious to review the available options and develop a recommendation and plan of action for management.

Bill Sullivan seized the momentary silence following Carbone's request for an analysis of the options to present his position. During informal conversations with Carbone and Pichet earlier in the week, he had come to realize that neither of them was initially inclined to attempt to reinstitute the contractual relationship which Finnco had terminated in February. Therefore, he knew that he faced an uphill battle to persuade management of the wisdom of continuing work with Finnco, at least on this contract.

BILL SULLIVAN: "Yesterday I spoke with Messrs. Lattisla and Satosaki (Finnco's managing director and his program assistant, respectively) and they have indicated to me that the work being done by the Finnish substitute supplier, Skiberg, is proceeding very slowly and Finnco is extremely disappointed with the quality of work performed by Skiberg thus far. In addition, he disclosed to me that Skiberg's inability to meet certain timetables would ultimately prove very costly to Finnco. I believe that he left the door wide open for us to come back in and complete the project."

FRANK CARBONE: "Bill, surely you're not suggesting that we now pick up the pieces, more than ten months later, and attempt to complete the project as planned. Even if we could somehow gear up to do this, I'm not at all certain that this course of action would be in our best interests financially."

Red McWhinney couldn't resist the opportunity which Carbone had laid before him:

"Not in our best interests! Actually, my analysis indicates that even if Amco had been able to hit every delivery date and we had encountered no unusual development or manufacturing obstacles, the rising costs of materials and labor and the enormous management and transportation costs (associated with Finnco's delay and the political and logistical problems for the project stemming from the Afghanistan problem), when contrasted with an extremely low bid and contract price on the project, probably would have resulted in Amco being denied its usual healthy profit on such projects."

BILL SULLIVAN: "That's absurd. While I'd admit the margins were not as fat as we would normally expect, there was still a reasonable profit to be made on the project. Red, quite frankly, I think that's terribly irresponsible to be making those assertions without a full and proper analysis of the contract."

RED MCWHINNEY: (To Frank Carbone) "You want my full and proper analysis? I have two boxes of computer runs and a dozen different spread sheets using different assumptions—all of which support my conclusion. I'd suggest that we try to negotiate as favorable a settlement as possible and be willing to accept a percentage—a substantial percentage—of our out-of-pocket expenses in an attempt to put this matter behind us."

BILL SULLIVAN: "Hold on, we're getting off the point. My proposal is that we go back to Finnco and attempt to renegotiate the deal. They need Amco's expertise and they should be willing to pay for it. Specifically, I'd suggest that we recommence the contract with Finnco but only on the condition that Amco be immediately reimbursed for all expenses incurred through February 1980. A mutually agreed-upon timetable for project completion should be agreed to. In addition, Finnco should be willing to pay Amco a substantial bonus for satisfactory completion of the project pursuant to the to-be-agreed-upon timetable. The bonus would be in recognition of Amco's willingness to reenter the contract at this stage as well as its completion of the project in a timely manner."

FRANK CARBONE: "That's an interesting concept; do you really think Finnco would agree to those conditions, Bill?"

BILL SULLIVAN: "It certainly won't hurt to ask."

MIKE PICHET: "Frank, I've held off commenting until now but I'll have to disagree with Bill's last statement. As MSD's matter, for us to either commence negotiations to reinitiate the contract (and in that context reveal that we wish to negotiate a better deal) or to reach a reasonable settlement, as Red has suggested, both of these approaches place Amco in a position of weakness. Rather, I would strongly urge that we immediately commence arbitration by serving notice on Finnco's in-house counsel, Matti Kerkola, of our intention to commence arbitration in The Hague. By the way, this will not come as a surprise to Kerkola, as he has already mentioned to our country manager, Matti Lesslo, that he expected the parties might go to arbitration.

Moreover, I think Amco must demonstrate to Finnco and our other contracting parties that we will not, now or in the future, accept premature termination on such flimsy grounds. This is becoming increasingly important as the global political atmosphere grows more unstable, and any political hiccup may serve as an opportunity for a contractor to simply cancel our contracts, without penalty of any kind."

FRANK CARBONE: "Mike, while I understand the precedent-setting nature of Amco's commencing and, hopefully, succeeding with an arbitration, I must tell you at the outset that I am skeptical about arbitration as a mechanism to resolve this problem. How soon can we actually get the parties to start the arbitration process? How long will it be before the arbitration actually starts and how long will it last? What is your best guess as to an award that might be forthcoming and how do we collect an award if one is directed in our favor?"

MIKE PICHET: "Allow me to respond to those questions, Frank. They're fair and astute ones to be asked.

We expect the arbitration process to work as follows. First, we believe that the Governing Law and Arbitration clause of the contract with Finnco provides a good basis upon which to bind the parties to proceed to arbitration. We also feel that Finnco may want to proceed to arbitration to make its own claim against Amco for the return of its $630,000 down payment. We believe that if we commence arbitration, they will counterclaim against us. The worst thing that could happen would be for Finnco to simply ignore our demand for arbitration, but we are investigating international treaties that we feel confident would force them into arbitration.

Frank, we expect to commence the arbitration process rather quickly. After the parties agree to proceed, I would envision the selection of arbitrators would take two months—Amco and Finnco would each select a neutral arbitrator with the understanding that those two would select a third who would serve as chairman. Following the selections of the arbitrators, we would, in consultation with the arbitral panel, agree to governing rules and a timetable for discovery (the fact-finding portion of the process), and then proceed to conduct discovery and prepare briefs which outline our position to the arbitrators. This stage of the process might stretch out another three to four months, depending on the number of briefs which are permitted by the arbitral panel. Following final submission of the briefs, we should be prepared to start the actual arbitration within about a month.

Therefore, Frank, we are looking at about a seven-month process before the arbitration is complete and perhaps another two to three months before an award is announced. Obviously, by comparison to litigation or dispute resolution in the United States or elsewhere, this is a very speedy procedure. I expect the actual arbitration would last about two weeks by the time both sides present their respective cases and witnesses and have the opportunity to cross-examine the other.

Frank, you have asked what the size of an award might be on behalf of Amco. You have assumed that we will prevail—which is something that I cannot assure you of. One of the drawbacks of arbitration (unlike most civil court systems) is that no prior history exists with respect to this arbitral panel so that it is impossible to predict how they will react. Moreover, unlike most legal proceedings in civil law countries, a body of law has not developed which provides a precedent of similar cases from which we can take guidance. Rather, we must rely on our ability to convince the arbitrators of the equities of our position which dictate an award in our favor.

I'm quite confident that Amco's position is a very strong one and that we will prevail, but you should also realize that the panel, being somewhat Solomonic in their approach, would probably award Amco perhaps half of the $1.6 it is seeking with some recognition of Finnco's prior payment of $630,000. I feel confident that once an award is made that both Amco and Finnco, as two legitimate and well-known international companies, will feel bound to honor this obligation."

Frank Carbone was reeling somewhat from Mike Pichet's minilesson in arbitration. The arbitration procedure is obviously adversarial which in itself was at odds with Carbone's belief that Finnco was basically a reputable company and, in light of being one of the largest industrial product companies in Finland, was one he still hoped to do business with, notwithstanding its actions on this project. He also felt that while relations had obviously chilled temporarily with the Soviet Union, due to the Afghanistan invasion and the ongoing Iran hostage debacle, MSD could realize enormous potential in sales to the Soviet Union and the East bloc countries of some of MSD's lower-level equipment. This lower-level equipment is sufficiently advanced to be of interest to the East bloc but not sophisticated enough to concern the U.S. government—at least until the president's temporary license suspension of last January. Of course, with Ronald Reagan taking office in one month, everyone is a bit uncertain of the political climate which may exist between the East and West blocs. Also, how would his recommendation of a plan and its implementation impact on his consideration for the position as president of Amco-Europe?

The options which had been raised were diverse and each offered interesting but not altogether satisfactory ways of resolving the outstanding indebtedness owed by Finnco. However, a recommendation must be made—and made quickly.

Exhibit 1 Sequence of Events

Date	To	From	Key Statements/Subject
27 Sept. '79	Finnco	Amco	Amco requests increase in termination liability since Sovietco approval had not been received and indicates it will continue in good faith unless Finnco notifies it otherwise.
28 Sept. '79	Finnco	Amco	Sovietco approval had not yet been received, and thus requested termination liability be increased to $450,000 to cover activity thru Oct. 1979.
5 Oct. '79	Finnco	Amco	Amco asks for response to its telex of Sept. 28. re. termination liability.
8 Oct. '79	Finnco	Amco	Amco requests assurance that Finnco would pay actual expenses up to $450,000 should Sovietco decline to approve Amco as supplier of D.P.
18 Oct. '79	Finnco	Amco	Amco informs Finnco it is continuing to work with the understanding that Finnco concurs and would cover termination liability as stated in Sept. 28 telex.
22 Oct. '79	Amco	Finnco	Finnco requests data to counter Skiberg arguments to Sovietco.
31 Oct. '79	Finnco	Amco	Amco again informs Finnco that work on the contract continues with the understanding that Finnco concurs and will cover full termination costs in the event Sovietco forces reprocurement from our competitor.
6 Nov. '79	Amco	Finnco	Finnco responding to 10–31 telex from Amco. Indicates "we do not see any reason for interrupting your work in this project."
3 Dec. '79	Finnco	Amco	Letter from Amco discusses unanticipated delays in obtaining Sovietco's approval, which was due on 30 Sept. and states Finnco has asked Amco to continue to satisfy its contractual obligations, which has been done. Amco puts Finnco on notice that this has involved a substantial growth in the funds required and by the end of December 1979, expenses will be at a $1.6 million level. Amco requests Finnco to put on paper its requests to continue working, confirming the several phone calls, and so forth that have taken place in the proceeding months, that the termination liability should be increased to $1.6 million. Reason for the concern is clearly identified as the failure of Sovietco to either approve or disapprove.
5 Dec. '79	Amco	Finnco	Finnco alerts Amco to possible participation in a meeting in Moscow to support its case with the Russians.
6 Dec. '79	Finnco	Amco	Amco clears up details on the visit to Russia to try to influence Sovietco.

(continued)

Exhibit 1 (*Continued*)

Date	To	From	Key Statements/Subject
10 Dec. '79	Amco	Finnco	Sets up meeting in Moscow Dec. 18, 1979. No decision yet from Sovietco. Asks for Amco assistance.
13 Dec. '79			Another confirmation of meeting in Moscow December 17.
27 Dec. '79	Finnco	Amco	Amco expresses concern to Finnco over the lack of Sovietco approval. Asks for increase in termination liability, identifies $1.6 million termination liability by the end of December, $2.6 million by the end of January 1980. Puts Finnco on notice that Amco is going to make the decision to stop work on 31 December unless these matters are resolved.
4 Jan. '80	Finnco	Amco	Amco suggests language for the inclusion in response to Amco 31 Dec. letter. Suggests following options: increase termination liability to $1.6 million, direct Amco to suspend operations, make the second installment of payment.
4 Jan. '80	Amco	Finnco	Finnco reference discussions with Amco on Jan. 3 1980. Requests Amco stop all work except the design work for taut wire system; also indicating that at this stage, termination liability should not be changed because Sovietco approval was imminent. Indicates concern that the changed world political situation might affect the Russians' decision.
9 Jan. '80	Finnco	Amco	Amco acknowledges stop work of 4 January, except for the taut wire, indicates it has suspended work, asks for concurrence that the stop-work costs will be paid by Finnco. Refers to the deteriorating international situation etc. Indicates Finnco has not received any indication that Amco export license is in jeopardy.
10 Jan. '80	Finnco	Amco	Amco indicates that on Jan. 9 the U.S. President issued an order to review all exports for Russian equipment. Expected a delay of four to six weeks, stated that there is, in Amco's opinion, not a force majeure situation yet since its performance is not affected.
11 Jan. '80	Amco	Finnco	Finnco repeats stop work direction, citing Sovietco failure to approve, and also citing President Carter's export prohibition to the USSR. Also denies responsibility for costs of stop work because it is not dependent upon them. After the situation has been clarified it promises to discuss prolongation of delivery time.

(*continued*)

Exhibit 1 *(Continued)*

Date	To	From	Key Statements/Subject
12 Jan. '80	Amco	U.S. Govt.	Mailgram announcing suspension of all existing validation Export Licenses (including Amco's temporary) issued for shipment to USSR and requiring that Export License be returned to the U.S. government. Further disposition of licenses to be provided as soon as possible.
12 Jan. '80	Finnco	Amco	Amco acknowledges receipt of Finnco's message of 11 January, again confirms it has stopped work, again indicates it is not a force majeure situation and that Amco does not have deliveries scheduled soon. Puts Finnco on notice that the costs are theirs to absorb.
1 Feb. '80	Finnco	Amco	Informs Finnco that a review of the export license is in process. Indicated that Amco would take all reasonable steps to attempt to obtain the required authorization to ship, points out that the deliveries are a long way away.
8 Feb. '80	Amco	Finnco	Finnco responding to Amco telex of 1 February, indicates Amco has not yet given satisfactory evidence that it would be able to meet the delivery times of the contract, citing the US government boycott and citing that Amco is unable to give them a clear answer and guarantee that the delivery of the equipment will be on time without delaying the building of the drilling vessel. Therefore, in accordance with Finnish law, it notifies cancellation of the purchase order and demands immediate return of the down payment.
13 Feb. '80	Finnco	Amco	Amco responding to Finnco telex of 8 February, again discusses the US government situation; asks that Finnco confirm the $1.6 million termination liability amount and asks for immediate payment of $630,000 as payment no. 2.
31 March '80	U.S. Govt.	Amco	Letter from Amco withdrawing Export License A 282592 from further consideration as contract had been terminated by Finnco.
17 April '80	Amco	Finnco	Finnco states that a continuing force majeure situation existed on 8 Feb. 1980 and that Finnco had the right under Finnish law to cancel the purchase order. Demands return of funds.
25 Nov. '80	Amco	Finnco	Finnco requests again repayment of $630,000.
28 Nov. '80	Amco	Finnco	Finnco provides Amco a copy of a January 18, 1980 telex, in Russian, from Sovietco to Finnco purporting to approve Amco as the oil drilling equipment supplier.

Exhibit 2

29 March 1979

Finnco
Pori Finland

Attn: Mr. V. Veroken

Amco has learned that you have been awarded the Russian Drillship Program. Congratulations.

We are pleased for you. We trust that our tender for the dynamic positioning systems for these ships satisfies your requirements. We recognize the importance of proven performance and operational reliability for exploration drillings. Our hardware fulfills these requirements.

Amco is committed to support this important program. The export license obstacle has now been resolved. The various United States government agencies have given their approval and the Department of Commerce will provide us a letter stating this. Only the routine approval endorsement by the second committee in Paris remains.

We are prepared to offer a no-cost cancellation contract to your good selves as a protection until the final committee action has been taken.

We trust our latest wire contained the information desired. We look forward to providing you with our updated fare offer including these new system elements.

We are prepared to revisit Finland to work out final technical details and consummate a contractual agreement. Our Finnish subsidiary director will contact you to make these arrangements.

Look forward to working with you on this exciting project.

Best regards,

F. Carbone
Vice President, Marketing
Amco Offshore Operations

Exhibit 3

13 April 1979

To: Finnco
Pori Finland
Attn: Mr. L. Lattisla
cc: Amco Stockholm
Attn: Mr. L. Larsen

Telex Message

We understand that you plan to be at forthcoming OTC exhibition in Houston in May. We look forward to the opportunity to see you there and discuss our offer for the CP systems on the Russian Drillships. Please stop by our booth 2333 at the show so a convenient time can be arranged. We are staying at the Marriott West Loop Hotel.

We hope to have a copy of the export approval confirmation at that time. All of our top management personnel will be at the show for you to meet.

We look forward to these discussions.

Best regards,

W. Sullivan
Offshore Operations

Exhibit 4 AMCO

M. Lesslo
Managing Director

June 1, 1979

Finnco
Finnluoto
28880 Port 88

Attn: Mr. Lattisla

Dear Mr. Lattisla:

On behalf of Amco, we would like to thank you for the hospitality and interest shown to our engineering team in Pori. We appreciate your giving us an opportunity to review our quotation and technical specification. We feel we are extremely well qualified to be your oil drilling system contractor, and we are confident of doing an excellent job.

It is particularly advantageous for Finnco to have an accredited Amco office in Moscow under Mr. Sullivan's leadership and the local liaison and coordination provided by Mr. Lesslo and Amco Finland. We are sure this arrangement will greatly improve our day-to-day communications with the shipyard. We also have local access in the United States to the subsea equipment suppliers you recently selected in Houston.

To review our offer regarding the assistance of Mr. John Walter in Oslo, let us reiterate our points again:

1. We would like to receive a letter of intent from Finnco as soon as possible, expressing your willingness to select Amco as the oil drilling equipment contractor.
2. The letter of intent would be valid for sixty days, during which time Amco is obliged to deliver the formal export license documentation for the oil drilling equipment.
3. Amco would make the services of a senior systems engineer, Mr. John Walters, available to Finnco immediately, and as necessary to provide technical liaison and assistance to the Finnco project team. There would be no cost to Finnco for this support. Mr. Walters is located in Oslo, Norway, and could travel to Pori as required.
4. Should Amco not be able to deliver the formal export license documentation within 60 days, the letter of intent would be rendered invalid, and Finnco would be under no further obligation to Amco.

We certainly hope you will select Amco as the oil drilling equipment contractor. We bring a long record of performance and a team of professional people experienced with the Penquin class drillship. Oil drilling equipment is our business, and you can be assured of a reliable system, delivered on time. Amco has many other interests in Finland and the USSR. The international team assigned to your project is dedicated to making the Finnco contract a success and maintaining Amco's reputation for excellence the world over.

Thank you again for your hospitality. We are looking forward to a long-term friendship with Finnco, and we hope to hear from you soon. Please do not hesitate to contact Mr. Lesslo at Tel. 99-81121 if you have any further questions.

Yours sincerely,

on behalf of F. Carbone

Exhibit 5

WIRE

27 December 1979

To: Finnco
Attn: Messrs Lattisla cc: M. Lesslo
Satosaki J. Walters
Veroken W. Sullivan

Would like to take this opportunity to thank you for your continuing support of Amco as discussions regarding Soviet drillship system continues. We are hopeful that meetings in Moscow have served to clear up any misunderstandings regarding our system.

I would like to know of my concern over several elements of our contract with your shipyard which require immediate resolution. As you are aware, we expected to have final Sovietco approval for Amco oil drilling systems by September 30, 1979. Since this date is now long past us, Amco has, at your direction, continued to maintain the original work schedule for the oil drilling systems in our contract, together with the cost responsibilities which the original contract schedule implies.

In order to formalize your direction in the various Telexes and phone calls over the past several weeks that increased the termination liability and resulting obligations of both parties under your order 903737 after September 30, 1979, we request you to modify the Termination Liability clause on page 5 of the Purchase Agreement by adding the following paragraph:

"In the event the owner (Sovietco) neither approves nor disapproves of this agreement by the end of September 1979, this agreement shall continue in full force and effect until such time as the purchaser (Finnco) notifies the seller (Amco), in writing, that the owner (Sovietco) has disapproved of Amco as the oil drilling equipment supplier. In the event of disapproval, the seller (Amco) shall be entitled to recover all costs plus a reasonable profit."

Amco is now at a point where we will be required to make substantial additional obligations for purchased material in order to maintain the original system schedule. As our correspondence of December 3 indicates, our commitment level on this project will reach 1.6 million U.S. dollars by December 31, 1979, and 2.6 million U.S. dollars by January 31, 1980. As good businessmen, we simply cannot obligate ourselves to these cost levels until the termination liability clause in our contract has been formally modified to reflect the intent and understanding of the parties.

I am communicating with your directly to request that you give us your position regarding the formal termination liability modification and your intentions with regard to the progress payment which is due on December 28. I would appreciate your answering by return Telex, as we are faced with a decision on December 31 to suspend work on the project temporarily until these important matters are resolved. We are naturally reluctant to take such action, but we feel that Amco has continued in good faith to uphold our obligation without a formal statement of our contractual position in the event of termination.

Please be assured that Amco continues to be vitally interested in your project and we are prepared to meet all of our contractual obligations as before. It is my hope that the formalization of termination liability and progress payment issues can be resolved quickly and that we can proceed without any schedule delay. I look forward to your prompt reply.

Best regards, and our deepest appreciation again for your support during the Moscow meetings.

F. Carbone

Exhibit 6

3 January 1980

Attn: L. Lattisla
cc: T. Satosaki

Suggest you include the following points in your telex to Frank Carbone covering the actions resulting from our meeting on 3 January 1980.

1. Finnco agrees to cover Amco costs on the systems ordered under P.O. No. 903737 in the event Finnco must cancel contract at Sovietco's direction. Acknowledges Amco's cost, including material commitments to January 1980, is 1.6 million U.S. dollars.
2. Finnco directs Amco to suspend material procurement on a temporary basis until Sovietco has made final decision on who they want as the oil drilling equipment supplier. During this partial work suspension, Amco is authorized to continue labor expenditure, complete design finalization of the taut wire system. Amco's labor expenditures will not exceed 50,000 U.S. dollars per week during January 1980. Finnco agrees to reevaluate this partial work suspension on 1 February 1980 and advise Amco what actions should be taken after this date.
3. Finnco will make payment on the 2nd installment upon receipt of a dimensioned outline drawing for the proposed taut wire final design from Amco.
4. Finnco agrees that the temporary work suspension will impact Amco's cost and schedule and agrees to renegotiate these elements in order 903737 upon resumption of work.

I have talked with Frank Carbone since our discussions and it is of the utmost importance that we have Finnco position in writing on the above points.

A telex on 4 January 1980 to Seattle will be satisfactory. My suitcase arrived at Helsinki so we have the additional document for your submittal to Dr. Russianov.

I can be reached at Amco's office in Helsinki if you have any questions.

Regards,

Bill Sullivan

Exhibit 7

4 January 1980

Attn: Mr. Carbone
cc: Mr. Sullivan
Mr. Lesslo, Amco oy, Helsinki

In reference to the discussion of January 3rd, 1980, at our office, we inform at Mr. Sullivan's suggestion that the following was agreed;

- All the works concerning our order no. MTO 903737 will be stopped for the present except the design work for the taut wire system.
- RR would not like to make any modification in the clause "termination liability" at this stage because Sovietco decision in regard to oil drilling equipment will be obtained in the near future.

We are afraid that the changed world political situation might have effect on the Russian decision concerning the oil drilling system.

Regards,

Finnco
Finnluoto works/Leo Lattisla

Exhibit 8

10 January 1980

Amco Sea
Attn: Messrs. Lattisla, Satosaki, Veroken
cc: Matti Lesslo—Amco Finland

Yesterday, 9 January 1980, President Carter issued an order for review of export licenses for equipment to Russia. The review is expected to last 4–6 weeks. During the review period, no shipments are to take place. Since we do not have any planned equipment shipments during the announced review period, there is not yet a force majeure situation as far as our contract is concerned. We will advise you as soon as possible of anything which would affect the validity of our current export license.

Regards,

F. Carbone
Amco, Inc.
Seattle, WA

Exhibit 9

11 January 1980

Attn: Mr. F. Carbone
Our Order No. MTO 903737

As response to your telex of January 10th, 1980, we repeat that you have to stop the work for our above order at least for the present. The reason for this is that the owner (V/O Sovietco) has not yet given the final approval for your equipment and specially due to President Carter's export prohibition to the USSR concerning this kind of equipment. We consider that we are not responsible for the costs due to stopping of the work, because the reasons for this do not depend on us. After the situation has been changed we are ready to discuss with you for instance prolongation of the delivery time.

We regret the troubles caused by the changed circumstances in our cooperation which started so pleasantly.

Regards,

Finnco
Finnluoto Works/Leo Lattisla

Exhibit 10

28 January 1980

Attn: Mr. F. Carbone/Mr. W. Sullivan
Our Order MTO 903737

In your telex of January 10, 1980 you mentioned that the review of export licenses for equipment to Russia will take four to six weeks. Now, according to our understanding, the political situation between USA and USSR is more difficult than in the beginning of January. Therefore, we ask you to kindly give us a completely clear answer if you have an export license or not and what kind of guarantee you are able to give us for that license.

We need your answer as soon as possible, latest by Monday, February 4, 1980.

Regards,

Finnco

Exhibit 11

1 February 1980

Attn: Matti Kerkola
To: Finnco
Attn: L. Lattisla
cc: Amco Finland
Attn: M. Lesslo
Reference: (1) Telex of 28 January from Finnco to F. Carbone/W. Sullivan concerning export license status

(2) Telex from F. Carbone to Finnco dated 10 January 1980 (message number 8085)

As indicated in reference (2), a review of our export license is in process. Effective 12 noon est January 11, 1980 the U.S. Office of Export Administration suspended shipments to the Soviet Union. At their request, we returned our existing license. We were informed in writing that quote "you will be notified as soon as possible regarding the further disposition of your licenses and authorizations."

Contacts with our Amco Washington, D.C. office indicate that the status is unknown at this time and the review is still in process. We will continue to follow up and keep you informed. Since export authorizations are not in our control, Amco cannot predict the future concerning a fully validated license for the deliveries of three shipsets. Amco will continue to make reasonable attempts to obtain the required authorizations. As you know, no deliveries were planned before 30 September 1980 and by the time deliveries could be made, the situation will probably be clarified and, in our opinion, it is possible that we could.

We have learned that shipments to intermediate consignees have been permitted where consignee press to obtain approval from US before shipment to USSR.

Regards,

F. Carbone
Vice President
Amco, Inc.
Seattle, WA

Exhibit 12

Attn: Mr. F. Carbone/W. Sullivan

We have received your telex of February 1, 1980. We have to state that you have not given satisfactory evidence, that you will be able to meet delivery times which are mentioned on purchase agreements. Because the boycott of the US government concerning high level technical equipment to USSR is now valid and you are unable to give us clear answer and guarantee that you will deliver the equipment on time without delaying the building schedule of drilling vessels.

Therefore and according to the Finnish law, we cancel the purchase order no. MTO 903737 made between Finnco oy and Amco Inc. on August 3, 1979.

We ask you immediately return all payments made by us amounting to US dollars 630,000—to our bank Kansallis-Osake-Pankki, Helsinki, Aleksanteri Street 42, Finland USD account No. 202343-2421(2).

Regards,

Finnco
Satosaki & Kerkola

cc: Amco Finland—Mr. Lesslo

5

MANAGING INTER-GOVERNMENTAL CONFLICTS

One of the most difficult, complex situations a multinational corporation can face is being caught between two governments engaged in some sort of political conflict or disagreement. Such a situation is particularly difficult when one of the countries involved is the company's home government. As one analyst observed, international businesses are often confronted with "a series of clashes between United States policy and that of other nations, in which the corporation has on occasion been something like the bird in a badminton game."[1]

How international firms can manage the conflicting demands, laws and regulations of two governments has become an issue in several areas, such as anti-boycott laws, antitrust provisions, and basic foreign policy disputes. But perhaps this problem has been faced most frequently and controversially in the field of export controls regulating East-West trade. The United States government has the authority to prevent trade with "enemy countries" and to deny certain U.S. goods or technology to other countries for foreign policy purposes. Under the Trading with the Enemy Act, the Treasury Department can forbid all transactions between "any person" under U.S. jurisdiction and foreign nationals affiliated with an enemy country (North Korea, Vietnam, Cambodia, Laos, and Cuba). Under the Export Control Act, U.S. firms must gain a license from the Commerce Department for the export of controlled products and technology to certain countries, principally those ruled by communist governments. The State Department regulates the export of military weapons. The total cost of all U.S. export controls on East-West trade was an estimated $4 billion in lost sales to American companies in the 1982 to 1987 period alone.[2]

These laws and regulations have thus caused U.S. firms tremendous problems. Besides the potential for lost sales, there can be lengthy delays in having any licensing request approved. Even more frustrating, an item not on the controlled list could be added at a subsequent date because of foreign policy developments. As a result, a firm could be caught in the middle of a contract, when a product is being produced but not yet delivered, and thereby victimized by shifts in the political climate, which have been considerable in East-West relations. Of course, the most dangerous of all situations is for a multinational to face conflicting demands by two governments, one insisting that products be shipped according to contract and the other threatening sanctions if delivery occurs. Such a dilemma for American firms has arisen because the U.S. government insists upon the extraterritorial extension of its laws, much to the consternation of foreign governments.

Typically, U.S. companies have attempted to manage such crises by seeking "middle-ground solutions."[3] The objective here is to find areas of compromise or to delay decisions until policies are changed. The ability of the firm to manage such outcomes successfully is a function of both the determination of each government to meet its policy objectives and the government-relations and negotiation skills of the company's managers.

In certain instances, however, middle-ground solutions cannot be found, and the firm is confronted with making a painful but clear-cut choice. The paramount importance of bargaining power analysis, negotiation skills, and understanding legal options is particularly felt at this point. How such conflicts can be best managed, moreover, is a dynamic problem, for stakes and relative bargaining power often shift during the crisis. A firm's negotiation and conflict-management tactics thus should be approached on a sequential and contingency basis.

Besides suggestions of how to manage the crisis of being caught in the middle of a intergovernmental conflict, multinational corporations can position themselves better to cope with a crisis before it occurs. One precrisis recommendation is the company should institutionalize the function of managing government relations and export controls, particularly if East-West trade is a significant part of the business. In particular, the company should have an in-house expert on export controls, and this individual should develop and maintain very close contacts with key government officials. This will allow the company to gauge government policy better. Developing personal relationships may also result in more favorable and expeditious rulings on licensing requests. In addition, the company should institute a review program or internal audit on business subject to export controls, and this audit should be conducted by managers not responsible for marketing. Such a review may catch potential problems before a crisis ensues. Lastly, it is important to contingency-plan and factor in time delays given your product/market target. Anticipating problems and developing action plans accordingly are important to all areas of international business, but experience has shown this to be particularly true in the case of East-West trade.

NOTES

1. Seymour J. Rubin, "The Multinational Enterprise and the 'Home' State," in *Global Companies*, ed. George W. Ball (Englewood Cliffs, N.J.: Prentice-Hall, 1975), p. 48.
2. Stanley D. Nollen, "Business Costs and Business Policy for Export Controls," *Journal of International Business Studies*, 18 (Spring 1987), p. 8.
3. Thomas N. Gladwin and Ingo Walter, *Multinationals Under Fire: Lessons in the Management of Conflict*, (New York: John Wiley & Sons, 1980) p. 157.

Dresser and the Soviet Pipeline Controversy (A)

On August 18, 1982, Rock Grundman, Government/Business Affairs Counsel for Dresser Industries, was awakened in the middle of the night by an urgent long-distance phone call from the company's French subsidiary.

Mr. Grundman's caller hurriedly related the latest chain of events and concluded by saying that a ship named the "Borodin" was en route to the French port of Le Havre to load three completed compressors for the Soviet pipeline. The situation was critical. Since June 18, 1982, when President Reagan had announced his expanded embargo, communications between the parent and its subsidiary had been consciously limited. A new embargo had extended the one of December 30, 1981, to include the foreign subsidiaries of U.S. firms who were producing equipment under U.S. licenses. The president's action in June meant that Dresser's French subsidiary could honor its Soviet pipeline contract only at the risk of U.S. government sanctions or blacklisting. This action not only put Dresser in a difficult position, it put a strain on relations between the United States and its European trading partners, who would be beneficiaries of the Soviet pipeline. (See Exhibit 1 for a chronology of events.) The French government had requested that they be shipped on time. Arrival time of the ship was uncertain, but its likely departure date was late August.

Mr. Grundman saw Dresser as being "between a rock and hard place." If the company honored the U.S. president's directive, it would alienate the French government. If the company responded to the French government's request for shipment, the company could face repercussions from the U.S. government. Whichever direction the company took, the offended government could initiate civil or criminal action.

As he hung up the phone, Mr. Grundman pondered the significance of the ship's name, "Borodin." Aleksandr Borodin was a famous Russian composer in the mid-1800s. Were the Russians trying to get Dresser to dance to their music by sending the "Borodin" to France?

Over his first cup of coffee, Mr. Grundman notified officials of the U.S. State and Commerce Departments and the U.S. Trade Representative of the reported destination and name of the ship. These actions were followed by a call to France so that the French government would be fully informed as well. After these calls were completed, he wondered what the ultimate consequences of this dilemma to Dresser would be and what the company could do in response.

DRESSER INDUSTRIES

Dresser was founded in 1880 as a producer of new types of lead-free pipe couplings. The company grew during the 1960s through acquisitions and became a leading supplier of engineered products and technical services to energy and natural resources industries throughout the world.

In 1981 Dresser Industries was divided into five industry segments: petroleum operations, energy processing and conversion equipment, refractories and minerals operations, mining and construction equipment, and industrial specialty products. Total sales and service revenues amounted to $4.6 billion in 1981, with earnings of $317 million. These levels reflected an increase over the previous year of 15 percent and 21 percent, respectively. Carefully developed functional policies, sophisticated planning and control, effective marketing programs, and a high level of capital and technical spending contributed to the achievement of this performance. Proprietary products and services in the energy-related markets were also important to maintaining Dresser's leading position in the world.

Headquartered in Dallas, Texas, Dresser employed over 57,000 people and operated in more than 100 countries. Dresser, in fact, had $1.5 billion in export sales in 1981. With this extensive network, the company and its subsidiaries had captured 20 percent to 30 percent of the world's market for compressors. Through advanced technology development, compressors continued to be one of the company's key strategic products, accounting for 86 percent of the energy-processing segment's sales, which totaled $900 million in 1981.

Dresser-France, one of the company's divisions within the Dresser Compressor Group, was owned by Dresser A.G. (Vaduz), a Liechtenstein corporation. Dresser Industries owned Dresser A.G. The French subsidiary contributed about $492 million in annual sales in 1981 and exported about 92 percent of its output. Gas compressors and other devices built in its plant were based on the technology developed by the Dresser-Clark Division in Olean, New York, and other U.S.-based divisions. Several of the company's other international manufacturing operations had similar licensing agreements to build identical compressors.

DRESSER AND THE SOVIET CONNECTION

Dresser began exporting compressors to the USSR in the 1930s, and during the political cold war of 1949–1963, continued to conduct business with the Soviet Union without U.S. government intervention. As relations between the Soviet and U.S. governments thawed in the late 1960s, sales in general between the two countries accelerated. Western exports of manufactured goods flowed east, and eastern exports of mineral raw materials and labor-intensive goods flowed west. Transfer of western technology, in particular, grew dramatically. In fact, international sales of U.S. licenses increased three times faster than merchandise exports.

To encourage this favorable flow of trade, Congress passed the Export Administration Act of 1969 as a successor to the Export Control Act of 1949. The new act reduced restrictions of exports to communist countries of goods and technology for economic development. (Exports for military development were still prohibited.) The new legislation was further amended during the early 1970s (the Nixon *detente* years) so as to allow U.S. companies to compete for Soviet business on an equal basis with Western European counterparts.

The Soviets were anxious to purchase foreign equipment and technology to develop their oil and gas industry. In 1975 they initiated negotiations with Dresser for a $144 million contract to help them build a plant to manufacture drill bits. After careful reviews in the Department of Defense, the export license was finally issued in May 1978.

Support in Washington for liberalization of trade with the Soviets began to erode at about the same time. Incidents such as the trials of Soviet dissidents Shcharansky and Ginzberg, the Soviet support of insurrection in Africa, and the Soviet invasion of Afghanistan in 1979 ended the climate of *detente* between the two countries. With President Carter's ensuing export embargo, the Dresser drill-bit license was revoked. By this time, however, all the necessary goods had been shipped, and only the final phase of limited Soviet technical training remained. Similarly, General Electric's turbine technology had already been delivered to four European countries. That contract was the heart of the Soviet pipeline project.

THE SOVIET PIPELINE

In the 1960s, the Soviet Union discovered a vast reserve of natural gas in the province of Urengoi in Siberia. A six-tube pipeline was initially planned to carry up to 65 billion cubic meters (bcm) per year to Western Europe, 3,700 miles away. (The length of this pipeline was four times longer than the Alaskan pipeline.) Contracted delivery of gas was later scaled down to 35 bcm/year, beginning with 10 bcm in 1984.

As the worldwide oil crisis had developed in the 1970s, consumers conserved energy and looked for alternative energy sources. Natural gas proved to be a cheaper alternative, with price differentials widening to 50 percent between 1974 and 1977. Gas consumption within the EEC countries grew sharply and was expected to reach 400 bcm by the end of the century. Because European production could not supply the total projected demand, other sources of natural gas supply were analyzed on the basis of cost, reliability, and potential impact on balance of payments. European leaders believed that the USSR was the only country that could reasonably satisfy their requirements. They were confident that the EEC would not become overly dependent on the Soviets because, despite the fact that the new Soviet pipeline would supply 20 percent of the EEC's total natural gas needs, only 5 percent of total energy supplies would be sourced from the Soviets. Furthermore, the Europeans were optimistic about the jobs that would be created to support the pipeline, since the countries were facing rising unemployment and inflation.

The pipeline project was the largest commercial transaction ever attempted between the East and the West. Originally, costs of construction were estimated to be $11 billion. Productive life of the pipeline was said to be 25 years, beginning in 1984.

Construction of the pipeline would require the cooperation of twelve nations, dozen of companies, and more than 120,000 Soviet workers. Financing of the project, including the imported equipment and pipe, would be negotiated through the Western European beneficiaries. The final costs were reestimated to be $25–$30 billion because of unforeseen problems and delays.

The French engineering firm Creusot-Loire was selected as the contractor for approximately eighty compressors valued at $1 billion. GE licensees in the EEC received the orders for the turbines to drive all 120 or so compressors in the pipeline project. On September 28, 1981, Dresser-France signed a contract with Creusot-Loire and the USSR for one group of twenty-two compressors to be powered by the GE turbines. The $20 million order required 20 percent of Dresser-France's total operations and represented a substantial portion of its annual workload in Le Havre. Deliveries were scheduled to begin in May 1982.

Previous energy projects with the USSR had been profitable for European businesses. Most of the ventures had been a type of countertrade known as compensation agreements: western exports were compensated with credits that the Soviets would repay, wholly or partly, in goods at some future time. Transfer of foreign exchange was minimal. In the new pipeline agreement, however, transfer of foreign exchange would flow in exchange for the natural gas.

U.S. OPPOSITION TO THE URENGOI PIPELINE

The U.S. government objected to the Soviet-EEC deal mainly from a political standpoint. The Reagan Administration believed that European dependency on Soviet oil threatened European security and increased Europe's vulnerability. Resistance to Soviet aggression might be weakened by actual or potential interruption of supplies. Such interruptions had been experienced before, but never during an international crisis, and supplies had always been restored.

Another argument addressed the sale of technologically advanced equipment that could strengthen the Soviet strategic position. Gas exports to Western Europe could earn the USSR $10–$15 billion in hard currency annually by the 1990s, which could be used to bolster its military forces.

The Reagan Administration argued that such a Soviet military buildup directly threatened U.S. national security. Therefore, building U.S. military forces and applying economic pressure against the Soviet Union became a top priority with some within the administration.

Export controls were believed to be effective only under certain conditions. An example of ineffective controls cited by some observers was the grain sales embargo imposed by President Carter in 1979. The desired effect was not achieved because other suppliers were readily available. On the other hand, when hard currency was used for grain purchases, that money was not available for arms purchases. This choice between guns and butter was believed to put effective pressure on Soviet action. "U.S. grain sales make the Russians dependent on us and force them to give up their hard currency every year," said one Reagan advisor. "The pipeline does just the opposite, it makes the Europeans dependent on the Russians." Such was the Reagan Administration's answer to European charges of hypocrisy when the U.S. president announced his pipeline sanctions policy while still allowing wheat sales to the Soviets.

THE SANCTIONS

Precipitated by the Polish government's declaration of martial law on December 13, 1981, on December 30, President Reagan announced new economic sanctions against the Soviet Union. These sanctions expanded the 1978 restricted list of oil and gas equipment exports by domestic companies to include oil and gas transmission and related goods. It also restricted further issuance or renewal of validated licenses for export to the USSR of high-technology products, technical data, and oil and gas equipment and technology.

The proclamation had immediate implications for U.S.-based companies that had supply contracts for the Soviet pipeline. GE had a $175 million contract for the 125 turbine rotors; only twenty-three sets had been supplied so far. (Companies in France, the United Kingdom, and Italy were to build the turbines.) Caterpillar, which was already experiencing financial difficulties, had a $90 million contract for pipe-laying tractors. Other domestic companies also had outstanding contracts that might be denied licenses.

Prior to the December sanctions, Dresser Industries had conferred with the administration to verify the government's position on U.S.-Soviet business. Dresser had asked if the U.S. government had any strong objections to the compressor contract. The government gave a neutral reaction, neither a yes or no answer. Based on this response, Dresser signed the compressor contract in September 1981.

When the sanctions were announced three months later, all necessary technology and information had already been transferred to Dresser-France from Dresser-Clark. Mr. Grundman recounted those events this way:

> At that time, I was on vacation in Sante Fe, New Mexico. I was advised while in Santa Fe of what the president had done, and I discussed it with the operating units and lawyers involved and made sure that no data was transmitted to France subsequent to that date. In effect, we put a wall between the U.S. and Dresser-France from that day forward, but that was easier said than done, because we had just transmitted by mail another set of technical drawings, which was unnecessary to the completion of the contract. We actually required Dresser-France to return them unopened. I jokingly vowed never to go on vacation again.

Communications with the Reagan Administration were continuous at the same time. Dresser wanted to express its intentions clearly and to understand the interpretation of the government's regulations. Most importantly, Dresser did not want the U.S. government to act against its interests based on rumor or incorrect facts. Dresser thus took a proactive stance with the government. As Mr. Grundman described it:

> Immediately after New Year's weekend, I arranged a meeting with an assistant secretary of Commerce to give an interpretation of the regulation. I needed to be sure we could lawfully proceed with the contract or at least determine where we stood from a legal standpoint in order to make an informed business decision. The end result, however, was that the assistant secretary was noncommittal and gave no response to my inquiry as to whether the regulations applied retroactively or were intended to. Therefore, we had to rely on our legal judgment that they did not apply retroactively, and they knew that would be our interpretation.

On the international front, the EEC remained committed to participating in the natural gas pipeline despite the economic sanctions against the project. The countries contended that growth in trade with Eastern Europe and the USSR was necessary to maintain Western Europe's economy. West German industry officials indicated that more serious problems could arise if the Reagan Administration prohibited American companies from delivering parts and components to European manufacturers supplying equipment for the pipeline. A search for other suppliers was one option that was contemplated.

As far as Dresser was concerned, the spring of 1982 was business as usual. As Mr. Grundman recounted:

> Nothing happened except normal business. The commercial decision to proceed was made, with Dresser-France in the position to proceed without any further help from the United States. We understood that the regulations were not retroactive.

Reagan's "trade war" with the Soviets, however, was one of the top issues that consumed the Versailles summit meetings in June 1982, among the United States, United Kingdom, France, West Germany, Japan, Italy, and Canada. Their discussions were concluded with a loosely worded, hard-to-interpret agreement whereby the countries would proceed "prudently" in their economic approach to the Soviet Bloc. The European leaders left the summit believing that Reagan would ease his embargo policy in exchange for their agreement to review credit terms to Eastern Europe in the future.

A few days after the accord, France was the first to announce publicly its interpretation of the Versailles agreement. President Mitterrand expressed his intent to continue the current credit policy with the USSR. Therefore, in response to Europe's refusal to eradicate the policy of interest-rate subsidization for the pipeline, on June 18 President Reagan announced extensions to the sanctions effective as of June 22, 1982. The extensions covered foreign subsidiaries and licensees of U.S. companies.

The decision had been formulated in a National Security Council meeting. On Friday, June 18, Bo Denysyk, a Deputy Assistant Secretary of Commerce, called Rock Grundman to ask what the proposed sanctions would do to the Dresser-France contract. "Halt it" was the reply. Fifteen minutes later, the sanctions were announced.

Mr. Grundman was told that the sanctions would be retroactive, making it unlawful to transfer anything that was made with the assistance of U.S. technology. He immediately advised Dresser's president, Jim Brown, who sent a telex to Dresser-France on June 19 advising them to cease work on the contract and not to ship the three completed compressors to the Soviet Union.

Under the Export Administration Act of 1979 (see Exhibit 2), the President of the United States could initiate civil, criminal, and administrative penalties against violators of his trade sanctions, including placing the offending firm on a denial or "blacklist." U.S. export controls were implemented by the Commerce Department's International Trade Administration (see Exhibit 3). Any blacklisted company could be denied authority to export goods or technology, and other companies could be denied any transactions with that company. Such penalties could be targeted at either U.S. corporations as a whole, their overseas subsidiaries only, or foreign-owned companies. As Lionel H. Olmer, Under Secretary of Commerce for International Trade Administration, explained:

> We are putting our shoulder to the wheel to make these sanctions as effective as possible . . . denial list (companies) could be prohibited from receiving any export of any good or data from the United States, irrespective of whether it's related to oil or gas.

Olmer, moreover, predicted that President Reagan's actions would delay the pipeline project by at least two years and might even cause the project to collapse. He also estimated that the sanctions would result in roughly $1.2 billion in lost sales for U.S. companies. When asked what the Commerce Department's reaction would be if France passed a law barring companies from complying with U.S. regulations, Olmer stated: "It would be a contentious matter. I hope it won't arise."[1]

A week after the sanctions were announced, President Mitterrand made a public statement requesting that all French-based companies honor their original contracts. Several weeks later, the French government sent a letter to Dresser-France asking the company to ship the three completed compressors on schedule and resume work on the remaining ones. On August 23rd, once the "Borodin" had arrived in Le Havre, the French government issued an "Order du Requisition" to Dresser-France requiring completion of the compressor contract with the USSR. Such orders by the French government could not be challenged in the French judicial system. Dresser now was caught squarely in between two governments. Noncompliance with the French order could cost the French affiliate and its managers $60,000 and up to twelve months in jail, in addition to a contractual penalty not to exceed 8 percent of the total contract price for failure to deliver.[2] Even nationalization of Dresser-France's facilities was considered a real possibility by managers in Dallas.

The reactions of other European governments were swift and angry as well. British Prime Minister Margaret Thatcher, who was considered a close friend and ally of President Reagan, was in fact the first European leader to condemn the June 18th sanctions. Like the government of France, she invoked a UK law, the Protection of Trading Interests Act, which compelled three British firms with compressor contracts to ignore American export controls. The governments of West Germany and Italy also urged their firms to honor pipeline contracts, thereby defying the U.S. embargo. The foreign ministers of the ten European Economic Community countries, moreover, issued a joint statement, which said: "The action, taken with-

[1]*The New York Times,* June 24, 1982, p. 1.
[2]*Oil and Gas Journal,* August 30, 1982, p. 74.

out consultation with the Community, implies an extraterritorial extension of U.S. jurisdiction, which in the circumstances is contrary to the principles of international law."

Mr. Grundman described the circumstances under which he managed this situation:

> Curiously enough, when the first shoe dropped, I was in Sante Fe. When the second shoe dropped, I was on my way to my last two-week duty in the Air Force reserve. Conducting business by express mail and pay telephone while at Maxwell Air Force Base during the last two weeks of June was interesting, but of course, the most important thing had been taken care of already—the telex to Dresser-France had been sent. Then, after I returned from reserve duty, President Jim Brown died. When Chairman J. V. James resumed the role of the president, he called me into his office and said he wanted me to handle the Dresser-France situation. The immediate thing to do was to make sure that nothing was done precipitously by either the U.S. or French governments. The first decision was to keep them both informed completely, which we did.

Mr. Grundman told both governments about continued communications between Dresser-Headquarters and Dresser-France and with each respective government. Copies of formal correspondence were cross-issued to both governments. The U.S. government acknowledged the information but remained noncommittal in its response. Through informal discussions with many senior officers in the administration, Mr. Grundman argued that the sanction policy was harmful to the health of the companies involved as well as the countries. Some senior officials agreed with him privately, but not always publicly. The press reported:

> Some officials sympathized with Dresser's position noting that if the company is successful in stopping the shipment, its French executives face severe penalties. If, on the other hand, the shipment is delivered, the American parent company faces severe sanctions under the Export Administration Act.[3]

Unfortunately for Dresser, many administration officials were not sympathetic to the company's situation. In addition, the legal position of the Reagan Administration was strong. The law gave the president total discretion in implementing export controls for foreign policy reasons. Dresser's only viable legal argument was that in spite of any foreign policy rationale, Reagan's sanctions violated the intent of the Export Administration Act since sanctions were imposed retroactively and on companies outside U.S. jurisdiction. Nevertheless, as the "Borodin" approached Le Havre, it became clear that the Reagan Administration was going to react strongly if Dresser-France loaded those compressors. As reported in the press on August 23rd:

> Administration officials said yesterday that an interdepartmental working group of the National Security Council began last Friday to map out a strategy for legal and administrative actions against Dresser Industries, should the loading occur, as well as stern diplomatic messages to the French government. The group was chaired by Treasury Secretary Donald T. Regan . . . . Another administration official said yes-

[3]*Washington Post,* August 23, 1982, p. A1.

> terday that two specific options thus far studied by the working group are seeking a temporary restraining order in U.S. District Court against the Dresser subsidiary's shipment and taking administrative action against Dresser, perhaps going so far as to cut off its French subsidiary from future equipment supplies.[4]

Even the possibility of placing Dresser as a whole on a denial list was not out of the question.

BORODIN STARTS THE MUSIC

Since late July when the chairman and president of Dresser had given Mr. Grundman the lead role in managing the pipeline crisis, few other senior executives had been privy to the details of the situation. The General Counsel was not involved at this stage, because he was in Europe on other business. After Mr. Grundman received the phonecall from Dresser-France on August 18 informing him of the "Borodin" being en route to Le Havre, the days passed very quickly and the pressure mounted enormously. Unfortunately, Dresser was victimized by being the first test case of a foreign policy dispute between the U.S. and European governments. Other firms would face a similar dilemma in a few days, particularly a British firm, John Brown Engineering Ltd., whose compressors were scheduled for shipment before the end of the month. Nevertheless, Dresser was first, and on August 23rd, the most pressing decision now rested on an accurate understanding of the company's possible options. Did the French subsidiary have any choice but to obey Mitterrand's order? If the French order was obeyed, the U.S. government had made it clear that a blacklisting of Dresser-France would probably follow. Given this threat, could headquarters close its eyes and let the French subsidiary make its own choice? Alternatively, should Dresser again order their subsidiary to ship or not to ship the compressors? Or should Mr. Grundman, keeping the Logan Act in mind,[5] request the U.S. government to allow headquarters to negotiate directly with the French government? Should Dresser take legal action against the U.S. government by challenging the President's authority in the Export Administration Act of 1979? Apparently challenging the French government's "Order du Requisition" was not an option. Since the ship was to be loaded with the compressors in a couple of days, Dresser would have to make its decisions quickly.

Certainly, the U.S. government had its preference. As reported in the press:

> "The hope is to go the diplomatic route," said one senior official, who emphasized that the president is adamant about not backing off from the sanctions. At the same time, this official said that no decision has been made on what course to take if the first loading occurs at Le Havre. He ruled out any American attempt to physically interfere with the loading. The official said that lawyers from the State, Defense, Commerce and Justice departments are still hopeful that Dresser officials can be persuaded to take additional steps to stop the shipment. Moreover, the official said,

[4]*Ibid.*

[5]Logan Act forbids U.S. private citizens from negotiating with a foreign government about U.S. foreign policy, unless prior approval by the government has been given.

> the administration is planning to tell the French government through the State Department that Reagan takes the export ban seriously and intends to enforce it.[6]

Another administration official, however, stated that:

> Dresser officials already have done most of what a court order would require them to do to stop the shipment. This official said that Dresser's top management in Dallas has already ordered the French-based Dresser executives to stop the shipment. Those (French) executives, in turn, told the freight handling company in an August 11 letter that ". . . All shipment is forbidden until further instructions are given to you in writing . . ."[7]

[6] *Washington Post,* August 23, 1982.
[7] *Ibid.*

Exhibit 1 Chronology of Events

June 1978	Contract for drill bit plant signed.
December 1979	Invasion of Afghanistan by Soviet troops.
January 1980	President Carter imposes sanctions and denies export licenses of technology transfer.
September 1981	Contract signed with Creusot-Loire, SA, and Machinoimport to manufacture and sell 21 compressors.
December 13, 1981	Martial law in Poland.
December 29, 1981	Last technical document to Dresser-France sent.
December 30, 1981	President Reagan imposes embargo.
June 18, 1982	President Reagan makes embargo retroactive, effective June 22, 1982.
June 20, 1982	Mr. Grundman flies to Maxwell Air Force Base for two-week reserve duty.
June 25, 1982	President Mitterrand makes public speech requesting completion and shipment of compressors.
July 3, 1982	Mr. Grundman returns from reserve duty.
July 25, 1982	President and chairman of Dresser puts Mr. Grundman in charge of situation.
August 10, 1982	President of Dresser-France receives letter from French Minister of Research and Industry stating that Soviet contract would be honored.
August 18, 1982	Mr. Grundman informed of "Borodin" destination.
August 23, 1982	French government issues legally enforceable requisition order to ship compressors.

Exhibit 2 Export Administration Act Regulations, Excerpts

387.1 Sanctions

(a) Criminal

(1) Violations of Export Administration Act.

1. *General.* . . . whoever knowingly violates the Export Administration Act ("the Act") or any regulation, order, or license issued under the Act is punishable for each violation by a fine of not more than five times the value of the exports involved or $50,000, whichever is greater, or by imprisonment for not more than five years, or both.

2. *Willful violations.* Whoever willfully exports anything contrary to any provision of the Act or any regulation, order, or license issued under the Act, with the knowledge that such exports will be used for the benefit of any country to which exports are restricted for national security or foreign policy purposes except in the case of an individual, shall be fined not more than five times the value of the exports involved or $1,000,000, whichever is greater; and in the case of the individual, shall be fined not more than $250,000, or imprisoned not more than 10 years, or both. . . .

(b) Administrative

1. Denial of export privileges. Whoever violates any law, regulation, order, or license relating to export controls or restrictive trade practices and boycotts is also subject to administrative action which may result in suspension, revocation, or denial of export privileges conferred under the Export Administration Act.

2. Civil penalty. A civil penalty may be imposed for each violation of the Export Administration Act or any regulation, order, or license issued under the Act either in addition to, or instead of, any other liability or penalty which may be imposed. The civil penalty may not exceed $10,000 for each violation except that the civil penalty for each violation involving national security controls imposed under Section 5 of the Act may not exceed $100,000.

Source: Export Administration Regulations, January 25, 1983.

Exhibit 3 Commerce Department—International Trade Administration

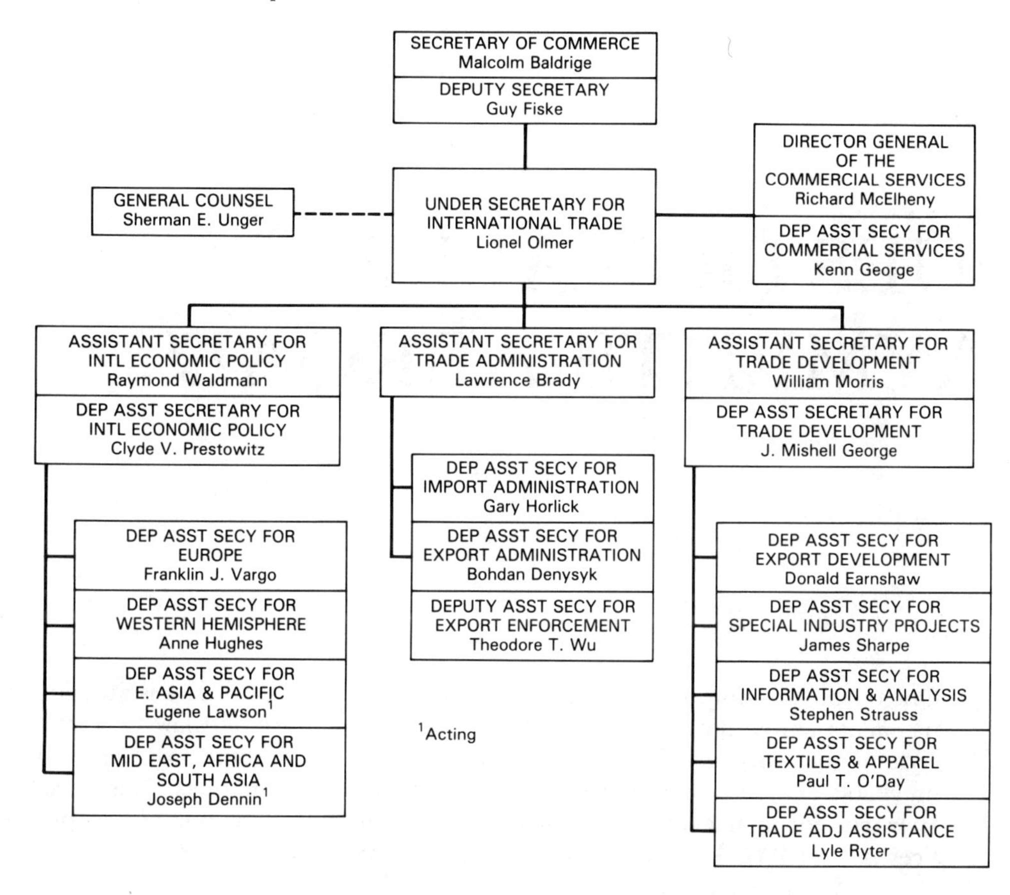

6

QUESTIONABLE PAYMENTS ABROAD

One of the most important issues international managers must face is questionable payments abroad. What is acceptable in terms of culture and law varies greatly around the world (see Appendix), and managers must come to grips with the inevitable demands that will be placed on them in foreign markets. This is particularly true for managers of U.S. corporations because of the Foreign Corrupt Practices Act (FCPA). A detailed understanding of this issue is necessary.

In the early 1970s, the Securities and Exchange Commission conducted a program of voluntary disclosure in which a number of American companies revealed spending significant sums of money for questionable or illegal payments to foreign officials over the years. In its final report to Congress in 1976, the SEC indicated that some eighty-nine corporations had filed disclosure statements identifying such payments.[1]

Subsequent congressional hearings in 1976 demonstrated that foreign corrupt practices were even more widespread than the SEC report had determined. Executives from more than 400 U.S. corporations—including 117 of the Fortune 500—voluntarily admitted having made more than $300 million in questionable payments to foreign government officials, politicians, and political parties. Exxon disclosed payments of $59.4 million; Lockheed, $55 million; Boeing, $50.4 million; and Northrop, $34.3 million.

To address the situation, Congress enacted the FCPA in December 1977. The Senate Committee which drafted this legislation offered the following as its rationale for recommending the bill:

> Corporate bribery is bad business. In our free market system, it is basic that the sale of products should take place on the basis of price, quality, and service. Corporate

> bribery is fundamentally destructive of this basic tenet. . . . Foreign bribery affects the very stability of our overseas business. Foreign corporate bribes also affect our domestic competitive climate when domestic firms engage in such practices as a substitute for healthy competition for foreign business.[2]

The FCPA attacks the problem of corporate bribery abroad in a twofold approach: first by banning certain types of foreign payments and second by requiring U.S. firms to keep accurate records and to maintain adequate internal accounting controls. The antibribery provisions of the Act prohibit firms from paying foreign officials in order to obtain or retain business. The accounting provisions deter bribery by imposing an affirmative requirement on firms and managers to keep books and records which accurately reflect an entity's transactions (including any questionable payments) and to maintain an adequate system of internal controls to assure that the entity's assets are used for proper corporate purposes. Individuals violating the antibribery or the accounting provisions can be fined up to $100,000, imprisoned for up to five years, or both for each offense. Corporations, on the other hand, can be fined up to $2,000,000 for criminal violations of the Act.

This chapter will describe the antibribery and accounting provisions of the FCPA, as amended by the Omnibus Trade and Competitiveness Act of 1988. In addition, the enforcement measures taken by the SEC and the Department of Justice will be detailed. The chapter will also outline some of the steps managers can take to ensure their firms' compliance with the FCPA.

THE ANTIBRIBERY PROVISIONS

Foreign political payments have been most common in oligopolistic industries handling large, capital-intensive products—industries such as aerospace, construction, and energy development. U.S. firms have bought political influence in several ways. The most common method is to pay exorbitant commissions to foreign "sales agents" or "consultants," who pass along some or most of the money to government officials with influence on contract negotiations. In a refinement on the process, the foreign agents may pay kickbacks to U.S. executives.

The payments may be laundered through foreign subsidiaries, numbered Swiss bank accounts, or transfers to nonexistent companies. Alternatively, the bribes may be paid directly from off-the-book bank accounts. A 1978 study of 109 companies that voluntarily admitted "questionable" payments made before the FCPA's enactment reported that these firms had maintained more than $63.1 million in secret bank accounts or slush funds.[3]

Where does the money come from? The phony discount is one way to raise money off the record. Purchasers pay full prices while the books record discounted sales; the difference goes to a slush fund or directly to a bribetaker. The 1978 study found that $14.2 million in sensitive payments were financed through overbilling and $3.3 million via fake invoices. Inflated expense accounts raised about $500,000, chiefly for executives' personal political contributions.

The antibribery provisions of the Foreign Corrupt Practices Act criminalize such payments. The provisions apply to all corporations with reporting obligations to the SEC or whose securities are registered with the SEC *and* to all "domestic concerns." The FCPA defines "domestic concerns" as all citizens, nationals, or residents of the United States and all business entities organized under the laws of any state, territory, or possession, *or* having their principal place of business in the United States.

This definition would appear to exclude from the jurisdiction of the FCPA foreign subsidiaries of American corporations organized under the laws of a foreign country and which have their principal place of business outside the United States. However, the FCPA as amended in 1988 makes it unlawful to make, offer, or authorize payments to "any person while knowing that all or a portion of such money or thing will be offered or given, or promised, directly or indirectly, to any foreign official . . . for purposes of . . . influencing any act or decision of such foreign official."[4] Since "knowing is defined as specific awareness or "willful blindness," U.S. corporations will typically be held responsible for illegal payments made by their foreign subsidiaries, particularly those that are wholly or majority-owned. For minority-owned subsidiaries, on the other hand, the corporation must act in good faith to use its influence on the subsidiary to comply with the law. As the Conference Report on the 1988 amendments stated in regard to the law's accounting provisions:

> It is unrealistic to expect a minority owner to exert a disproportionate influence over the accounting practices of a subsidiary. While the relative degree of ownership is obviously one factor, other factors may be important in determining whether an issuer [a SEC reporting company] has demonstrated good faith efforts to use its influence.[5]

Besides defining the scope of the law in terms of the party making the payment, the FCPA also addresses the issue of who is being paid and why. If payments are made to foreign officials in order to expedite routine government action, such a payment is legal under the FCPA. Routine government action is defined as an action which is ordinarily and commonly performed by a foreign official in—

1. obtaining permits, licenses or other official documents to qualify a person to do business in a foreign country;
2. processing government papers such as visas and work orders;
3. providing police protection, mail pickup and delivery or scheduling inspections associated with contract performance or inspections related to transit of goods across country;
4. providing phone service, power and water supply, loading and unloading cargo or protecting perishable products or commodities from deterioration; or
5. actions of similar nature.[6]

The Conference Report, however, specifically excluded from routine action any decision that had the functional equivalent of "obtaining or retaining business for or with or directing business to any person."[7] For example, payments to a ministry official responsible for authorizing price increases for a product would still be illegal under the FCPA because that would constitute an attempt to influence the discretionary power of a foreign official in order to gain or retain business.

Thus, the intent of the law is that payments must be made "corruptly" in order to be considered a violation; an individual or entity making a payment would be held liable under the Act only if he or she were found to possess "an evil motive or purpose [or] an intent to wrongfully influence the recipient."[8] In addition, the legislative history behind the Act indicates that "true extortion situations would not be covered by this provision since a payment to keep an oil rig from being dynamited should not be held to be made with the requisite corrupt purpose."[9] The drafters of the FCPA considered as "extortionary" any threats of violence to people or to existing facilities. Two corporation lawyers advise managers subjected to demands they believe extortionary that "the only safe course is to report the demand to the Justice Department—which routinely advises extortion victims—before any payment is made."[10]

The FCPA identifies three classes of foreign individuals or entities to whom payments are prohibited, unless they are for expediting routine government action; these individuals are:

1. any foreign official;
2. any foreign political party or official thereof or any candidate for foreign political office;
3. *any* person, when a company knows . . . that person will give, promise or offer all or part of the company's payment to a third party who is a foreign official, political party or candidate for political office.[11]

The FCPA defines a "foreign official" as

> any officer or employee of a foreign government or any department, agency, or instrumentality thereof, or any person acting in an official capacity for or on behalf of any such government or department, agency, or instrumentality. Such term does not include any employee of a foreign government or any department, agency, or instrumentality thereof whose duties are essentially ministerial or clerical.[12]

By excluding from its definition of "foreign officials" those persons "whose duties are essentially ministerial or clerical," Congress apparently intended to allow under the FCPA so-called "facilitating" or "grease" payments made to minor functionaries to persuade them to carry out their customary tasks—such as allowing shipments through customs, issuing construction permits, or giving police protection.

The FCPA thus would not bar large payments to minor officials—as long as their duties are "ministerial or clerical." In addition, the 1988 amendments provide areas of affirmative defense against charges of FCPA violations. For example, a firm could defend itself on the basis that "the payment of a gift, offer, or promise of anything of value that was made was lawful under the written laws and regulations of the foreign official's, political party's, party official's or candidate's country."[13] In addition, the 1988 amendments provide an affirmative defense that

> the payment, gift, offer or promise of value that was made was a reasonable bona fide expenditure, such as travel and lodging expenses . . . directly related to—

1. the promotion, demonstration, or explanation of products or services; or
2. the execution or performance of a contract with a foreign government or agency thereof.[14]

The Conference Report, however, explicitly stated that if a gift or payment is corruptly made to obtain or retain business then such a defense would not be acceptable.[15]

ENFORCEMENT OF ANTIBRIBERY PROVISIONS

Most of the enforcement proceedings under the antibribery provisions of the FCPA have involved direct and corrupting payments by corporations or individuals to foreign officials. Only nine months after the passage of the FCPA, the SEC filed suit against an oil company, Katy Industries, its chairman, and one of its directors, for agreeing to pay an Indonesian oil official a percentage of the profits of an oil production sharing contract which the official had arranged. Katy and the two individuals involved settled the case by agreeing to an injunction forbidding them from future securities laws violations and by agreeing to establish a committee of outside directors that would review the SEC's allegations and file a full report. Since Katy had issued prospectuses in connection with a public sale of stock and had disseminated proxy materials to shareholders during the time it was making payments to the Indonesian official, the SEC also charged that Katy had committed fraud against its stockholders by failing to mention its illegal payments in these documents. Katy thereby opened itself up to a multitude of private lawsuits by disgruntled stockholders for its illegal conduct.

Another oil company, which had advanced $1.5 million to the Director of Petroleum Affairs in Qatar in order to obtain certain oil concessions for the company, was forced to submit to a similar injunction in *United States v. Carver,* as were a Dallas construction company and two of its directors who had paid $1.4 million to foreign officials to obtain construction contracts. In other cases, the SEC has sought more serious treatment for payments to foreign officials. In *SEC v. International Systems & Controls Corporation,* the SEC asked the court to appoint a receiver to take control of the assets and to oversee the business activities of a Houston-based energy development firm which had paid more than $23 million in bribes to foreign officials in various countries.

Bribes by several U.S. companies to officials of the Mexican national oil company PEMEX resulted in a number of enforcement proceedings against the parties involved. The president of Crawford Enterprises, Inc., an oilfield supply company, agreed to pay kickbacks of between five and ten percent of the purchase-order value of any compression equipment contracts which PEMEX awarded to Crawford. Three other companies, the C. E. Miller Corporation, Ruston Gas Turbines, Inc., and the Solar Turbine Division of International Harvester, Inc., also competed vigorously for PEMEX's compression business; so Crawford enlisted agents from these companies to join Crawford in its kickback scheme. Eventually, this unusual joint venture, which involved bid-rigging as well as bribery, unraveled after collecting orders totaling $225 million and paying nearly $10 million in kickbacks. Ruston quickly plea-bargained with the SEC and agreed to pay $750,000 in fines; Crawford was brought to trial and convicted of forty-six violations of the FCPA, thereby being subjected to possible fines of $46 million. Many individuals from all the companies involved suffered criminal convictions for their roles in the scheme. Crawford's president, for example, was convicted of forty-six counts of bribery and faced a possible sentence of up to 236 years in prison and fines of up to $470,000; the vice president of Ruston was convicted of forty-four violations of the FCPA.

While most of the enforcement actions under the FCPA have dealt with cases such as these, involving direct payment by American companies to foreign officials, the government has also brought enforcement proceedings against companies which have employed "agents" or "consultants" to make indirect payments to foreign officials. In *SEC v. Clark Oil Refining Corporation,* the SEC charge that a wholly owned subsidiary of a refining company had arranged commissions to a Liechtenstein corporation, which was to contact the state-owned oil company of the Emirate of Abu Dhabi in order to obtain price reductions on contracts to purchase crude oil. The refining company, in a consent decree, agreed to avoid future violations of the FCPA, to include a description of the SEC allegations in its next quarterly report, and to devise a system of internal accounting controls to prevent future violations.

In 1986, the SEC brought an action against Ashland Oil and its former CEO for alleged indirect payments to officials of the government of Oman. In April 1980, Ashland Oil paid approximately $29 million for a majority interest in a Zimbabwean mining operation which had been controlled by an Omani government official. The mining operation did not prove to be profitable, and Ashland wrote off its entire investment in the enterprise in 1982. In September 1980, however, the Omani government awarded Ashland a crude oil contract for 20,000 barrels a day for a year at a $3-per-barrel discount from the regular selling price. Ashland and its former CEO agreed to an SEC consent injunction.

These cases help illustrate the breadth of the FCPA's prohibition against making payments to *any* person when a company knows that person will pass the payment along to a foreign official. The *Ashland Oil* case shows the willingness of the SEC to look behind an ostensibly legitimate business deal and take action if it sees what looks like a cover-up for a bribe. The *Clark Oil Refining Corporation* case demonstrates that a parent company can be charged with violating the FCPA if one of its subsidiaries makes an illegal payment. This rule will probably hold true even where a foreign subsidiary is not itself subject to the FCPA. The key considerations are that the parent company *is* subject to the FCPA and knows that its subsidiary is making illegal payments. The same standard applies to the activities of consultants or foreign-sales agents. In addition, it should be stressed that the "knowing" provision in the amended Act does not excuse "deliberate avoidance of knowledge."[16] Thus, a particularly risk-averse company may wish to avoid any unusual transactions. One commentator suggested that:

> a risk-averse company certainly would want to investigate any rumor that an agent was involved in making payments to foreign officials . . . . A company might even want to hire local counsel to confirm agents' assertions regarding the legality of certain payments. Indeed, the company might also wish to seek assurances regarding an agent's understanding of and compliance with the FCPA's antibribery provisions.[17]

THE ACCOUNTING PROVISIONS

Whereas the antibribery provisions apply to all "domestic concerns," whether these are businesses registered with the SEC or not, the accounting provisions cover only companies subject to securities laws—that is, only public companies. In a sense, however, the accounting provisions have a wider scope than the antibribery statutes. Bribery is a rare event, compared to recordkeeping and control, which are day-to-day activities. In fact, a former SEC staff member has called the accounting provisions "the most extensive application of federal law into international corporate affairs since the passage of the 1933 and 1934 [Securities] Acts."[18]

The SEC proposed the FCPA's accounting provisions to Congress. In its investigation of more than 500 companies that had made illegal foreign and domestic political payments, the SEC described as "devastating" the "fact that and the extent to which some companies falsified entries in their own books and records." The Commission concluded that the "almost universal characteristic" of the cases investigated was the "frustration of our system of corporate accountability, which has been designed to assure that there is proper accounting of the use of corporate funds, and that documents filed with the Commission and circulated to shareholders do not omit or misrepresent material facts."[19]

While questionable payments abroad by American corporations led to the passage of the FCPA accounting provisions, the accounting provisions regulate *all* of the recordkeeping and control activities of companies which report to the SEC—not just those activities relating to their foreign operations. Indeed, much of the SEC's enforcement of the accounting provisions has involved domestic rather than foreign conduct.

The accounting provisions as amended in 1988 have the following features. First, the law limits criminal liability for violating the accounting provisions to those who "knowingly circumvent" the system of internal accounting controls or who "knowingly falsify" accounting records or transactions. This legal standard conforms to the earlier SEC announcement that "if a violation was committed by a low-level employee, without the knowledge of top management, with an adequate system of internal controls, and with appropriate corrective action taken by the issuer, we do not believe that any action against the company would be called for."[20] Moreover, the SEC had earlier assured companies that it would not bring enforcement proceedings for inadvertent recordkeeping mistakes or falsifications unknown to management, despite their theoretical liability under the original Act. As the SEC stated:

> The Act's principal purpose is to reach knowing or reckless misconduct . . . . Neither its text and legislative history nor its purposes suggests that occasional, inadvertent errors were the kind of problem that Congress sought to remedy in passing the Act. No rational federal interest in punishing insignificant mistakes has been articulated.[21]

The SEC had also articulated certain suggestions as to what kinds of control systems will survive scrutiny under the Act:

> The test of a company's control system is not whether occasional failings can occur. Those will happen in the most ideally managed company. But, an adequate system of international controls means that, when such breaches do arise, they will be isolated rather than systemic, and they will be subject to a reasonable likelihood of being uncovered in a timely manner and then remedied promptly.[22]

The SEC suggests that independent directors, audit committees, and internal auditors may help a control system satisfy the legal requirement for reasonableness—a standard which the SEC equates with sound business practice.

This is the second area addressed by the 1988 amendments, which explicitly define both the "reasonable detail" in which firms must keep their books and the "reasonable assurance" that management has control over corporate assets. The definition employed is "such a level of detail and degree of assurance as would satisfy prudent officials in the conduct of their own affairs, having in mind a comparison between benefits to be obtained and costs to be incurred in obtaining such benefits."[23] Again, this definition mirrors earlier SEC statements or interpretations that guided enforcement under the FCPA.

It should be noted that a limited national security exemption to the accounting provisions exists in the original and amended law. The provision permits firms involved in U.S. intelligence activities abroad to falsify books and records—only to the extent necessary to conceal that involvement—provided that the falsification is "done upon the specific written directive" of a federal agency responsible for intelligence activities. The president must authorize these agencies to issue directives, and the agencies must submit to the House and Senate intelligence committees yearly summaries of all matters covered by the directives. The directives expire in one year, unless renewed in writing. The exemption was probably intended to permit concealment of foreign-based employees who are actually undercover agents. The exemption applies only to the recordkeeping provisions of the FCPA.

ENFORCEMENT OF THE ACCOUNTING PROVISIONS

A number of civil enforcement actions under the FCPA's accounting provisions have been brought by the SEC since 1978; no criminal cases have appeared under the accounting provisions. The vast majority of these enforcement actions has been settled by consent decrees or in administrative actions rather than through litigation.

The greatest number of cases has involved situations in which books and records were falsified in order to conceal a questionable payments scheme. In *SEC v. Page Airways,* the SEC alleged that Page and six of its officers had paid more than $7.5 million to officials of several African nations to advance the sales of Gulfstream II aircraft. The SEC also charged that Page had made false, misleading, and incomplete statements in the company's reports to shareholders and had maintained inadequate controls over the use of corporate assets. The case was settled by a consent decree in which Page's management agreed to a permanent injunction barring Page from further violations of SEC's reporting and proxy soliciting requirements. In addition, Page agreed to retain a Cornell law professor to conduct an internal investigation of the alleged payment and to disclose the results of this investigation to its shareholders.

While *SEC v. Page Airways* is an example of a case in which the SEC has attacked a bribery scheme by means of the FCPA's accounting provisions alone, the SEC has often brought actions under both the antibribery and the accounting provisions. In the *SEC v. Clark Oil Refining Corporation* and *SEC v. International Systems & Controls Corporation* cases discussed previously, the SEC added allegations of falsified accounting records to its charges of bribes and kickbacks. Likewise, in *SEC v. Sam P. Wallace Company, Inc.*, the SEC brought suit against a Dallas mechanical contracting firm and its chief officers under the FCPA's accounting and antibribery provisions and under federal securities reporting, proxy soliciting, and antifraud statutes. In a consent decree, the company agreed to an injunction prohibiting future violations and to an investigation of the SEC's allegations by a nonmanagement committee of directors.

ENFORCEMENT JURISDICTIONS UNDER THE FCPA

The Justice Department and the SEC are charged with enforcing the FCPA. The SEC is required to conduct investigations, to bring civil injunctive suits or administrative proceedings against alleged violators, and to refer criminal cases to the Justice Department. The Justice Department is also responsible for investigating bribery by "domestic concerns" that do not report to the SEC. Testimony made during the Congressional hearings indicated that one-third or 9,000 of the U.S. companies doing business overseas report to the SEC. The other two-thirds (about 21,000) are privately held.

In addition to prosecution by the SEC and the Justice Department, there remains a third enforcement possibility. Private parties, including a company's shareholders or competing firms, could bring suits for damages under the FCPA. The question of whether private parties can sue under the FCPA has not yet been settled by the courts. Self-regulation by private litigants would be far more efficient and less expensive than government enforcement; on the other hand, private firms could use FCPA lawsuits to harass competitors.

Because of some uncertainties surrounding the law, business executives have requested interpretive and enforcement guidelines from the SEC and the Justice Department. Although rigid guidelines have not been forthcoming, the Justice Department has agreed to conduct case-by-case reviews of specific proposed transactions and to issue advisory letters, covering only the FCPA's antibribery provisions to the requesting companies within 60 days. Under the Justice Department's FCPA Review Procedure, a company seeking advice on the legality of its planned activities must provide the Department with a detailed description of its intentions. The Justice Department may refuse to comment. If the Department does respond to a request, it and the company will be bound by the response. In addition, the SEC has informally agreed to take no enforcement action in cases where the Justice Department has preapproved a transaction. The Justice Department may still prosecute a company for violations of other federal statutes, even if it has granted a favorable response to an FCPA guidance request.

The Review Procedure has been used only a few times. Critics blame the scant number of requests for review on a provision which allows the Justice Department to keep and "use the governmental purposes" the documents provided by a requestor. These documents might be subject to disclosure to the public—and to a firm's competitors—under the Freedom of Information Act.

COMPLIANCE WITH THE ACT

What should managers do if they suspect their firms have violated the FCPA? Probably the least painful course for companies discovering their own violations is the SEC's voluntary disclosure program, which started in 1975. Companies discovering possible violations of securities laws can conduct internal investigations, publicly file the material facts (usually on Form 8-K, filed with the SEC), and adopt preventative measures. The SEC requires that the internal investigation be conducted by independent members of the board of directors, with help from the firm's regular external auditing firm. Preventive measures include strengthened internal controls and a corporate policy statement from the board of directors. The policy statement is intended to prevent illegal foreign and domestic political payments as well as false or incomplete books and records.

Two corporation lawyers offer the following advice.[24] If managers or auditors of public companies discover possible violations, they should inform inside counsel and the audit committee (or the board itself, if the company has no audit committee) and seek advice from outside counsel. If the lawyers believe that the violations may be significant, the audit committee or the board should authorize an internal inquiry. Investigators should include outside counsel and outside auditors, and they should report directly to the board or to the audit committee. When the inquiry is complete, the audit committee can determine whether a corrective Form 8-K must be filed with the SEC. At this point, the company will be able to negotiate with the SEC. The manner of resolution acceptable to the SEC will depend on the seriousness of the violation and the degree of participation by senior managers. A. Clarence Sampson, the SEC's former chief accountant, has stated that the SEC would look more kindly on companies that make timely disclosures and take preventive actions on their own.[25] Privately held companies should follow similar internal procedures, conferring instead with the Justice Department on the best means of resolution.

What sorts of preventive measures are possible? Most lawyers urge that a company's first step should be to set up an audit committee of independent and energetic outside directors. Secondly, managers should review existing controls—to avoid violating either the recordkeeping or the controls provisions. Such a review could begin with the external auditor's criticisms and suggestions. Thus, senior managers, internal counsel, and internal auditors should carefully examine the auditor's suggestions. If managers choose not to make any of the proposed changes, they should record the reasons for that decision.

Controls of certain sensitive transactions should be carefully reviewed, whether external auditors are critical of them or not. Such transactions include the following: political contributions; transfers of funds outside of the country; use of tangible corporate assets, such as aircraft, boats, apartments and estates; and possible insider-dealings, such as sales to firms owned in part by corporate officials. In all these instances it is particularly important that the records show not only the amounts but the circumstances and true purposes of all transactions.

Allowable facilitating payments must also be carefully documented and controlled, to comply with the accounting provisions as well as to ensure that employees do not escalate purported grease payments into bribes. Castle and Cook, Inc., a Honolulu-based diversified food company, has described its methods of controlling facilitating payments. Robert Moore, vice president and general counsel, says that the firm draws up careful budgets for all "specially regulated costs." No grease payments may be made unless they have been budgeted. The total budget for facilitating payments is usually over $200,000 per year; the money is used to get local army and policy personnel to guard warehouses, to move shipments through customs, and to get ships out of port. Each division's budget for such payments is screened by internal and external legal counsel in the host countries to determine that the payments are legal under local laws. The division's treasurer must certify that the payments are used for the purposes specified. Then the budgets pass up through the ranks to be approved by group managers, internal auditors, general counsel, and the vice president of finance.[26]

Auditors also recommend that certain types of accounts and assets are particularly vulnerable to misappropriation and therefore require stringent controls. For example, political payments have often been made from accounts without tangible assets—such as accounts for consulting expenses, for sales expenses (advertising, commissions, discounts), or for employee remuneration (bonuses, travel, entertainment). Accounts payable have also been drained. Other endangered assets are those that are unrecorded and readily converted to cash—such as scrap, vending machine revenue, sales samples, marketing plans and data lists (lists of stockholders, employees, or customers).

In addition to reviewing existing controls and strengthening them if necessary, managers will want to consider whether the firm's organization fosters compliance. For example, internal auditors are less likely to be influenced if they report directly to the audit committee or to the board than if they report to senior financial managers. Similarly, internal auditors of divisions and subsidiaries are less susceptible if they report to central auditors rather than to divisional or subsidiary managers—although the latter procedure is more often the case. In general, the more decentralized the company and the greater a unit's distance from headquarters, the greater the chances that the unit will disregard corporate controls if they seem to be a nuisance. Because corporations can be held liable for subsidiaries' actions, some companies are now requiring from their subsidiaries quarterly reports documenting and explaining financial conditions, sensitive payments, and irregularities in internal controls.

Managers will also want to consider whether the firm's climate subtly persuades employees to override controls and resort to creative accounting or bribes. Sometimes overly optimistic forecasts motivate executives to manipulate accounts and falsify reports. Other pressures might include excess capacity, obsolete product lines, unrealistic demands for more profits, and sales dependent on a few customers or transactions.

Finally, writers on the FCPA agree that written corporate-conduct codes will help employees to understand the law and to resist temptation.

> While companies will never be able to eliminate completely the dealings of dishonest employees, it is crucial that management document its affirmative disapproval of such dishonest activities in corporate minutes, memos, and elsewhere. . . . The secret of living with the new law's provisions lies . . . in the ability of American business to convey to its employees that unethical practices are not tolerated.[27]

IMPACT OF THE FCPA ON U.S. BUSINESS

The FCPA generated a tremendous amount of criticism after its passage in 1977, especially among firms with extensive international dealings. Several surveys of business executives in firms affected by the FCPA reported widespread disapproval of the Act. A 1980 survey by the Commerce Department, for example, observed that "the uncertainty perceived by U.S. businessmen and the lack of clear guidelines in the Act hindered doing business abroad . . . businessmen often tended to err on the side of caution, forgoing potential export sales rather than risk litigation."[28] A 1981 survey by the Government Accounting Office (GAO) disclosed that nearly 55 percent of the companies affected by the Act believed that efforts to comply with the FCPA cost more than the benefits received.[29] These criticisms led to the successful effort to amend the law.

Other critics have questioned the need for substantial amendment to the FCPA. One commentator disputed the surveys of business executives which indicated that the FCPA has had a negative impact on American exporters. His study determined quantitatively that the FCPA has had no appreciable effect on the share of trade of U.S. exporters in any industry or in any country in which improper payments are allegedly prevalent. He concludes that:

> Legislators must be careful to avoid emasculating the law. Despite the complaints of business leaders and the anecdotal evidence they provide, analysis of empirical data simply does not support their claims that the FCPA places American exporters at a competitive disadvantage relative to exporters from other nations.[30]

The GAO study which reported widespread disaffection with the Act among businessmen also concluded that the Act had served its purpose well. The report stated:

> The act's accounting and antibribery provisions have generated substantial changes in corporate activities. Overall, these changes should strengthen the system of corporate accountability and reduce the occurrence of questionable corporate payments . . . [For example,] the act has . . . caused almost all respondents to review the adequacy of their systems of internal accounting control . . . Extensive changes

> have been made in documenting and testing internal accounting control systems and in strengthening internal auditing.[31]

Yet another observer has hypothesized that improper payments are often ineffective in the short run (noting that the unscrupulous government officials who would accept bribes are sometimes likely to refuse to change their actions despite a bribe or to auction themselves to the highest briber) and particularly damaging in the long run.

> The immediate economic gains that might be derived from engaging in [questionable payments and bribes] can be greatly offset by future losses, costs, and penalties. It is far wiser, from an opportunity-cost standpoint, for companies to focus on strengthening their legitimate competitive advantages internationally, rather than to drain off considerable energy, creativity, and resources in deciding whether or not, and how, to engage in questionable acts without getting caught.[32]

To a certain extent, this debate about the FCPA has run its course, for the law was amended in 1988 as part of the Omnibus Trade and Competitiveness Act. These amendments were intended to clarify certain provisions, reduce paperwork and alleviate some concerns about criminal liability. In particular, the changes in the law limit criminal liability for violations of accounting standards to those who "knowingly circumvent" accounting controls or "knowingly falsify" records. In addition, the "reasonable detail" that is required in bookkeeping is described in greater detail, and how payments can be legally made to procure its performance of certain routine governmental actions is clarified. The impact these changes will have on the behavior of U.S. managers abroad remains to be seen.

APPENDIX

The following list of states which prohibit various forms of bribery is meant to be exemplative only and does not proport to be complete. The source* reported that "all of the [states'] statutes examined prohibited bribes."

A. *Liability of Persons*

1. States in which the recipient of a bribe must be a public official in order to be liable for bribery:
   Bolivia
   People's Republic of China
   Colombia
   El Salvador
   France
   Federal Republic of Germany
   Ghana
   India
   Jordan

*SOURCE: Jefferi Joan Hamilton, "The Foreign Corrupt Practices Act of 1977: A Solution or a Problem?" *California Western International Law Journal,* Vol. 11, No. 1, Winter 1981, pp. 129–134.

Netherlands
Paraguay
Saudi Arabia
Senegal
Sweden
Switzerland
Tanzania
Thailand
United Kingdom
Zaire
Zambia

2. States in which business persons or agents also may be liable for receiving bribes:
Netherlands
Sweden
United Kingdom

B. *Kinds of Illegal Payments*

1. States which expressly prohibit bribes where a transaction is pending or likely to be pending before a public official:
People's Republic of China
Colombia
France
India
Saudi Arabia
Senegal
Sweden
Tanzania
Thailand
United Kingdom
Zambia

2. States which refer generally to the prohibition of bribes to public officials and employers:
Bolivia
El Salvador
Ghana
Jordan
Netherlands
Paraguay
Switzerland
Zaire

3. States which prohibit threats or acts of violence to procure payments from individuals:
Federal Republic of Germany
France
Ghana
Netherlands
People's Republic of China
Saudi Arabia
Senegal
Sweden
Switzerland
United Kingdom
Zaire

4. States which prohibit facilitating or "grease" payments:
Bolivia

Colombia
El Salvador
Federal Republic of Germany
France
Ghana
India
Jordan
Netherlands
Saudi Arabia
Senegal
Sweden
Switzerland
Tanzania
Thailand
United Kingdom
Zaire
Zambia

5. States which prohibit "kickbacks" by prohibiting monies paid to public officials during, before, or after a transaction:
   Colombia
   India
   Senegal
   Tanzania
   Thailand
   Zambia

NOTES

1. This chapter, in part, is extracted from "Technical Note on the Foreign Corrupt Practices Act," UVA-G-320, which was prepared by John Quarterman, Darden MBA/JD '87, under the supervision of Charles R. Kennedy, Jr. Associate Professor of Business Administration.
2. U.S. Senate Committee on Banking, Housing and Urban Affairs, *Foreign Corrupt Practices Act of 1977,* Senate Rept. No. 114, 95th Congress, 1st Session, 1977, p. 3 (hereinafter cited as Senate Rept. 95-114), reprinted in *1977 U.S. Code Congressional and Administrative News.* p. 4101.
3. The study, titled *An Examination of Questionable Payments and Practices,* was made by Charles E. Simon and Company, a Washington, D.C. research firm. See summary in "Study Reveals Methods Used for Questionable Payments," *Journal of Accountancy,* May 1978, pp. 7–8.
4. Quoted by Adam Fremantle and Sherman Katz, "The Foreign Corrupt Practices Act Amendments of 1988," *The International Lawyer,* 23 (Fall 1989), p. 760.
5. *Ibid.,* p. 766.
6. *Ibid.,* p. 762.
7. *Ibid.,* p. 762.
8. Senate Rept. 95-144, p. 10, reprinted in *1977 U.S. Code Congressional and Administrative News,* p. 4108.
9. *Ibid.,* p. 11.
10. John S. Estey and David W. Marston, "Pitfalls (and Loopholes) in Foreign Bribery Law," *Fortune,* October 9, 1978, p. 184.
11. *Foreign Corrupt Practices Act of 1977* sections 104(a)(1), 104(a)(2), and 104(a)(3), *United States Code,* title 15, sections 78dd-1(a)(1), 78dd-2(a)(2), and 78dd(a)(3).
12. *Foreign Corrupt Practices Act of 1977* section 104(d)(2), *United States Code,* title 15, section 78dd-2(d)(2).
13. Fremantle and Katz, "Amendments of 1988", pp. 762–763.
14. *Ibid.,* p. 763.
15. *Ibid.,* p. 763.

16. *Ibid.*, p. 761.
17. Rafael A. Porrata-Doria, Jr., "Amending the Foreign Corrupt Practices Act of 1977: Repeating the Mistakes of the Past?", *Rutgers Law Review,* 38 (Fall 1985), p. 44.
18. Alan B. Levenson, former Director of the SEC's Division of Corporation Finance, quoted in David L. Goelzer, "The Accounting Provisions of the Foreign Corrupt Practices Act—the Federalization of Corporate Recordkeeping and Internal Control," *Journal of Corporation Law,* 5 (Fall 1979), pp. 21–22.
19. U.S. Senate Committee on Banking, Housing and Urban Affairs, 94th Congress, 2d session, *Report of the Securities and Exchange Commission on Questionable and Illegal Corporate Payments and Practices,* (hereinafter cited as 1976 SEC Report).
20. SEC Report No. 17,500, p. 17,233-10.
21. *Ibid.*, p. 17,233-10.
22. *Ibid.*, p. 17,233-11.
23. Fremantle and Katz, "Amendments of 1988," p. 765.
24. Dennis J. Block and Ellen J. Odoner, "Enforcing the Accounting Standards Provisions of the Foreign Corrupt Practices Act," *Financial Executive,* July 1979, p. 23.
25. *Securities Regulation and Law Report* (BNA), No. 517, August 22, 1979, p. D-5.
26. "Misinterpreting the Antibribery Law," *Business Week,* September 3, 1979, p. 150.
27. Edward P. Ballinger and Jesse F. Dillard, "The Foreign Corrupt Practices Act," *CPA Journal,* February 1980, p. 46.
28. U.S. Department of Commerce, *Report of the President on Export Promotion Functions and Potential Export Disincentives,* September 1980, pp. C-6 to C-14, quoted in John L. Graham, "Foreign Corrupt Practice: A Manager's Guide," *Columbia Journal of World Business,* 18 (Fall 1983), p. 91.
29. GAO Report, pp. 13, 58–59, reprinted in *Federal Securities Law Reporter* (CCH), 1981 Transfer Binder, paragraph 82,841, p. 84,113.
30. Graham, "A Manager's Guide," p. 94.
31. GAO Report, 1981 Transfer Binder, paragraph 82,841, p. 84, 112–113.
32. Barry Richman, "Can We Prevent Questionable Foreign Payments?", *Business Horizons,* 22 (June 1979), pp. 14–15.

Questionable Payments Under FCPA

The following caselets* are reflective of actual events or managerial decisions under the FCPA. All situations have been disguised.

1. A U.S. oil executive during negotiations with the head of the Ministry of Petroleum Affairs in a Middle Eastern country is told that an oil concession is more likely if their discussions are postponed until a later date. The government official suggests that the oil executive make all the arrangements for a meeting in Innsbruck, Austria, including ski accommodations and other amenities.

2. The head of an American beverage company is negotiating the production and sale of a product within an Asian country. His in-house legal counsel knows a local law firm with two American-trained partners, but a German manager with operations in the country suggests that the brother of the director of the Foreign Investment Review Board be hired instead. The brother, who is a lawyer, charges a 200 percent premium over the other law firm's rate. The director must eventually approve any negotiated agreement.

3. The country manager for an American petrochemical company receives a notice from the Ministry of Economic Affairs in a Middle Eastern country that all foreign investment contracts will be reviewed and that changes in taxes and royalty payments are possible. A lawyer, who is the nephew of the Minister of Economic Affairs, contacts the country manager and offers to represent the firm in upcoming negotiations. His fees are 20 percent higher than asked by other law firms.

4. A U.S. company is competing for a $50 million telecommunications contract in a Latin American country. A Lichtenstein consultant has offered to represent the company to help secure the contract, which will be awarded in one month. His fee is $1 million.

5. A subsidiary manager of a U.S. company has been kidnapped by a political terrorist group in Latin America, and a ransom of $1 million is demanded for his safe return.

6. An import license for an important shipment of raw materials has been denied by a middle-level bureaucrat in an African country and local supplies are almost depleted. The bureaucrat suggests that the American company's country manager should deposit $500 per import license in a numbered Swiss bank account. All payments to government officials are illegal in this country, even though corruption is known to be widespread.

7. The allocation of foreign exchange for the purchase of a needed import is being denied by a middle-level bureaucrat in a Latin American central bank. The

*These caselets were prepared by Associate Professor Charles R. Kennedy, Jr., Babcock Graduate School of Management, Wake Forest University, 1989.

bureaucrat suggests that the American company's country manager should pay him $100 for the number of a Swiss bank account, which the bureaucrat says belongs to the head of the central bank, who reportedly wants $1,000 for the foreign exchange allocation.

8. The country manager of a U.S. wholly owned subsidiary discovers that his marketing manager has paid $1,000 to a government official in the Patent and Trademark Office of a Asian country to get a product's brand name approved for local sales. The payment was recorded as a marketing expense on the advertising budget.

9. A U.S. consumer-products company had formed a minority-owned joint venture in an Asian country five years ago. The U.S. representative in the joint venture recently discovered that the marketing manager, who was a local national, had regularly made payments to government officials in the Patent and Trademark Office to get brand-name approval for local sales. The payments were recorded as marketing expenses on the advertising budget.

10. A new country manager of a U.S. company in Asia was told by the outgoing country manager that certain practices were required in order to conduct normal business in the country. In particular, key government bureaucrats in various ministries should be entertained two or three times a year at parties which included beautiful and "willing" females.

11. The executive vice president who headed the international division of a U.S. multinational corporation received a letter from a new marketing manager in an overseas subsidiary. He complained of being pressured by the country manager to pay "bribes" to government officials in order to secure sales of their industrial equipment. The marketing manager said he suspected such payments had been routinely made in the past.

12. The new captain of a U.S. Merchant Marine vessel is told by the veteran first-mate that one should pay port officials in a certain Middle East country in order to get priority treatment in terms of docking facilities. Otherwise, the ship would have to wait countless days before unloading its cargo.

7

ORGANIZING FOR POLITICAL RISK

The most recent comprehensive study of how major U.S. corporations have organized for political risk assessment and management was conducted in 1983.[1] Of the sixty-one large multinationals studied, forty-five had institutionalized the political risk function by giving some individual or department the formal responsibility for assessing the macroeconomic and sociopolitical environment. Most of these companies, moreover, had created the current area of focused responsibility after 1978, indicating some increase in attention given to political risk after the Iranian revolution, as reported by the media.[2] This conclusion is reinforced by comparing these results with research conducted under the auspices of the Conference Board in 1978.[3] The Conference Board study, headed by Stephen Kobrin, reported that 55 percent of a 193-firm sample had a formal, systematic approach to political risk, versus the 1983 study's 74 percent. Clearly, major U.S. firms have continued to stress the importance of managing political risk.

There are also indications that the way political risk is managed is changing, thus reflecting its increasing importance. For instance, there is a noticeable trend toward placing the political risk function in the corporate planning department. The 1983 study indicated that 75 percent of firms with a formal approach to political risk had institutionalized the function in corporate planning, whereas the most popular locations in the Conference Board study were the international division or finance-economics departments. This suggests that political risk considerations are becoming more integrated into strategic decision making.

Another indication that political risk is viewed as an increasingly important managerial function is the rise in the number of full-time versus part-time jobs devoted to macroeconomic and sociopolitical assessment. In the 1970s, nearly nine out of ten political risk analysts in major corporations had duties other than assessing the external environment. By the mid-1980s, most managers assigned to the political risk function were given full-time responsibilities in this area.[4]

There is also a trend toward concentrating the political risk function in one individual or department, as opposed to dispersing the responsibility in multiple locations. For example, every firm in the 1983 study that had institutionalized political risk since the Iranian revolution had focused the function in only one area or department. Conversely, of the firms that had a formal approach to political risk in the 1970s, one-third had multiple locations for such assessments; one wonders how effective and coordinated the management of political risk can be under such circumstances.

The trends in how the political risk function is organized at the corporate level are clear; it is increasingly located and focused in the planning department as a full-time duty of some staff member. Despite these general trends, however, there are significant variations in how corporate headquarters interacts with operational managers in the field, particularly heads of foreign subsidiaries. The extent of political risk responsibilities placed on country and line managers varies greatly even among corporations with a full-time political risk analyst housed in corporate planning. These differences are also reflected in the way political risk information is reported from the field to corporate headquarters. Some reports are offered only on an ad hoc basis; others are regular parts of quarterly reviews or the annual strategic planning process. In some corporations, country or subsidiary managers are required to submit separate and lengthy political risk assessments on a periodic basis.

There is perhaps no one correct or best way the political risk function can be organized and managed throughout the entire corporation. Instead one has to match the firm's organizational approach in the area of political risk to its competitive-industry structure, culture, management values, history and operational structure.[5] Of course, the same point is true for organizational issues in general.[6]

NOTES

1. Charles R. Kennedy, Jr., "The External Environment-Strategic Planning Interface: U.S. Multinational Corporate Practices in the 1980s," *Journal of International Business Studies,* 15 (Fall 1984), pp. 99–108.
2. "The Post-Shah Surge in Political Risk Studies," *Business Week,* December 1, 1980, p. 69; Louis Kraar, "The Multinationals Get Smarter About Political Risks," *Fortune,* March 24, 1980, p. 26; Ronald Alsop, "More Firms Are Hiring Own Political Analysts to Limit Risks Abroad," *Wall Street Journal,* March 30, 1981, p. 1; Peter Stone, "Boom Days for Political Risk Consultants," *The New York Times,* August 7, 1983, p. 1.
3. Stephen J. Kobrin, John Basek, Stephen Blank, and Joseph La Palombara, "The Assessment and Evaluation of Noneconomic Environments by American Firms: A Preliminary Report," *Journal of International Business Studies,* 11 (Spring/Summer 1980), pp. 32–47.
4. Kennedy, "External Environment-Strategic Planning Interface," p. 101.
5. Amir Mahini, *Making Decisions in Multinational Corporations: Managing Relations with Sovereign Governments* (New York: John Wiley & Sons), 1988, pp. 189–200.
6. William H. Davidson and Philippe Haspeslagh, "Shaping a Global Product Organization," *Harvard Business Review,* 60 (July–August 1982), pp. 131–132.

Political Risk Management at American Chemical Company

At American Chemical Company (ACC), President and Chairman of the Board Robert M. Deaton was considering a reorganization within his company. With foreign investments in over thirty countries, he was concerned that the company's present approach to political risk was inadequate. A couple of recent incidents in Brazil and Nigeria had raised a red flag in front of Deaton's eyes. In both countries, changes in trade and foreign exchange regulations had adversely affected ACC's subsidiaries. These developments, moreover, came as a complete surprise to those responsible for political risk assessment at ACC. Deaton was convinced that the firm could do a better job of managing these kinds of risks in the future.

AMERICAN CHEMICAL COMPANY

American Chemical Company had been one of the first companies to enter the petrochemical business in the 1920s, and by the 1980s, ACC remained a major player in that industry. Although chemicals and plastics constituted the plurality of the company's sales, ACC was well diversified (see Exhibit I).

Besides product diversification, the company was geographically dispersed as well, with foreign direct investment in 32 countries. These included petrochemical, gas or metal operations in India, Indonesia, Korea, Malaysia, Philippines, Taiwan, Argentina, Brazil, Colombia, Ecuador, Peru, Venezuela, and South Africa. Extensive battery operations also existed in Egypt, Ghana, Ivory Coast, Kenya, Nigeria, and Sudan. Thus, the company had many important investments in relatively unstable and risky Third World countries, although Europe was the company's largest international market (see Exhibit 2). In fact, major expansions or investments had been made recently in Brazil, Korea, Philippines, Ivory Coast, Kenya, and Sudan.

Most of the company's operations in Third World countries were majority-controlled joint ventures, although a few were 100 percent subsidiaries or minority-share joint ventures. Country managers were focal points in a product-area matrix that made up the company's organizational structure. At corporate headquarters, an international division headed by an executive vice president had existed since the 1920s, when expansion into Europe began. Within the international division, regional vice presidents headed their respective areas and had primary authority over country managers, who also reported in a dotted-line relationship to global

This case was prepared by Charles R. Kennedy, Jr., Associate Professor of Business Administration.

product coordinators within each domestic product division. These coordinators carried the title of vice president and had the authority to seek arbitration if disputes with area vice presidents arose; they could appeal disputes to the strategic planning department. Executive vice presidents, who headed the international division and each domestic product division, could naturally appeal any dispute to the executive committee, composed of the five executive vice presidents and the president and chairman of the board.

The planning process was embedded in the matrix organization. Operating, line managers were the primary planners at ACC. Both country and product managers developed annual strategic plans under the guidance of the planning department. Ultimately, the strategic planning department made recommendations to the executive committee based on their portfolio/strategic business unit analysis. Country and product managers could formally challenge or oppose these recommendations before the executive committee, but typically, strategic goals and management-by-objective standards were successfully negotiated between operating, line managers and the strategic planning department before disputes were appealed to the executive committee.

POLITICAL RISK MANAGEMENT AT ACC

A formal and systematic approach to political risk assessment had been based in the strategic planning department at ACC since the mid-1970s. Of the five full-time professionals within the planning department, one was given the responsibility for assessing the macroeconomic and sociopolitical environment. Essentially long-range scenarios were developed for planning purposes.

In developing these assessments and scenarios, very little information from line and country managers was used. In fact, there was no attempt to rigorously and systematically solicit country managers' views about local political risks. Information supplied by outside consultants and experts was used to a much greater extent. The planning department's annual report on scenarios was highly qualitative and very central to the development of final strategic recommendations to the executive committee.

Robert Deaton, who had assumed the position of president and chairman of the board two years ago, was concerned that the job of assessing global economic and sociopolitical risks was too big and important for one professional analyst in the planning department to handle. In early 1985, therefore, Deaton solicited recommendations from top managers in both the strategic planning department and the international division, who gave the chairman quick responses (see Exhibits 3 and 4). Deaton wanted to make a decision soon, so he commissioned a report by a political risk consultant as well (see Exhibit 5).

Exhibit 1 Sales and Operating Profits for Business Segments (in millions of dollars)

Sales	**1984**	**1983**	**1982**	**1981**	**1980**
Chemicals and Plastics	2150	2079	2132	2559	3015
Batteries and Auto Products	1756	1673	1789	1758	1581
Gases and Related Products	1311	1341	1528	1598	1324
Metals and Carbons	864	898	942	1180	1334
Operating Profits	**1984**	**1983**	**1982**	**1981**	**1980**
Chemicals and Plastics	198	60	65	234	318
Batteries and Auto Plastics	201	198	199	192	182
Gases and Related Products	236	189	195	264	257
Metals and Carbons	29	(15)	48	198	256

Exhibit 2 Sales and Operating Profits by Geographic Region (in millions of dollars)

Sales	**1984**	**1983**	**1982**	**1981**	**1980**
Europe	861	840	851	903	999
Latin America	564	561	698	700	634
Asia	636	703	751	749	682
Canada	498	522	525	30	75
Africa/Middle East	110	98	115	114	117
Operating Profits	**1984**	**1983**	**1982**	**1981**	**1980**
Europe	69	61	84	72	85
Latin America	127	101	103	116	121
Asia	50	63	74	73	82
Canada	10	10	(25)	39	74
Africa/Middle East	12	2	9	4	16

Exhibit 3 Memorandum

TO: Robert M. Deaton, President and Chairman of the Board
FROM: William Stevens, Assistant Director of Strategic Planning
RE: Political Risk and Macroeconomic Forecasting
DATE: January 30, 1985

I was pleased to hear that you had the view that more resources were needed for political analysis and macroeconomic forecasting. I couldn't agree with you more and have thought of several ways this activity could be improved. I propose we hire three to four full-time professionals to work with me in our department. With the new people on board, the forecasting function could be greatly improved and more tailored to the needs of our company.

Several other companies have organized the political-economic analysis function in the way I propose. For example, American Can has a unit attempting to generate original, independent risk forecasts. The company has three full-time professionals attached to corporate planning who operate a model called the "Primary Risk Investment Screening Matrix" (PRISM). PRISM, which was started in 1978, is basically a mathematical computer model that screens over 50 countries in terms of American Can's particular interests. The model reduces around 200 variables into two indices: economic desirability and risk payback. The company considers investments only in those dozen countries with the best PRISM ratings.

I would like to build a similar system and model at ACC.

Exhibit 4 Memorandum

TO: Robert M. Deaton, President and Chairman of the Board
FROM: William Parker, Executive Vice President, International Division
RE: Political Risk Reorganization
DATE: February 5, 1985

I certainly agree with the need to devote more resources to political risk analysis. I would also argue that the company should completely reorganize the political risk function. At present, the function is formally housed in the strategic planning department, with one full-time professional devoted to this sort of analysis. I object to the present system because their political-economic assessments are made in isolation of what our managers on the scene say. It makes sense that overseas managers who know the business well should be a primary source of information about local political and economic risks.

With the goal of increasing the role of local, subsidiary managers in mind, the following proposal about political risk reorganization is made. The international division will create a "Political Risk Assessment Department" (PRAD), which will design, administer, and interpret political risk reports from overseas managers. This information along with external data from consultants, academic publications, government contacts, and so forth, will be used to form a political risk report. The timing of the report will coincide with the annual strategic review process. A team of three full-time professionals should be able to do the job well.

Similar approaches to political risk analysis exist elsewhere. At General Motors, for example, the International Economic Policy Group surveys overseas managers through an extremely long, sophisticated questionnaire. The questionnaire comes in three parts. In "Part One: Assessment of Factors," line managers are asked to rate 45 variables or considerations along a seven-point continuum. The questions are very future- or forecast-oriented; 32 (71 percent) of the questions ask line managers to make prediction's about future developments. In "Part Two: Policy Issues" and "Part Three: Policy Environment," the questions are also forecast-oriented and follow an approach similar to the "Prince System" of World Political Risk Forecasts. Although the information collected from the line does not dominate decision making, it does have a significant impact on final political risk ratings. These ratings take the form of scores between zero and 100 for over 50 countries. The higher the number, the lower the political risk. These ratings are supplied to GM's chief financial officer and to other interested parties, such as strategic planners within the company.

The company should rely on overseas managers more in the area of political risk, and the GM system is a good, systematic way to integrate line managers in the political risk process. The administration of such a system should also be housed in the international division, where country managers directly report. Political risk assessments by PRAD, moreover, would be promptly distributed to all interested and pertinent parties, like the strategic planning department, which can certainly retain their present approach to political risk. This proposal is not in substitution for the present system. It is instead viewed as a valuably needed supplement.

Exhibit 5 Confidential Report

TO: Robert Deaton, President and Chairman of the Board, American Chemical Company
FROM: Cyrus R. Kilpatrick
RE: Approaches to Political Risk Management
DATE: February 1, 1985

I have been asked to provide a report on the various approaches major companies have taken toward political risk without making specific recommendations for your company. The following report should suffice.

There are perhaps five generic approaches to the management of political risk, and they were first described by the director of international relations at Xerox, who called them by their initials models R, S, K, B, and C. In model R, for "reactive," a firm has no formal structure or organization to assess political risks. Although managers of subsidiaries are the primary source of information about political risks, there is no standardized or systematic approach to how that information is reported to corporate headquarters; it is reported ad hoc. At the corporate level, moreover, no individual or department has been given the formal responsibility to assess political risk. The management of political risk thus tends to be a reactive exercise.

In model S, however, for "sherpa" (those who help mountain climbers to the summit), the level of corporate political risk institutionalization is high, but the degree of dependency on country or line managers for political risk information is low. At corporate headquarters, moreover, a staff of economic and political risk specialists attempts to generate original forecasts about the external environment. In effect, they are trying to create a political intelligence unit, but in the process of generating their forecasts, these units typically rely little or not at all on country or line managers for political risk information. Such an approach towards overseas managers, who are often local nationals, is generally followed because the opinions of overseas managers are not trusted and there is a disregard for their training and ability to do a good political risk job. In other words, country and line managers are seen as unavoidably biased because of local interests and perspectives.

In model K, for "Henry Kissenger," the lack of information from line management is more the product of a low level of stress on formal and ongoing political risk analysis at corporate headquarters than it is of a general attitude by corporate staff about overseas managers. In essence, the model K corporation relies heavily on external consultants, such as Henry Kissenger, and/or on international advisory boards composed of prominent former government officials and experts on various countries. Usually only top management meets with these advisory boards, perhaps only once or twice a year. The exact impact this approach has on corporate decision making is unclear, but it is probably tenuous at best because the political risk function has no permanent, internal push for these kinds of issues to be taken seriously.

In model B, for "bottom-up," on the other hand, the level of corporate emphasis on political risk is high. An individual or department at corporate headquarters has been given the formal responsibility for managing political risk. In the collection, assessment, and recommendation phases of the process, country and line managers are heavily involved; they are also rewarded for good political risk work within the bonus/performance evaluation system. Such an approach makes maximum and systematic use of all the advantages that line managers can bring to the management of political risks, but it does so at the expense of accentuating the disadvantages of a line-driven system.

These disadvantages are the same concerns voiced by corporate political intelligence units: if one relies too heavily on country and line managers, the corporation runs the risk of being blinded by biased information. Model B also tends to downplay or ignore the real value that external expert advice and internal objective analysis by corporate staff can bring to the management of political risks.

In model C, for "combination," some elements of the "sherpa" and "bottom-up" approaches are found. In all three models (S, B, and C), full-time political risk managers exist at corporate headquarters, but their role in each model differs. Model C is when political risk coordinators try to blend external and internal sources of information into a comprehensive report. Final political risk recommendations to top management are thus the ultimate responsibility of the political risk coordinator. Unlike model B, line managers do not directly participate in corporate decisions about political risks. As a result, the dependency on line managers for information about political risks is lower for model C relative model B firms. Political risk coordinators, however, integrate line managers into the process of assessing political risk to a much greater extent than political intelligence units.

Given these general comments, a few detailed examples of each model might be instructive. Occidental is a good example of the model R approach. The company has not given anyone at corporate headquarters the formal responsibility to assess political risk full-time and relies heavily on country and line managers for political risk information. Top corporate managers, however, are generally expected to look at such risks as an intrinsic part of their overall responsibilities. Of course, no one represents this managerial model better than Armand Hammer, Occidental's long-time chairman of the board.

If the management system at Occidental is evaluated in terms of performance, one would have to give the company high marks. Occidental has been able to find and produce oil in a number of politically risky countries without having experienced any major political disasters. My knowledge of Occidental's line managers, who are responsible for political risk assessment, also suggests that the company has an effective approach to the management of these risks.

Occidental's country and line managers collectively realize that their political risk responsibilities are very important to the firm, with these responsibilities primarily focused on the accurate and comprehensive reporting of information to corporate headquarters. The reporting of political risk information, however, was mostly ad hoc and unstructured, for no corporatewide and standardized reporting format existed. Occidental's managers, moreover, were generally satisfied with how well they were rewarded for their political risk duties.

Both model K and model S firms are unlike Occidental in that line and country managers are virtually excluded from the political risk process. At United Technologies Corporation, for example, country and line managers have a relatively small role to play in political risk management. Most political risk concerns are handled by consultants and top management within the International Advisory Council, chaired by the president of United Technologies (Alexander Haig, when it was first formed in June 1983). To some extent, the corporate strategic planning staff also had a part-time duty to assess political risks, but over time the relative importance of the International Advisory Council has increased. Managers at United Technologies describe political risk management there as very "top-down." This is typical of a model K firm.

Many model S firms, on the other hand, create mathematical computer models, like the PRISM system at American Can, but this is not always the case. At Atlantic Richfield Company (ARCO), for example, two full-time professionals within the strategic planning department attempt to develop highly qualitative scenarios for the company's ongoing and prospective projects. Corporate staff essentially produces a lengthy narrative report or a one-page summary that details key political variables and the most likely scenario for a particular project. During the process of developing "future-oriented" and "project-related" reports, little information from line managers is used. Unlike the typical analyst within a political intelligence unit, however, the head of ARCO's political risk operation views the lack of line management input as a weakness in the system, but organizational and cultural constraints within the company are considered serious obstacles to integrating line managers further into the political risk process.

Model B and C firms, on the other hand, strongly utilize country and line managers in the political risk assessment process, which is supervised by a full-time corporate political risk manager. Model B and C firms differ simply on the relative stress placed on line and country managers for information relative to other sources.

At Xerox, for example, the organizational structure and culture require a strong "bottom-up" approach. Historically, Xerox has had a significant number of important 50-50 joint ventures around the globe, some of which became 51 percent owned by Xerox over time. In essence, foreign subsidiaries of Xerox have a strong tradition of local autonomy; joint venture partners also had a significant managerial role within the company. Thus, when the Xerox approach to political risk management was developed, country and overseas managers had to play a major role in order for the system to work effectively.

At Xerox, the political risk system is called the Issues Monitoring System (IMS) and is headed by the director of international relations, who is attached to the corporate planning department. As part of IMS, country and line managers not only report the bulk of the company's political risk information but are involved in a series of negotiations with regional and corporate personnel over specific political risk objectives. Significantly, the promotion, evaluation, and bonus/incentive system is in part tied to these objectives.

One other company includes political risk objectives within its personnel evaluation and bonus system. Pepsico does so within its strategic review and planning process. As a result, country managers are very involved in the management of political risk. These managers are responsible for narrative reviews on the company's risk profile and for achieving certain political risk objectives. These activities are coordinated by the international strategic planning department, which contains three full-time analysts working on specific political risk projects.

Dow Chemical has also significantly integrated line managers into the evaluation and assessment process, albeit not to the same extent as Xerox and Pepsico. At Dow, a political risk coordinator collects information from line managers and external contacts and then writes a political risk evaluation. Dow's approach to political risk management is called the Economic, Social, and Political (ESP) Risk Assessment Program and is headed by the manager of the international business environment. This corporatewide position was created in 1980, although the ESP approach had been used in the Latin American region since 1971. The manager of the international business environment is essentially a political risk coordinator who organizes periodic country reviews and constantly monitors the international scene on a full-time basis.

The ESP system is operated through teamwork among different levels of Dow employees and is typically triggered when the manager of the international business environment initiates a country review by forming a team of between six and eight Dow employees. The team usually includes the local country manager and two or three of his or her key people, plus "outsiders" from regional and corporate headquarters. The manager of the international business environment heads the team during week-long brainstorming sessions in the country being reviewed. After a rough consensus within the team is reached, the team disbands, and the manager of the international business environment writes a country risk report.

I hope this report is useful. It gives you an overview of the various organizational approaches that companies have taken toward the management of political risks. If you require any additional information or advice on this or any other political risk matter, I will be glad to provide it.

CK/mtd

8

MANAGING INTERNATIONAL COMPETITION

In the eyes of most business leaders and government officials around the world, U.S. industry has suffered significant competitive setbacks in the last three decades.[1] The causes of this deterioration in U.S. competitiveness are varied, and several recommendations can be made as to what managers of U.S. corporations should do to address the competitive problem. Before making these recommendations, however, a brief look at the history of the United State's competitive decline will be useful in order to understand better how the problem can be tackled in the future.

The first comprehensive examination of the decline in U.S. competitiveness was made in 1971 by Peter Peterson, then Secretary of Commerce under President Nixon.[2] In the so-called Peterson Report, issued in April of that year, the Commerce Secretary predicted the first U.S. merchandise trade deficit since 1893. For Peterson, this deficit was a manifestation of declining U.S. international competitiveness. According to the report, this competitive decline had several primary causes: an increase in the capabilities of competitors, particularly in Japan and Western Europe; trade barriers abroad; an overvalued dollar; a long-term decline in U.S. productivity gains; a corresponding increase in U.S. unit labor costs; and the lack of attention toward enhancing the nation's competitiveness by U.S. government leaders. Peterson, moreover, argued that U.S. domestic efforts to improve U.S. competitiveness were far more important than voluntary or induced actions by our trading partners.

During the 1970s and 1980s, the deterioration in U.S. competitiveness, as reflected in the trade balance, continued and intensified. This trend was particularly evident in the mid-to-late 1980s, when the trade deficit ballooned annually to over $150 billion. Basically, the same causes identified by Peterson in 1971 were still at work in 1985.

In February 1985, the President's Commission on Industrial Competitiveness issued its report.[3] The commission headed by John Young, CEO and chairman of Hewlett Packard, identified five major weaknesses in U.S. competitiveness: U.S. trade policy; international trade laws; exchange rates; labor and other human resource costs; and businesses' cost of investment capital, which caused lags in U.S. productivity. The Commission, like Peterson, argued for a domestic focus in restoring U.S. competitiveness. These efforts should center on improvements in the rate of U.S. savings, investment, and productivity, which were best stimulated by changes in macroeconomics policies by the federal government. Of course, these efforts should not obscure the need to open foreign markets to U.S. goods or to get exchange rates to levels that more closely approximated their true purchasing power.

These recommendations, moreover, should not mislead business leaders to think that the burden of improving U.S. competitiveness lies in the hands of government officials. To the contrary, the major responsibility for such improvements is arguably centered on the corporate community. This is particularly true in the U.S. political context, where institutional and ideological factors probably preclude the kind of government-led industrial policies seen in Japan. If industrial policies to improve U.S. competitiveness are to emerge, it will probably be an industry-led effort. As Bruce Scott argued:

> Business leaders, and leaders in the various knowledge occupations on which business depends, will have to take primary responsibility for changing U.S. economic strategy. The alternative is slow decline and ultimately crisis. . . . Congress cannot lead on an issue as complex as U.S. competitiveness. Congress has 535 members, each with a narrow constituency that votes regularly. . . . The president, of course, could lead. But . . . competitiveness vies with other priorities for the time of any president. As a long-term consideration, it will normally be deferred while short-term crises are dealt with. If competitiveness is to achieve the priority it deserves, business leaders . . . must take the lead.[4]

The ways in which business leaders can take the lead are varied, but they can be divided into internal and external actions. Corporate managers should never ignore what they can do on their own to improve the firm's competitiveness. Such actions include certain business fundamentals which are sometimes forgotten. These fundamentals are: the need to be customer-oriented; the importance of corporate culture and shared values in producing a committed and productive workforce; the crucial nature of product quality in meeting consumer needs and in reducing overall costs; the advantages of gaining market share; and the key role investment and research-and-development spending play in the long-term competitiveness of any firm.

Such actions, however, may be necessary conditions for restoring the competitiveness of U.S. corporations, but they are not sufficient. As long as American companies are burdened by an uneven playing field, created by government policies here and abroad, probably no amount of internal change will reverse the competitive decline of American industry. Corporate leaders by necessity must address and help change government policies in order to foster a fairer and more supportive competitive environment. As a result, the government-relations function and political strategies employed by American firms will become increasingly important, and although corporate efforts can be aimed at foreign governments directly, most of their attention must be focused on leaders in Washington,D.C.

As in negotiations in general, the most effective companies are those actively involved in the political process, particularly on a behind-the-scenes, informal basis. In this way, a firm can more effectively communicate its concerns and positions. At the same time, government allies and enemies can be better identified. Subsequently, a corporation's announced preferences in public policy should be crafted to maximize the support of its allies in government, while simultaneously minimizing the opposition of its foes. In addition, it is often wise to form collective efforts with other companies, but such industry-wide lobbying should not entirely replace the direct intervention of corporate heads in the political process. The personal involvement of corporate chairmen, CEOs and presidents in public-policy issues is critically important.[5]

At the industry-wide level, the example of the Semiconductor Industry Association (SIA) is noteworthy for other trade associations to follow.[6] SIA successfully lobbied for trade action against Japan by the U.S. government in 1986–87, followed by the creation of Sematech, a research consortium of SIA members which receives $100 million a year from the Defense Department in support of semiconductor research. At the company level, the success of Motorola Corporation should symbolize what is possible in restoring the competitiveness of U.S. industry.[7] In addition to making a massive internal commitment to product quality, a renewed corporate culture, and to investment and research-and-development expenditures, Motorola's top executives have been aggressive in pursuing a more open market in Japan and more competitive policies in Washington. These efforts have had enormous payoffs in profitability, market position worldwide, and changes in public policies favorable to the firm. Other American companies should take notice and study these cases, for they demonstrate the value of implementing the recommendations just discussed.

NOTES

1. Bruce R. Scott, *et. al*, "Competitiveness: 23 Leaders Speak out," *Harvard Business Review*, 65 (July–August 1987), pp. 106–123.
2. Peter G. Peterson, *The United States in the Changing World Economy* (Washington, D.C.: U.S. Government Printing Office, 1971).
3. President's Commission on Industrial Competitiveness, *Global Competition: The New Reality* (Washington, D.C.: U.S. Government Printing Office, 1985).
4. Bruce R. Scott, "Competitiveness: Self-Help for a Worsening Problem," *Harvard Business Review*, 67 (July–August 1989), p. 121.
5. David B. Yoffie, "How an Industry Builds Political Advantage," *Harvard Business Review*, 66 (May–June 1988), p. 83.
6. *Ibid.*, pp. 82–89 and see Harvard Business School case, "The Semiconductor Industry Associa-

tion and The Trade Dispute with Japan (A)," 9-387-205, Rev. 10/87, written by John J. Coleman, under the supervision of David B. Yoffie.

7. "The Rival Japan Respects—Motorola's Secrets: Strong R & D, Built-in Quality, and Zealous Service," *Business Week,* November 18, 1989, pp. 108–118; and see Harvard Business School case, "Motorola's Japan Strategy," 9-387-093, Rev. 4/87, written by John J. Coleman, under the supervision of David B. Yoffie.

The State of the U.S. Steel Industry: 1985

The year 1985 was a crossroads for the officials whose decisions affected the fate of the U.S. steel industry. The industry was still in trouble despite a continuing three-year recovery of the economy, major restructuring by steel companies, changes in labor relations, and a number of government policies implemented. Foreign competition remained strong in this truly global industry. Labor leaders called the first strike on a major company (Wheeling-Pittsburgh) since 1959. Industry employment stood at only a little over one-half of its 1977 level.

The U.S. government had no intentions to develop a specific industrial policy for steel. Yet the numerous policies adopted by the government had endangered their relations with a number of countries, particularly with the European Community (EC). The year 1985 was a difficult one for the Reagan Administration with stumbling blocks having emerged in tax reform, foreign policy, trade relations, and macroeconomic management, among other areas. Was it a good time to launch policies that could solve steel's long-term problems? Could a free market president support protectionist policies? Or would such measures merely provide a remedy to unfair trade practices by other nations? Even if such policies could be implemented, would labor and management undertake actions designed to achieve a long-term solution?

Labor faced renegotiation of contracts in early 1986. The United Steel Workers of America (USWA) president, Lynn Williams, was facing an election in November 1985, but was running without opposition. Management had taken a hard line with labor recently. When the U.S.W.A. offered wage concessions to ailing companies, the big companies demanded equal treatment. What options did Williams have when his constituency was diminishing with layoffs and plant closures as management claimed that wage levels were noncompetitive with foreign companies and with smaller companies receiving wage concessions?

Companies were rethinking their strategies. Diversification into nonsteel activities had been taking place. U.S. Steel only obtained 35 percent of its revenue in 1984 from steel making, for example. World steel capacity was well beyond the levels required by world demand. Was it wise to invest in an industry plagued by worldwide overcapacity? Even if the supply-demand situation could be tamed, would labor and government cooperate to allow the companies enough assurance that investments might eventually produce an acceptable return on investment?

This case was written by Grace Tumang, Research Assistant, and Alan R. Beckenstein, Professor of Business Administration. The advice and cooperation of officials of the American Iron and Steel Institute and World Steel Dynamics are gratefully acknowledged.

INDUSTRY COMPETITION

Until the 1970s, the U.S. industry had always been a classic example of a domestically controlled oligopoly. Imports had achieved a penetration of less than 13 percent by 1970 (Exhibit 1). The top four firms accounted for between 45 and 55 percent of shipments between 1950 and 1970, a figure that had dropped to below 40 percent by 1981.

The pre-1970s concern for the vigor of competition due to industry structure evolved by the 1980s into a concern for the survival of the U.S. companies due to foreign competition. "Globalization" became the most popular descriptor of the changes in the industry. Despite significant transportation costs, steel mill products were being shipped around the world. Imports into the United States had increased from around 12 million tons (13.5 percent of the market) in 1975 to over 26 million tons (26.4 percent) in 1984 (Exhibit 2). Much of the increase in imports during recent years did not come from Japan and other Asian countries, as popularly believed, but came from Europe (Exhibit 3).

The U.S. steel producers suffered from a cost disadvantage relative to their foreign competitors. Exhibit 4 displays costs per metric ton shipped (at actual operating rates) for five countries in the years 1980 through 1985 (first half). Dramatic changes took place in the ranks of these competitors over the five-year period. Even more dramatic changes took place in the cost components and how they varied over time in different countries.

The numbers in Exhibit 4 are expressed in dollars. The dramatic changes in exchange rates over the period 1980–85 affected the numbers significantly. Exhibit 5 displays the effect of fluctuations of the four foreign currencies against the dollar. Clearly, the appreciation of the dollar during the period hurt the competitiveness of U.S. producers.

The U.S. domestic producers had long been criticized for operating outmoded plants. Yet, between 1982 and mid-1985, costs per ton declined about $105 per ton, a 16.5 percent drop. Nonetheless, comparisons with Japan, the U.K., France, and West Germany remained unfavorable in mid-1985. This was true despite importers incurring, as of late 1983, transportation costs and duties of $74.61 for Japan and $70.76 for EEC countries.[1] Newly industrialized countries such as South Korea and Brazil were reputed to be even lower cost competitors. For example, the Pohang Works in South Korea was reputed to be one of the most cost-efficient producers in the world. The principal Brazilian and Korean carbon steel producers were state-owned facilities, built as part of state-established steel plants and financed at favorable capital costs.

Labor costs per ton were affected by both wage rates and productivity. Exhibit 6 displays comparative unit labor costs for 1980–85 (first half) as derived from labor costs per hour and manhours per ton shipped (a productivity measure). With the exception of the U.K., the United States experienced the greatest decrease in manhours per ton shipped among the countries compared. Unit labor

[1]AISI Response to CBO Study.

cost declines were less spectacular because foreign wage levels, expressed in appreciated dollars, were very low.

Labor costs per ton shipped accounted for 26 percent of total production costs in the United States during early 1985 compared to Japanese and British figures of only 20 percent and 18 percent, respectively. The premium paid in early 1985 to steelworkers was reflected in the differential between steel industry and total manufacturing sector average wage levels:[2]

United States	60 percent premium
Europe	20 percent premium

The Experimental Negotiating Agreement (ENA) of 1973 was largely responsible for the large wage differential. Concluded before significant technological gains were made by foreign steel producers, the ENA provided generous wage and employment cost increases under the condition that steelworkers gave up their right to strike. Between 1973 and 1981, employment costs rose faster than inflation rates.

For integrated carbon steel production, the U.S. steel industry ranked as the most productive among the major industrialized countries requiring only 6.02 manhours per ton shipped as of the first half of 1985 versus 7.51 manhours per ton shipped in Japan (Exhibit 6). The U.S. productivity gains were largely due to the enormous drop in the employment level and technological improvements. Recent work-rule changes, such as smaller work crews, also improved productivity. However, more investment and capacity reductions were required to maintain the productivity gains. It was estimated that labor costs per ton could be reduced by $42 to $44 if a productivity level of 4 to 5 manhours per ton could be achieved.[3] Notwithstanding the consistently high productivity levels achieved by the United States, unit labor costs remained a burden because of the considerable difference in labor costs per hour between the United States and its international competitors.

Besides labor productivity and labor costs, other factors—such as the slow adaptation of cost-saving technology like continuous casting and the substantial appreciation of the U.S. dollar—determined U.S. cost-competitiveness. Also, since the steel industry was capital-intensive, total costs were highly sensitive to capacity utilization rates. Thus, the surge of imports displaced domestic steel sales, further aggravating the U.S. cost disadvantage reflected in the exhibits.

One startling comparison was in raw materials costs, including energy (Exhibit 4). During the 1970s and 1980s, U.S. prices for iron, coal, and steel scrap increased sharply. Energy costs escalated as well during the post-energy crisis period (after late 1973). Japan had successfully located cheap supplies of raw materials in such places as Australia and Brazil, engaging in long-term contracts. The U.S. industry mainly stuck to its traditional North American sources. (Iron ore, limestone, and coal were principally supplied through company-owned or joint-venture operations.) By mid-1985, Japanese material costs were 27 percent lower than U.S. costs, a differential that exceeded the labor cost differential ($87.48 vs.

[2]World Steel Dynamics, *Steel Strategist #10.*
[3]Hogan, *World Steel in the 1980s,* p. 125).

$56.05 per ton) between the two countries (even though much of the Japanese raw materials costs were dollar-denominated.) Similar comparisons could be made with the European producers.

A cost study by World Steel Dynamics forecasted the domestic cost disadvantage to persist even if the U.S. dollar declined relative to foreign currencies. The study[4] forecasted that by 1987, U.S. pretax costs would be $641 per ton as contrasted to $503 per ton in Japan and between $437 and $482 per ton in the EC. With the pressures of limited funds and expensive labor, the U.S. steel industry was still struggling for means to regain competitiveness.

SUPPLY AND DEMAND

Until the global recession of 1974–75, it had been acknowledged that steel experienced a fairly predictable business cycle. Given substantial fixed costs in steelmaking, the pressure to cut prices during recessions, when capacity utilization was low, was very strong.

After the U.S. economy recovered, steel did not follow very well. While domestic shipments increased slowly (Exhibit 7) from 1975 through 1979, imports increased and shipments were still almost 10 percent below 1973–74 levels in 1979. What followed was a large decline in 1980 and an even larger decline in 1982. By 1985, shipments were still more than 30 percent below 1973–74 levels (peak years in both the United States and the world).

Capacity utilization levels (Exhibit 8) tumbled in 1982 to 48 percent in the United States and 70 percent in the western world. By 1984, these figures had improved to 70 percent and 80 percent respectively. The poor world supply-demand situation put pressure on foreign producers to export, particularly to the low-tariff-barrier U.S. market. Foreign firms built U.S. market share by undercutting domestic prices. Nonremunerative prices were supported by government ownership or subsidization of steel exports, according to U.S. producers. By 1985, 24 percent of western world capacity was partially or fully government-owned and much of the rest was government-guided, -directed, or -protected.[5]

The U.S. steel companies, faced with this unattractive situation from 1975–1985, suffered miserable financial performance (Exhibit 10). This hurt their ability to invest in modernization of facilities, further damaging their ability to compete with the surge of imports.[6] Hence, the comparative cost situation depicted above established the conditions for competition in 1985 as world and U.S. demand improved.

There also was a geographic shift in world steel markets for basic steel products (as opposed to specialty steel). The former growth markets of the United

[4]World Steel Dynamics, *op. cit.*

[5]*Ibid.*

[6]It should be noted that EC, LDC and Japanese steel producers also experienced poor financial performance during the same years. The Japanese industry, for example, operated at no time in the previous ten years above 70 percent of capacity.

States, EC and Japan matured. The fastest growth rates occurred in newly industrialized countries.

In the mature markets, steel employment dropped dramatically. Between 1970 and 1982, employment dropped 75 percent in the EC, 19 percent in Japan, and 46 percent in the United States.[7] Regional impacts were, of course, much greater, causing disastrous economic conditions in former steel towns. In France and Belgium, for example, riots occurred in connection with the announced shutdown of facilities and troops had to be called in to maintain order.

RESTRUCTURING IN THE U.S. STEEL INDUSTRY

Due to the ruinous price-cutting competition brought about by the increasing flow of imports starting in 1977, U.S. steel producers clamored for trade restrictions in order to rebuild themselves for future competitiveness. Aware that overcapacity was a global problem and that the U.S. market was the primary target of surplus steel, U.S. manufacturers painfully realized that restructuring was necessary. Indeed the U.S. steel industry by 1985 had dramatically modernized itself. Individual U.S. steel companies have pursued different restructuring options such as the closure of facilities, mergers, joint ventures, diversification, and investment in new technology.

Capacity Reduction

U.S. steel producers started to reduce capacity after the 1977 steel crisis. There was 160 million net tons of raw steel production capability in 1977. By early 1985, capacity was 134 million net tons. More closures were expected and a capacity of less than 120 million net tons was predicted by 1990.[8] Integrated companies accounted for most of the capacity reductions. These large-scale producers eliminated 14 million tons between 1977 and 1980—largely because of two bankruptcies—and phased out another 21 million net tons between 1981 and 1983.[9]

Closures

U.S. Steel, the world's second largest producer and the leading domestic steel company (Exhibit 1) abandoned numerous blast and basic-oxygen furnaces because of limited investment funds and to decrease its break-even capacity utilization level. In addition, it reduced its product line, withdrawing from the steel rod market. Between 1983 and 1984, U.S. Steel reduced its total steelmaking capacity by 5.6 million metric tons resulting in tremendous productivity improvement.[10] Thomas

[7]The United States has, however, suffered the largest percentage drop since 1981.
[8]Hogan, *op. cit.*, p. 37.
[9]*Ibid.*, p. 93.
[10]*Iron Age*, 1984 Top 50 World Steel Producers.

C. Graham, vice chairman of U.S. Steel, claimed that "We've reduced manhours per ton by about 45 percent in the past two years."[11] However, its effort to improve efficiency involved massive layoffs. U.S. Steel posted the biggest labor reductions among steel producing companies in the world in 1984. U.S. Steel's dismissal of 12,199 employees represented a 25.1 percent reduction from 1983's total employment. "We have halved the number of our management and nonexempt personnel in just over two years," said David M. Roderick, U.S. Steel chairman.[12]

Similarly, other integrated companies closed their uneconomic facilities. Bethlehem Steel Corporation, the second largest domestic producer, shut down its Lackawanna, N.Y. plant. Armco Inc. is gradually eliminating its production capacity in Houston, Texas. Republic Steel Corp. permanently abandoned its already idle plant in Buffalo, N.Y.

Domestic steel companies in the United States have closed or authorized shutdown of more than 600 manufacturing facilities from 1974 through 1985. Fifteen companies terminated operations during the same period.

Bankruptcies

Unfortunately, the industry was plagued with bankruptcies. The Wheeling-Pittsburgh case exposed the tragic and complex issues surrounding the U.S. steel industry crisis of the 1980s. After investing a grand total of $700 million in a new rail mill, several continuous casters, and on environmental control, Wheeling-Pittsburgh went bankrupt on April 16, 1985. It was ironic that a newly modernized and highly efficient Wheeling-Pittsburgh, ranked as no. 1 in the world for productivity improvement in 1984, filed for bankruptcy under Chapter 11. Wheeling-Pittsburgh's aggressive modernization program resulted in a remarkable 35.2 percent productivity improvement in 1984 at 238 tons per employee.

However, the falling market resulted in a depressed capacity utilization rate and continued losses between 1982 and 1984. After the United Steelworkers of America (USWA) refused to accept Wheeling-Pittsburgh's proposal for a wage reduction (from $21.40 per hour to $19.00 per hour), management had no choice but to declare bankruptcy.

Smaller steel companies experienced similar dead-end situations. After its German parent company went bankrupt, Korf Industries Inc. did the same in the United States. It was forced to sell its subsidiary, the Midrex Corporation, after successfully developing a labor-efficient (but high cost) direct-reduced iron (DRI) production process. In 1983, Guterl Specialty Steel Corporation of Lockport, N.Y. was forced by its creditors to sell its assets. McLouth Steel Corp. declared bankruptcy when the steel market collapsed in 1982. (In several cases the physical facilities were restarted by new owners operating with substantially reduced employment costs.)

[11] *Iron Age*, "Steel's Agony: How Steel Management is Coping."
[12] *Ibid.*

Mergers

In order to cut down excess capacity and reduce operating as well as investment costs, many large companies have considered mergers. Recently, the LTV Corporation merged its Jones & Laughlin Steel Corporation with Republic Steel Corporation to form LTV Steel Company. One object of the merger was to coordinate capacity reductions in plants, given that the two steel producers owned one-sixth of total U.S. raw steelmaking capacity. The merger also promised lower operating costs and savings on total capital expenditures required for modernization. Mergers were viewed as an efficient way of restructuring if they would result in leaner and cost-competitive operations. However, merging did not guarantee profits in the declining steel market. LTV idled much of its Aliquippa and Pittsburgh Works facilities indefinitely because of continued financial losses.

Joint Ventures

Other steel companies, like Bethlehem and Inland, resorted to joint ventures. The two integrated steel companies conducted joint efforts in building capacity for galvanized steel, the industry's fast-growing specialty market. Wheeling-Pittsburgh jointly developed a coating line with Nisshin Steel Company, which owns 10 percent of Wheeling-Pittsburgh. Similarly, LTV Steel invested jointly in an electrogalvanizing line with Sumitomo Metal Industries, Ltd. Foreign investors in domestic facilities provided much-needed investment funds.

Diversification

Instead of new investment in their steel segments, other steel companies opted to diversify into nonsteel activities. To protect themselves from the high risk associated with the steel industry, U.S. Steel, National Steel, LTV, and Armco invested in a multitude of areas such as oil, chemicals, aluminum, savings and loan associations, insurance, and even a shopping center. U.S. Steel had 63 percent of its assets devoted to steel production in 1975. By 1982, their steel business shrank to only 40 percent of total company assets. Armco Steel and National Steel Corporation placed such importance in their diversification strategies that they renamed themselves Armco Inc. and National Intergroup Inc. For financially troubled LTV, which incurred a net loss of $156.4 million in the first quarter of 1985, its lucrative aerospace and defense unit provided profits to offset partially its losses in the steel unit.

Adoption of New Technology

Long criticized as being slow to adapt to new steel production processes, the U.S. steel industry accelerated recently the replacement of its obsolete facilities. Steel producers significantly improved productivity and quality between 1983 and 1985.

Despite their enormous losses and high debt levels, steel companies found creative alternatives in soliciting sources for the required modernization funds.

Besides the aforementioned joint ventures with foreign investors, some companies have used "off-balance-sheet" financing. In 1983, Bethlehem arranged for the lease of two continuous casters from a consortium of financiers. Under the lease terms, incremental payments would be made by Bethlehem for every ton of steel produced. The financiers benefited from this arrangement by taking advantage of the depreciation and investment tax credit applied to steel capital investments. Future customers were another ingenious financing source. Several oil companies agreed to pay the financiers of U.S. Steel for the building of a seamless-pipe mill and a continuous caster provided they were guaranteed prompt deliveries of steel pipe products. As a result of modernization, some steel facilities such as Bethlehem's Burns Harbor Works, became world-competitive. However, steel companies still were short of investment funds in 1985.

During the past two decades, two major production trends—continuous casting and electric furnaces—emerged. Continuous casting proved to be superior to the traditional ingot-casting. By eliminating intermediate processes such as the rolling of thick steel ingots, continuous casting provided savings by using less time, energy, labor and by increasing yield (the proportion of finished products per ton of new steel produced). In 1984, 39.6 percent of total U.S. steel production was continuously cast as opposed to only 9.1 percent in 1974. However, compared to Japan and to the EC, where 80 percent and 53 percent, respectively, of total steel production was continuously cast by 1982, the U.S. steel industry was still lagging.

Electric furnaces have been increasingly used in the production of basic carbon steel. By 1984, 33.9 percent of U.S. raw steel was produced using electric furnaces, whereas in 1974 it was only 19.7 percent. Besides being adopted by large-scale producers, electric furnaces facilitated the development of minimills because of the relatively low capital costs required. Moreover, capacity could easily be increased in existing units by adding water-cooled side panels. Unlike the basic-oxygen furnaces, smaller, economical additions to capacity were possible. Though a growing trend, electric furnaces were not expected to replace completely basic-oxygen furnaces due to several limitations. Since the electric furnace utilized mostly steel scrap for its input, the level of contaminants present in scrap determined the quality of the end product. Thus, the electric furnace could not be applied to all steel products. Lastly, the increasing cost of power was another obstacle. In spite of these limitations, the use of electric furnaces was expected to grow because of their economical size and flexibility.

Minimills

Another positive development was the growth of minimills. Fully integrated producers spanned the complete production process, from the conversion of raw materials through the finishing processes. Minimills started the production process with steel scrap, thereby eliminating the coking and iron-making processes, as well as the actual conversion of iron ore into steel. The abbreviated production process in minimills allowed concentration on the more efficient electric furnaces (to melt and refine steel scrap) and continuous casting. Minimills offered many economical advantages, including much lower capital requirements (initial investments of 60 to

70 million dollars for the larger ones), lower material costs, and lower labor requirements. Also, because of their limited capacities and facilities, minimills had very narrow product lines such as steel construction bars and specialty steels like steel rods and bars. Because of greater efficiency in minimills, most integrated producers were displaced from the markets in which both competed.

Because of targeted marketing strategies of minimills, they were less vulnerable to sudden swings in demand. During the 1982 steel crisis, three minimills had greater production levels than some integrated companies. In that year, Nucor, Korf, and Florida Steel minimills were the tenth, eleventh, and fourteenth largest producers, respectively. Even minimills were hit by price, supply and demand problems. They were seen to be in an overcapacity situation for their market segments by 1985.[13]

RECENT CHANGES IN BUSINESS-LABOR RELATIONS

Bankruptcies have greatly strained business-labor relations, as in the Wheeling-Pittsburgh case in 1985. Under Chapter 11 of the Bankruptcy Code, Wheeling-Pittsburgh nullified its labor contract with the USWA. Management was able, with court approval, to set employment costs on its own. The union had permission to strike. When management decided to reduce employment costs to $17.50 per hour—an 18 percent reduction from the former $21.40 per hour—the company's 8,200 USWA workers walked out on July 21, 1985, and picketed outside the Monessen, Pa. plant. The breakdown of Wheeling-Pittsburgh's labor-management negotiations marked the first major strike in the U.S. steel industry since the nationwide strike of 1959. The aftermath was a significant impact on the rest of the industry. If concessions would be arranged, there would be greater downward pressure on wages, especially among integrated companies. If no compromise were to result, the newly modernized Wheeling-Pittsburgh would face the possibility of liquidation.

A closer look at the Wheeling-Pittsburgh walkout revealed another critical aspect of government labor policy. Monessen, Pa., once a booming town during the postwar era, had become haunted by its unknown future. A community priest commented, "We're very much concerned that this could turn into a ghost town." A waitress working in a restaurant near the plant said, "I don't care who's right and wrong on this thing. But if the plant goes down, everything here goes down. And then I'll lose my job, too."[14] Sooner or later, structural unemployment would have to be dealt with. Monessen, Pa., like other steel communities could have benefited from the entry of new industries, worker retraining, and relocation subsidies.

Successful concessions on the individual company level signaled the end of coordinated bargaining. In mid-1985, five major integrated companies, U.S. Steel, Bethlehem Steel, Armco, Inland Steel, and LTV, announced that they would termi-

[13]World Steel Dynamics, *op. cit.* p. 1.
[14]"Steel Strike Fosters Talk in Monessen About Better Days," *WSJ*, 7/22/85, pp. 3 & 7.

nate coordinated bargaining and warned the USWA that they would not tolerate unfavorably high wage rates as compared to smaller producers. Lynn Williams, president of the USWA, responded, "It wasn't our committee. It was theirs. Our basic objective will be the same. We will coordinate bargaining."[15] Thus, labor-management relations in the U.S. steel industry suffered from increasing strain. Yet, the new types of bargaining often offered lower employment costs. Whether wage concessions, or employee ownership as in Weirton Steel Corporation,[16] made the local steel industry internationally competitive or only perpetuated excess capacity was a much-debated issue.

INDUSTRIAL POLICY FOR STEEL?

U.S. government policy in the steel industry emphasized the objectives of rebuilding international competitiveness and easing the burdens of adjustment to changing market conditions. There was controversy on whether general policies or more specific industrial policies were the most efficient means for adjustment. Traditionally, U.S. industrial policy relied heavily on fiscal and monetary policies in response to cyclical pressures. With the decline of U.S. manufacturing industries and increasing foreign government intervention, business and labor called for more explicit governmental actions.

Should the government have retrained workers, reduced environmental regulation to ease the financial losses of steel companies or relaxed antitrust enforcement for the sake of efficient rationalization? Past U.S. government policies did not provide definitive answers. Laissez-faire doctrines were espoused, emphasizing the greater efficiency of the private sector and free-market incentives in the allocation of resources. There was no government coordinated and comprehensive industrial policy. In fact, there was no one central authority designated to perform such a function.

Historical relations between steel producers and the government were stormy. During the Truman administration, steel companies were seized for one month by the government when they refused to accept a contract with the United Steelworkers as arranged by the Federal Wage Stabilization Board. In 1962, President Kennedy denounced U.S. Steel President Blough's decision to raise steel prices. Kennedy also enforced antitrust laws against steel companies.

During the past decade, steel companies lobbied for strict enforcement of our dumping and countervailing duty laws and, failing that, for protection from imports, blaming foreign government subsidies for the unrestrained flow of low-priced imported steel. Recent bankruptcies and sustained losses strengthened the business demand for protectionism. Also, there emerged a strong coalition between business and labor in the bid for trade protection. Formerly labor clamored for labor adjustment assistance, with few results. Labor has since pushed for protectionism.

[15]"Newswatch: Major steelmakers put an end to coordinated bargaining," *Iron Age*, 6/7/85.

[16]The Weirton plant of National Steel was purchased by its employees through an employee stock ownership plan (ESOP). The Gadsden plant of LTV, required to be divested by LTV under a Department of Justice consent decree, was proposed to be owned under ESOP.

Trade Protectionism

Proponents of trade protection from steel imports argued that a protection period was necessary for optimal restructuring to take place, especially for new investment. They argued that protectionism would have eased the most painful problem of industrial adjustment: sectoral and regional unemployment.

Another rationale was the distant possibility of a steel shortage during periods of national emergency. As General Alton D. Slay, USAF (Ret.) testified in Senate hearings, "No basic industry is more critical to the defense of the United States than its domestic steel industry . . . given the essentiality of steel to the production of armaments and to the maintenance of infrastructure, it is inconceivable to me that we could tolerate a situation where we must depend on foreign suppliers for steel in times of international crisis. History demonstrates that we cannot be sure that friendly foreign governments would always consider it to be in their interest to help us."[17]

On the other hand, Robert Crandall suggested[18] that an inventory subsidy for semifinished steel would be less costly than maintaining surplus capacity. Crandall questioned the necessity and the required extent of U.S. self-sufficiency, given the increasing number of steel-producing countries and that current steel consumption uses could be postponed in case of a national defense emergency. Citing previous defense requirements, he noted that during World War II, roughly 40 percent of total industry production volume was used. During the height of the Vietnam conflict, only 2.2 percent of total U.S. shipments were required for those purposes.

The benefits of trade protection to the domestic steel industry were counterbalanced by the losses borne by domestic steel consumers in the form of higher steel prices. For steel-consuming industries, basic steel trade protection translated to higher costs of production and, therefore, declining competitiveness for products containing steel. This was reflected in the 1984 deficit of 6.4 million tons in U.S. indirect steel trade, such as in machinery products.[19] (It should be noted that this occurred during a period of falling prices.) Also, extreme forms of trade protection invited resistance and retaliation from trading partners, possibly penalizing other healthy U.S. export industries.

Steel public policy utilized various forms of trade protection. In June 1976, when U.S. specialty steel companies filed a complaint against imports under the 1974 Trade Act, the U.S. government put a specialty steel quota into effect until 1979 because it was unable to arrange an orderly marketing agreement (OMA) for specialty steels.

To maintain market share and regain competitiveness, domestic producers and the United Steelworkers lobbied the government to adopt voluntary restraint agreements (VRAs) between 1969 and 1974 with the EC and Japan to limit steel imports. According to a study conducted by Crandall, the VRAs resulted in higher

[17]AISI Annual Report, p. 7.
[18]Robert Crandall, *The U.S. Steel Industry in Recurrent Crisis.*
[19]AISI Annual Report, p. 12.

prices for steel imports, which increased by 6.3 percent to 8.3 percent between 1971 and 1972, and for domestic steel prices, which increased by 1.2 percent to 3.5 percent during the same period. The import penetration level was reduced by 25 percent from 17 percent of the total U.S. market between 1971 and 1972 to less than 13 percent between 1973 and 1974. This might have been due to the VRAs, but also might have been due to lower interest in exporting to the United States due to surging world demand. The industry's return on equity remained low. Since new investment was still unattractive, the protection period was not used to improve productivity and competitiveness.

In 1977, the U.S. steel industry and labor again clamored for protection from rising imports. A Congressional steel caucus pressed the government for new trade policy. The Carter administration initially encouraged the steel industry to file formal complaints to resolve "unfair" trade. By October 1977, nineteen antidumping (AD) cases had been brought against Japan and the EC since 1975, including the Gilmore Case, which culminated in a tentative resolution against Japan. The mounting tensions in U.S. steel trade negatively affected the then-ongoing Tokyo round of negotiations under the General Agreement on Tariffs and Trade (GATT).

A task force led by Undersecretary of the Treasury Anthony Solomon was formed to ease trade tensions and facilitate industrial adjustment. The Solomon Plan imposed a trigger-price system which provided an allegedly faster and more objective method of settling AD cases. The trigger-price system made use of a schedule of prices for steel imports based on Japanese total costs of production—Japan being the most cost-efficient producer at that time—including transportation costs and a reasonable profit margin. When the import price fell below the trigger price, such was considered prima facie evidence for AD investigations. The Solomon Plan also established the Steel Tripartite Advisory Committee—composed of government, industry, and labor representatives—to recommend policies and to monitor the Solomon Plan. There were also proposals for loan guarantee funds, shorter depreciation lives, government aid for afflicted steel communities, the reduction of environmental compliance costs, and the easing of antitrust laws.

Like the VRAs, the trigger-price mechanism (TPM), according to Crandall's study, raised both imported and domestic steel prices by approximately 10 percent and 1 percent, respectively. Overall, the weighted average increase in U.S. prices was about 2.7 percent resulting in a 1979 average price increase of $11.50 per ton. Crandall's cost/benefit analysis[20] of the TPM effects revealed that its major benefit was a decrease in the 1979 share of imports. However, by 1980, imports began to rise again. He estimated that the 1978–1979 trigger prices redistributed about $1 billion per year from consumers to domestic and foreign steel producers and labor. About $45 to $87 million per year accrued to approximately 12,400 steelworkers sustained by the TPM, excluding further wage hikes. The TPM, just like other protectionist measures, involved a hidden welfare cost in the form of inefficient allocation of resources to steel production. Because of the TPM, an

[20]Crandall, *op. cit.*

estimated 3.1 million tons of steel production was shifted from abroad to U.S. producers. Crandall estimated this welfare loss to be $22 million per year. It should be noted that foreign government trade practices—deemed "unfair" by domestic producers—also affect these same variables and any assessment of them.

The TPM was successful in preventing a full-blown import crisis in the short run. In spite of TPM's benefits, the U.S. steel industry was still unable to modernize fully because of the persistently low industry return on equity. It was alleged by U.S. producers that EC producers ignored TPM. The result was a wave of unfair trade cases, many of which were won by the U.S. industry. As a result, the TPM was suspended.

As evidenced by the VRAs and the TPM, trade protection did not solve the U.S. steel industry's structural problems. For this reason, trade protectionism had been criticized as being inefficient and an obstacle to restructuring. It was argued that, because of government protection, the industry's resistance to change had been indirectly encouraged by the government and that, otherwise, the free market would have allocated resources to more productive endeavors. The major complication is that these government effects came from a number of competing countries.

In October, 1982, the U.S.-EC Carbon/Alloy Arrangement was put into effect, limiting European steel imports to 5.4 percent of the U.S. market. The agreement was effective for "licensed" steel imports, as reflected in the 1984 import penetration levels of such products. However, for "consultation" products, EC imports exceeded the agreed levels by 216 percent. Accordingly, the U.S. called for a renegotiation and an extension of the agreement until 1989. The U.S. government started negotiations with the EC during early 1985 for two months, but the talks ended without major decisions. Negotiations were expected to resume in May 1985. Adding greater strain, the EC asked the U.S. for compensation for losses due to the U.S.-EC Carbon/Alloy Arrangement. Under Gatt ruling, countries negatively affected by protectionist measures could retaliate or demand compensation.

The domestic steel industry filed a section 301 petition in 1983 asserting that a trade agreement between Japan and the EC, wherein Japan agreed to restrain steel exports to the EC market, resulted in the surge of foreign steel into the U.S. market. However, the U.S. Trade Representative decided that evidence of damage to the U.S. steel industry was lacking.

In July 1983, President Reagan granted import relief to specialty steels for four years in the form of higher tariffs for stainless steel strips, sheets, and plates as well as global quotas for alloy tool steel and stainless steel bars and rods. The quotas succeeded in limiting imports, but higher tariffs failed to check the import surge of the affected products.

On November 19, 1984, after two years of EC imports of tubular steel exceeding its agreed limits, the U.S. government embargoed a steel pipe and tube shipment from the EC. Immediately, the U.S.-EC Pipe and Tube Arrangement was revised in January 1985.

The 1984 import crisis strengthened the business-labor coalition's bid for trade protection. When several U.S. producers and the United Steelworkers filed a petition under section 201 of the Trade Act, the U.S. International Trade Commission determined that the domestic steel industry had been injured by the 1984 import crisis. In early 1984, the "Fair Trade in Steel Act" was proposed in Congress, providing for a 15 percent steel import quota for five years.

On September 18, 1984, President Reagan denied remedies for the 201 injuries and came up instead with a five-year Comprehensive Fair Trade Program with the objective of limiting finished steel imports to 18.5 percent of the U.S. market, as well as a global quota on semifinished steel imports of 1.7 million tons. To fulfill this objective, the president sent U.S. Trade Representative William Brock to negotiate OMAs, also known as surge control arrangements, with steel producing countries not covered by the pact with the EC. Simultaneously, the Steel Import Stabilization Act was passed by Congress in October 1984. It authorized enforcement at the border of bilateral arrangements with ten steel exporting countries: Japan, South Korea, Brazil, Spain, South Africa, Mexico, Finland, Australia, Poland, and Czechoslovakia. These countries agreed to specific share limitations, resulting in an aggregate limit of 10.4 percent of the U.S. market for their finished steel imports, as contrasted to their aggregate 1984 U.S. market share of 14.5 percent.

The surge control arrangements were to last for five years and required export licenses for U.S. entry. For countries covered by the OMAs, the Commerce Department dropped pending antidumping (AD) and countervailing duties (CVD) cases. The Steel Import Stabilization Act provided for the enforcement of the law at the U.S. border under the jurisdiction of the U.S. Customs Service. Furthermore, the Act clearly provided that the large steel producers be required to invest substantially all their net cash flow in their steel segments or else forgo the import relief.

The global quota on semifinished steel contradicted the current industry trend of increasing dependence on low-cost imported semifinished steel. As more and more companies closed their melting operations, guaranteed sources of semifinished steel had become prerequisites for survival, especially in the long run.

The OMAs were by no means comprehensive as major producers like Argentina, Austria, Canada, Sweden, Venezuela, the Eastern Bloc, and some EC countries were left uncovered. AD and CVD cases were continued for such countries. Reagan's steel trade policy also sought to counteract foreign government subsidies such as export financing by initiating AD and CVD cases on "unfair" trade when necessary and by actively participating in the OECD Steel Committee.

With respect to tax policy, asset depreciation lives were shortened in recognition of heightened obsolescence. The Reagan Administration's 1981 Tax Equity Act provided for shorter depreciation lives for most manufacturing equipment and also for safe-harbor leasing, which granted the selling of tax credits by steel companies, thereby increasing cash flow.

Consistently a burden to steel producers, costly environmental regulations were deferred for three years by the Steel Industry Compliance Extension Act of 1981. The Clean Air Act was amended, postponing compliance dates, to complement modernization efforts. The government also pledged to ease antitrust laws to facilitate mergers that promise to rationalize operations.

The Keyworth Initiative was a modest effort named after Presidential Science Advisor Dr. George A. Keyworth to increase the competitiveness of the U.S.

steel industry. As a joint effort of the U.S. Government, Federal National Laboratories and domestic steel companies, the program was developing state-of-the art technology with the goal of cutting capital costs and reducing operating costs by as much as 30 percent.

POLICY OPTIONS FOR BUSINESS, LABOR, AND GOVERNMENT

The painful realities of layoffs, wage cuts, corporate restructuring, depressed regional economies, and poor financial performance made the ideological debates of free and fair trade seem rather distant. The behavior of business, labor, and government had been clear. Industry had sought and obtained protection from imports that were deemed unfair and/or injurious. The United States did, in fact, have a set of policies for steel, regardless of the ad hoc process by which they had evolved.

By late 1985, the policies and a rebounding market for steel had not eliminated the severe financial crisis in the industry. Imports were still a major problem. Great strides had been made in addressing the competitive problems faced by the industry, yet even greater strides would be needed to solve the problems permanently.

Each of the various challenges faced by the industry could have been categorized as structural or cyclical. Public policy solutions to these problems had both structural and cyclical effects. If a specific industrial policy were to be formulated by one or more of the three major "players"—labor, business, and government—it would be important that cyclical problems not defeat otherwise-sound structural solutions. If shorter term, cyclical policies were to be adopted, their acceptance would depend upon the longer-term prospects of a structurally sound industry.

The Reagan administration was particularly sensitive to the problems of long-run vs. short-run tradeoffs. The supply-side policies implemented during Reagan's first term did, after a "double-dip" recession, contribute to a long period of rapid growth. They also were alleged to have contributed strongly to the appreciation of the dollar to such an extent that many industries—steel included—were still noncompetitive with foreign competitors by 1985.

Was the strong dollar merely a cyclical problem? Could industry invest in modernization confident that the dollar would drop to "normal" levels soon? Or would dollar appreciation lead to capital outflows that exacerbated already-tight monetary conditions and produced a recession?

What was different about steel? Should the United States have developed a specific industrial policy for steel or was steel symptomatic of general manufacturing industry problems? The parties involved needed to assess whether steel possessed any special cyclical or structural characteristics demanding special attention.

Labor was positioned awkwardly in 1985. Most nonlabor partisans pointed to high compensation levels as a major problem. But why should labor attempt to save jobs through wage concessions when most forecasts for the industry pointed to the inevitability of a scaled-down industry anyway? Was employee compensation the primary structural impediment to a globally competitive industry in the United States? Who wanted to work for South Korean wage rates anyway?

Perhaps more importantly, could labor trust management and government to produce structurally sound, long-term policies which would justify a change in labor's strategy? Or could labor harness the issues of regional employment and unfair trade as short-term rallying points for favorable policies that obviated, or at least delayed, painful long-term adjustments.

Government officials had been reminded constantly over the previous decade that Japan, South Korea, and other governments had successful industrial policies that produced "champions" in selected industries. Even if an industrial policy could be developed, who would the champions be? U.S. steel companies had focused on diversification recently. Could the major companies be trusted to implement long-term solutions or would money spent merely go into financing corporate restructuring and reorganization?

Management had been frustrated by the lack of success of recent policies in preventing poor performance. Labor rates were high by international standards. Would dollar depreciation solve this problem? What could be offered to labor to produce jointly beneficial labor conditions? Trade restrictions had been proven ineffective during the 1980s. Various trade bills were before Congress in October 1985. Did steel require something extra? Could specific policies for steel—trade, investment, competition, environmental regulation—be requested? Could the major competitors even agree on the most desirable policies?

Even if the pessimistic scenario of a scaled-down, lower-wage industry producing mostly specialty steel were to be accepted by all parties, the problems of adjustment, and policies to assist such, were still formidable. Management, labor, and government each understood the painful reality of the situation in 1985. The question was who would take the lead in proposing the inevitable compromise that each foresaw?

Exhibit 1 Market Share by Firm

		1950 A	1950 B	1950 C	1960 A	1960 B	1960 C
U.S. Steel		22.6	28.4	28.0	18.7	26.3	25.2
Bethlehem		10.9	13.7	13.5	11.4	16.0	15.3
Republic		6.4	8.0	7.9	5.4	7.6	7.3
J&L	merged	6.8	8.5	8.4	7.0	9.8	9.4
Youngstown	1978						
National	merged	4.0	5.0	5.0	5.3	7.5	7.1
Granite City	1971						
Armco		3.0	3.8	3.7	5.0	7.0	6.7
Inland		3.3	4.1	4.1	5.1	7.2	6.9
Wheeling	merged						
Pittsburgh	1968	3.3	2.9	2.9	2.6	3.7	3.5
Total of above		60.3	74.5	73.5	60.5	85.1	81.4
Other domestic		20.3	25.5	25.2	10.6	14.9	14.3

		1970 A	1970 B	1970 C	1981 A	1981 B	1981 C
U.S. Steel		21.0	23.1	20.2	16.6	19.1	15.5
Bethlehem		13.8	15.2	13.2	11.6	13.3	10.9
Republic		6.7	7.4	6.4	6.5	7.5	6.1
J&L	merged	8.4	9.3	8.1	7.6	8.7	7.1
Youngstown	1978						
National	merged	7.3	8.0	7.0	6.6	7.6	6.2
Granite City	1971						
Armco		5.4	5.9	5.2	5.8	6.7	5.4
Inland		4.7	5.2	4.5	5.8	6.7	5.4
Wheeling	merged						
Pittsburgh	1968	2.9	3.2	2.8	2.1	2.4	2.0
Total of above		70.2	77.3	67.4	67.6	72.0	58.6
Other domestic		20.6	22.7	19.8	24.4	28.0	22.8

Note: A = Millions of Net Tons
B = Percent of Domestic Shipments
C = Percent of Domestic and Imported Shipments

Source: American Iron and Steel Institute (AISI) Annual Statistical Report—1984.

Exhibit 2 Imports

A. IMPORT LEVELS

	Imports, All Steel Mill Products (Thousands of Net Tons)	Market Penetration (Percent of Total Market)	Imports, Semi-Finished Steel* (Thousands of Net Tons)
1984	26,163	26.4%	1,516
1983	17,070	20.5%	822
1982	16,662	21.8%	717
1981	19,898	18.9%	790
1980	15,495	16.3%	155
1979	17,518	15.2%	345
1978	21,135	18.1%	414
1977	19,307	17.8%	298
1976	14,285	14.1%	240
1975	12,012	13.5%	243

B. PERCENT INCREASE (DECREASE)

	Imports, All Steel Mill Products	Imports, Semi-Finished Steel
1983–84	53.3%	84.4%
1982–83	2.4%	14.6%
1981–82	(16.3%)	(9.2%)
1980–81	28.4%	409.7%
1979–80	(11.5%)	(55.1%)
1978–79	(17.1%)	(16.7%)
1977–78	9.5%	38.9%
1976–77	35.2%	24.2%
1975–76	18.9%	(1.2%)

*Examples of semifinished steel are ingots, billets, and slabs.

Source: American Iron and Steel Institute (AISI) Annual Statistical Report—1984.

Exhibit 3 Imports By Countries of Origin

A. IMPORT VOLUME (Thousands of Net Tons)

	1984	1983	1982	1981	1980
Canada	3,167	2,379	1,844	2,899	2,370
Latin America	3,132	2,415	974	782	630
Europe	9,963	5,310	6,775	8,077	4,744
Asia & Africa	9,685	6,761	6,939	8,011	7,620
Australia & Oceania	216	206	130	129	132
Total Imports of Steel Mill Products	26,163	17,070	16,662	19,898	15,495

B. PERCENT OF TOTAL IMPORTS

	1984	1983	1982	1981	1980
Canada	12.1%	13.9%	11.1%	14.6%	15.3%
Latin America	12.0%	14.2%	5.8%	3.9%	4.1%
Europe	38.1%	31.1%	40.7%	40.6%	30.6%
Asia & Africa	37.0%	39.6%	41.6%	40.3%	49.2%
Australia & Oceania	0.8%	1.2%	0.8%	0.6%	0.8%
Total Imports of Steel Mill Products	100.0%	100.0%	100.0%	100.0%	100.0%

C. U.S. MARKET PENETRATION

	1984	1983	1982	1981	1980
Canada	3.2%	2.9%	2.4%	2.7%	2.5%
Latin America	3.2%	2.9%	1.3%	0.8%	0.7%
Europe	10.1%	6.4%	8.9%	7.7%	5.0%
Asia & Africa	9.8%	8.1%	9.1%	7.6%	8.0%
Australia & Oceania	0.2%	0.2%	0.2%	0.1%	0.1%
Total Imports of Steel Mill Products	26.4%	20.5%	21.8%	18.9%	16.3%

Source: AISI Annual Statistical Report, 1984.

Exhibit 4 International Comparative Cost Structure Costs per metric ton shipped (at actual operating rates)

1980	US	Japan	W. Germany	UK*	France
Revenue	**$507.24**	**$426.66**	**$506.96**	**$514.23**	**$501.61**
Labor	$175.11	$93.88	$164.56	$452.81	$172.87
Raw Materials	292.12	259.61	289.68	456.63	299.96
Financial Costs	39.93	82.85	63.04	159.57	105.53
Total Costs/Ton	$507.16	$436.33	$517.28	$1,069.02	$578.36
Exogenous Cost Factor				−342.70	
				$726.32	
Pretax Profit/Ton	$0.08	$26.32	($10.33)	($212.09)	($76.74)

* Strike year in the UK.

1981	US	Japan	W. Germany	UK	France
Revenue	**$574.28**	**$496.52**	**$440.60**	**$456.59**	**$433.64**
Labor	$185.19	$108.11	$145.10	$144.76	$143.14
Raw Materials	320.58	287.85	284.26	384.86	296.39
Financial Costs	39.76	93.32	57.28	77.06	90.60
Total Costs/Ton	$545.52	$489.28	$486.63	$606.68	$530.13
Pretax Profit/Ton	$28.75	$7.24	($46.03)	($150.10)	($96.49)

1982	US	Japan	W. Germany	UK	France
Revenue	**$581.17**	**$453.79**	**$463.15**	**$453.11**	**$447.73**
Labor	$214.54	$96.99	$162.08	$134.94	$146.08
Raw Materials	359.18	279.30	289.84	342.07	293.42
Financial Costs	65.34	84.04	66.03	76.32	94.33
Total Costs/Ton	$639.06	$460.33	$517.95	$553.32	$533.83
Pretax Profit/Ton	($57.89)	($6.54)	($54.80)	($100.21)	($86.10)

1983	US	Japan	W. Germany	UK	France
Revenue	**$533.37**	**$467.43**	**$436.64**	**$413.48**	**$419.49**
Labor	$173.08	$101.27	$152.94	$93.96	$156.80
Raw Materials	345.44	274.54	268.17	290.01	257.52
Financial Costs	64.62	96.08	60.86	53.40	91.47
Total Costs/Ton	$583.14	$471.89	$481.97	$437.36	$505.78
Pretax Profit/Ton	($49.77)	($4.47)	($45.33)	($23.89)	($86.29)

(continued)

Exhibit 4 *(Continued)*

	1984				
	US	Japan	W. Germany	UK	France
Revenue	**$542.56**	**$450.30**	**$405.02**	**$378.95**	**$387.79**
Labor	$149.10	$91.73	$117.18	$81.43	$128.20
Raw Materials	347.00	256.84	245.17	262.86	235.42
Financial Costs	66.85	88.71	46.63	46.21	72.77
Total Costs/Ton	$562.95	$437.28	$408.98	$390.51	$436.39
Pretax Profit/Ton	($20.39)	$13.02	($3.95)	($11.56)	($48.61)

	1985 (Jan.–June average)				
	US	Japan	W. Germany	UK	France
Revenue	**$523.90**	**$425.43**	**$387.11**	**$359.20**	**$368.03**
Labor	$139.10	$83.05	$95.33	$64.66	$105.44
Raw Materials	329.98	242.50	231.57	252.08	224.59
Financial Costs	64.85	82.34	39.17	36.33	57.25
Total Costs/Ton	$533.93	$407.89	$366.07	$353.07	$387.38
Pretax Profit/Ton	($10.03)	$17.54	$21.04	$6.14	($19.36)

Source: World Steel Dynamics (WSD) Price/Cost Monitor Report #7

Exhibit 5 1984 Pretax Costs, Foreign Exchange Rates, 1979 versus 1984 (U.S. versus foreign steel landed in Chicago area)

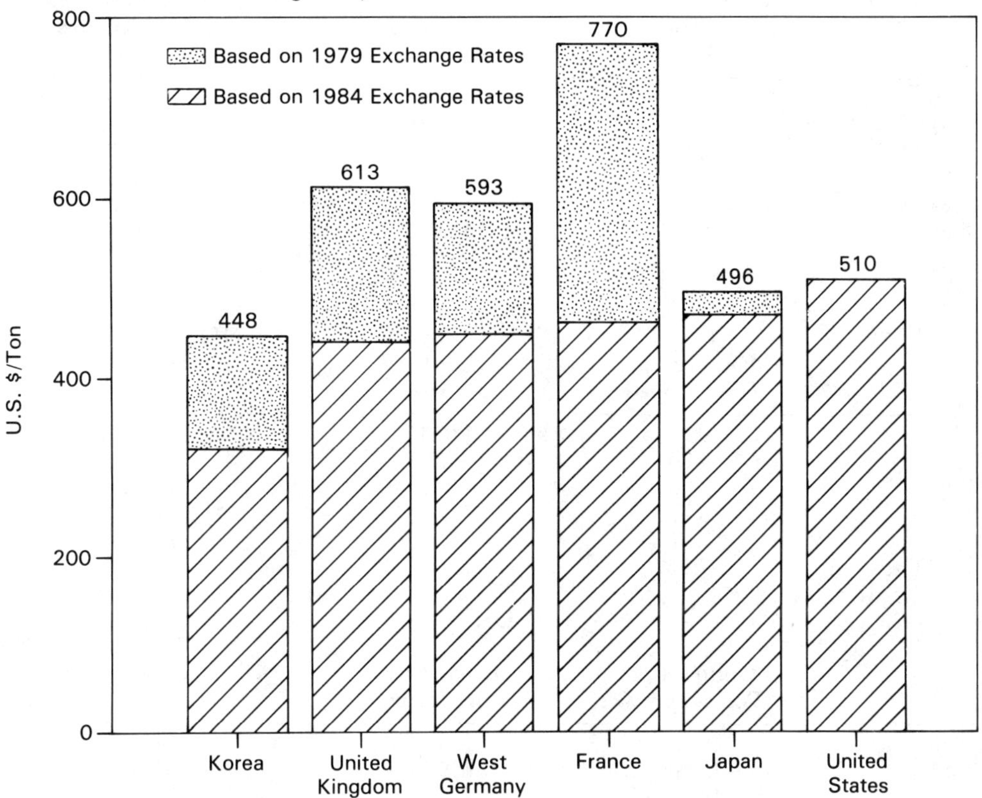

Sources: Morgan Guaranty Trust Co. and World Steel

Exhibit 6 International Comparative Unit Labor Costs (at actual operating rates) 1980–1985

US

	Manhours per Ton Shipped		Labor Cost per Hour		UNIT LABOR COST (Labor Cost per Ton Shipped)
1980	9.17	×	$19.06	=	$174.78
1981	8.90	×	$20.78	=	$184.94
1982	8.65	×	$24.67	=	$213.40
1983	7.28	×	$23.70	=	$172.54
1984	6.67	×	$22.36	=	$149.14
1985 (Jan–Jun)	6.02	×	$23.10	=	$139.06

Japan

	Manhours per Ton Shipped		Labor Cost per Hour		UNIT LABOR COST (Labor Cost per Ton Shipped)
1980	9.15	×	$10.25	=	$ 93.79
1981	9.36	×	$11.55	=	$108.11
1982	8.90	×	$10.90	=	$ 97.01
1983	8.47	×	$11.96	=	$101.30
1984	7.71	×	$11.89	=	$ 91.67
1985 (Jan–Jun)	7.51	×	$11.06	=	$ 83.06

UK

	Manhours per Ton Shipped		Labor Cost per Hour		UNIT LABOR COST (Labor Cost per Ton Shipped)
1980	46.02	×	$ 9.96	=	$458.36
1981	15.06	×	$ 9.57	=	$144.12
1982	14.86	×	$ 9.14	=	$135.82
1983	11.87	×	$ 7.92	=	$ 94.01
1984	11.68	×	$ 6.98	=	$ 81.53
1985 (Jan–Jun)	10.49	×	$ 6.18	=	$ 64.83

W. Germany

	Manhours per Ton Shipped		Labor Cost per Hour		UNIT LABOR COST (Labor Cost per Ton Shipped)
1980	11.04	×	$14.93	=	$164.83
1981	11.00	×	$13.19	=	$145.09
1982	12.26	×	$13.28	=	$162.81
1983	12.05	×	$12.71	=	$153.16
1984	10.21	×	$11.49	=	$117.31
1985 (Jan–Jun)	9.25	×	$10.30	=	$ 95.28

France

	Manhours per Ton Shipped		Labor Cost per Hour		UNIT LABOR COST (Labor Cost per Ton Shipped)
1980	11.22	×	$15.39	=	$172.68
1981	11.31	×	$12.66	=	$143.19

(continued)

Exhibit 6 *(Continued)*

1982	12.04	×	$12.15	=	$146.29
1983	12.14	×	$12.87	=	$156.24
1984	11.59	×	$11.01	=	$127.61
1985 (Jan–Jun)	10.86	×	$ 9.71	=	$105.45

Source: WSD Price/Cost Monitor Report #7.

Exhibit 7 World Crude Steel Production by Region (Millions of Metric Tons)

	US	JAPAN	EEC	BRAZIL	S. KOREA	USSR	TOTAL
1973	136.8	119.3	150.1	N.A.	N.A.	N.A.	N.A.
1974	132.2	117.1	155.6	7.5	1.9	136.2	703.8
1975	105.8	102.3	125.6	8.4	2.0	141.3	643.0
1976	116.1	107.4	134.1	9.2	3.5	144.8	675.5
1977	113.7	102.4	126.2	11.2	4.3	147.0	675.6
1978	124.3	102.1	132.7	12.2	5.0	151.4	717.2
1979	123.7	111.7	140.3	13.9	7.6	149.1	746.4
1980	101.5	111.4	127.8	15.3	8.6	147.9	716.0
1981	109.6	101.7	125.5	13.2	10.8	148.5	706.9
1982	67.6	99.5	110.5	13.0	11.8	147.2	645.2
1983	75.6	97.2	108.6	14.7	11.9	152.5	662.6
FORECAST							
1984E	85.8	104.1	119.9	18.3	12.9	171.4	740.4
1985E	95.0	110.0	127.0	N.A.	N.A.	N.A.	N.A.
1986E	102.0	120.0	130.0	N.A.	N.A.	N.A.	N.A.
1987E	79.0	115.0	123.0	N.A.	N.A.	N.A.	N.A.
1990E	85.0	125.0	120.0	N.A.	N.A.	N.A.	N.A.

Sources: World Steel Dynamics
International Iron and Steel Institute (as cited in the 1985 Iron Age Statistical Review)

Exhibit 8 World Production and Capacity Utilization, World Gross Capacity Utilization (Percent of Capacity)

	US	JAPAN	EEC	DEVELOPING WORLD	COMMUNIST WORLD
1973	97.0	88.4	85.8	65.7	89.7
1974	94.4	84.9	87.4	68.0	88.0
1975	76.8	73.1	63.5	68.4	88.5
1976	80.7	73.0	68.4	71.8	88.3
1977	79.0	64.9	62.1	70.2	87.2
1978	86.9	65.0	65.6	73.9	90.2
1979	87.9	71.5	69.2	78.1	87.4
1980	72.8	70.1	64.1	79.1	85.3
1981	77.5	63.9	63.7	72.5	81.1
1982	48.5	63.0	56.8	70.1	80.0
1983	55.3	61.6	59.0	67.6	83.1
FORECAST					
1984E	70.0	66.3	66.3	67.1	83.9
1985E	80.8	70.8	73.2	68.5	85.3
1986E	91.3	79.7	81.8	68.2	92.2
1987E	71.8	78.7	76.9	64.9	89.2
1990E	78.3	86.0	75.5	70.5	90.0

Exhibit 9 U.S. Steel Industry Highlights

	Net Domestic Shipments (Millions of Net Tons)	Finished Steel Average Composite Price (Cents per Pound)	Average Number of Employees
1984	73.7	27.313	236,002
1983	67.6	26.190	242,745
1982	61.6	25.271	289,437
1981	88.5	24.224	390,914
1980	83.9	21.655	398,829
1979	100.3	20.006	453,181
1978	97.9	17.940	449,197
1977	91.1	15.577	452,388
1976	89.4	14.213	454,128
1975	80.0	13.102	457,162
1974	N.A.	11.141	512,395
1973	N.A.	9.380	508,614
1972	N.A.	8.998	478,368
1971	N.A.	8.429	487,269
1970	N.A.	7.650	531,196

Sources: 1984 American Iron and Steel Institute (AISI) Annual Statistical Report
1985 Iron Age Statistical Review

Exhibit 10 Financial Highlights

	Total Sales (Millions)	Net Income* (Millions)	Return on Stockholder's Equity	Debt/ Equity Ratio	Total Dividends Paid (Millions)
1984	$55,192	($ 204)	−1.3%	99.3%	$526
1983	$48,449	($3,563)	−19.7%	97.9%	$439
1982	$52,083	($3,206)	−15.0%	83.5%	$582
1981	$60,173	$2,601	13.4%	43.8%	$689
1980	$52,829	$1,735	9.6%	50.3%	$630
1979	$55,140	$1,154	6.5%	48.3%	$593
1978	$49,033	$1,277	7.3%	49.5%	$536
1977	$39,400	$ 22	0.1%	45.5%	$555
1976	$36,093	$1,337	7.8%	38.9%	$637
1975	$33,144	$1,595	9.8%	33.1%	$658

*Net Income represents the results of total corporate activities including steel and nonsteel. It also includes unusual or extraordinary items affecting income or costs such as the sale of assets and plant closings.

Source: Steel and America, An Annual Report (AISI), May 1985.

U.S. Competitiveness and High-Definition Television (A)

In May of 1989, the American Electronics Association (AEA), the trade group representing major U.S. electronic companies, asked the U.S. government to provide $1.35 billion in grants, loans and guarantees to help develop high-definition television (HDTV). In particular, the Pentagon's Defense Advanced Research Projects Agency (DARPA) would spend $300 million over three years to develop new HDTV sets; the Commerce Department's National Institute of Standards and Technology would spend $50 million over three years to develop a new TV transmission standard; and the Commerce Department would also provide $500 million in low-interest loans and $500 million in loan guarantees to build new TV production facilities and for working capital. AEA also proposed the creation of an entity called the Advanced Television Corporation to manage government loans and to patent and license technology. In addition, the association said the electronics industry would match government funds on at least a dollar-for-dollar basis. Without government funding, AEA predicted that U.S. electronics companies would not enter the HDTV market because of the high risks and low profit margins. Furthermore, the association insisted that government support in HDTV was critical for the protection and development of the U.S. computer and semiconductor industries.

The proposal won the quick endorsement of Senator Ernest Hollings, chairman of the Senate Commerce Committee, who said, "We've got to get some money in there to get anything going."[1] On the other hand, officials in the Bush administration were not enthusiastic about AEA's proposal. Even Commerce Secretary Robert Mosbacher, who was sympathetic toward the need for some government support to the HDTV effort, criticized AEA's call for huge subsidies. As Mosbacher told the Senate Commerce Committee, "They're hoping Uncle Sugar will fund (HDTV). . . . I don't think they should depend on that."[2] Instead, Mosbacher favored an emphasis on giving American electronics companies antitrust exemptions, possible tax incentives and favorable government procurement. A limited amount of government funding would also be possible, such as DARPA's recent decision to spend $30 million on HDTV research. Such targeted policies were necessary for HDTV because, as Mosbacher exclaimed, HDTV could be "a major catalyst for technological progress."[3]

For the Mosbacher team at Commerce, however, the term "industrial policy" did not accurately describe the Commerce secretary's approach to HDTV. As

This case was prepared by Charles R. Kennedy, Jr., Associate Professor of Management, Babcock Graduate School of Management, Wake Forest University, Winston-Salem, North Carolina.

Wayne L. Berman, counselor to Mosbacher, insisted, "It's industry-led policy." In other words:

> We're not picking winners and losers in the sense that we're going to single out any particular HDTV technology over any other HDTV technology. We're not trying to pick one company's approach or standards over another company's.

Moreover, Berman went on to add, by turning down AEA's proposal to create an HDTV corporation, which would receive over a billion dollars in government funds, the Commerce Department had clearly rejected an "industrial policy" approach to HDTV. In characterizing AEA's proposal, Berman said, "That [would be] picking winners and losers big time."[4]

Others in the Bush administration were adamantly opposed to any targeted support for HDTV. Most prominent among these opponents were Michael Boskin, chairman of the Council of Economic Advisers, and Richard Darman, director of the Office of Management and Budget. For them, Mosbacher was too inclined to meddle in the marketplace via government protection and support. As William Niskanen, a member of the Council of Economic Advisers in the Reagan administration, observed, "Industrial policy seems to be in the walls at the Commerce Department."[5]

Other analysts outside the administration also pointed out the hazards of targeted industrial policies. As Paul Krugman, an MIT economist, remarked in regards to HDTV:

> There are lots of examples of things that sounded really good at the time they were put forward that turned out to be massive lemons for the governments that promoted them . . . The argument is that things will be chosen not because they're the right thing to choose, but because they have a constituency.[6]

Thus skepticism regarding prospects for HDTV could be found in many quarters, although they seemed to hold the minority viewpoint. As Julies Barnathan, president of broadcast operations and engineering at Capital Cities/ABC Inc., said: "Around here, we call [HDTV] the emperor's new clothes," but he admitted his view was "like speaking against motherhood and progress."[7] From another perspective, even if the HDTV market took off, the U.S. electronics industry would not be competitive against the Japanese. As Steven Jobs, CEO of Next Inc., insisted, "All this stuff about how the United States is going to participate [in HDTV] is a joke"; moreover, he predicted that the "computer industry will become a high enough consumer of semiconductors to dwarf HDTV."[8]

Thus the industrial policy debate and HDTV controversy raged inside and outside the Bush administration during the summer of 1989. The stakes involved seemed high, and decisions reached could set the tone and direction of U.S. competitiveness in manufacturing for decades to come.

HDTV MARKETS AND COMPETITORS

The potential global market for HDTV products, which includes advanced TV sets, VCRs and broadcast equipment, is huge—an estimated $50 billion by the turn of the century, according to a Department of Commerce study. In the United States alone, the market could reach $8 billion by the year 2000, which, on a per-capita basis, is low compared to Japan and Europe. This is due to the lag in the United States toward establishing a transmission standard for HDTV. Prices, however, are a major concern, for they will remain high in the United States on the bigger, more attractive HDTV sets well into the next century, as shown by an analysis of the Boston Consulting Group (BCG) in Exhibit 1. One should note that the average price of a new color TV set today is under $400, but if consumer demand and willingness to pay the higher HDTV prices are strong, the experience with color TV prices in the 1960s could be repeated (see Exhibit 2).

Consumer behavior is thus the major unknown in projecting the potential HDTV market. Certainly the technology to broadcast and receive HDTV signals is available, and consumers are attracted to the product. As BCG concludes after intensive interviews with American, European, and Japanese companies in the electronics industry:

A worldwide market for Advanced Television (ATV) products and services will emerge in the next decade.

- The technology is in hand.
- Europe and Japan are investing to create equipment *and program availability.*
- Price can reach acceptable price points once volume begins (< $1500 for a 27″ ATV).
- ATV has significant consumer appeal (although consumer reaction is the greatest unknown).
- U.S. market likely to reach $4–$8 billion by 2000, assuming a coherent U.S. ATV strategy is implemented.[9]

BCG's baseline forecast for market demand in the United States for HDTV products is shown in Exhibit 3.

The Japanese were the first to launch a HDTV research program. Starting in 1970, the Japan Broadcasting Corporation (NHK) coordinated a pooled research effort on HDTV that involved Sony, Toshiba, NEC, and other Japanese technology leaders. The program had a $500 million budget, and NHK, which is government supported, contributed 15 percent of the money. As a result of these research efforts, Japanese companies can now produce the full range of HDTV products—picture tubes, receivers, VCRs, programming on videotape, semiconductors, cameras, and transmission equipment. Of critical importance to the success of these efforts was the decision to establish a transmission standard in Japan early on so that product development could be guided and accelerated. The NHK transmission standard was called MUSE. It is a satellite-based system that will begin operations this year. The Japanese had hoped that Europe and the United States would adopt the MUSE system, thereby standardizing HDTV technology worldwide, but the Europeans in particular quickly dashed any such expectations.

Members of the European Community (EC) were alarmed at the prospect of the Japanese dominating this potentially rich industry. At the initiative of Thomson International of France and N.V. Philips of the Netherlands, Europe's two biggest consumer electronics companies, a pan-European effort was organized in 1986, which included eight countries and twenty-nine European corporations and research laboratories. With a budget of $200 million, a third of which comes from participating governments, the joint research effort produced a European transmission standard called HD-MAC, which was also satellite-based but not compatible with the Japanese system. In addition, European companies have made significant progress in product development and process technologies related to HDTV.

In the United States, no transmission standard has been established, but the Federal Communications Commission (FCC) has ruled that whatever standard is developed must be compatible with the existing stock of 140 million television sets owned by the approximately 90 million households in the United States. This ruling was greatly influenced by the U.S. broadcasting industry, which has a huge stake in terrestrial transmission systems. Moreover, given the FCC decision and the different broadcasting and telecommunications environments in the United States versus Japan and Europe, the probability is high that at least three distinct and incompatible HDTV transmission standards will be developed in the industrialized world.

Although a different transmission standard in the United States will slow down foreign companies in their penetration of the American HDTV market, it will hardly present insurmountable obstacles. Many foreign firms, particularly Sony, Thomson, and Philips, already have a significant manufacturing presence in the United States, and changes in hardware to conform to different transmission standards is not that difficult. Moreover, given the large size of the American market and technological advantages these firms already enjoy, Japanese and European companies will be formidable competitors in the U.S. marketplace for HDTV.

Compounding the competitive problem for the United States is that out of eighteen U.S. companies manufacturing TV sets twenty years ago, only one American-owned TV company still exists, Zenith Electronics. The company continues to lose money in consumer electronics; their computer business, however, is profitable. Nevertheless, Zenith faces severe competitive disadvantages relative to other companies that produce and sell televisions, as reflected in Exhibit 4. As a result, the advice from many Wall Street analysts and investors is for Zenith to exit the consumer electronics business. For these reasons and because of the absence of a broadcasting standard for HDTV in the United States, Zenith executives say a prototype for HDTV has not been developed. In addition, Zenith chairman Jerry Pearlman doubts the Department of Commerce's market estimates for HDTV; he says they are "way too optimistic."[10] Thus, for Zenith, the benefits relative to the risks make the company hesitant to incur on its own the major investments required for developing HDTV products and process technologies.

Chairman John Roach of Tandy Corporation has a similar view. Because of the United State's weak base in consumer electronics and the uncertain return on investment, American companies will not develop HDTV products on their own. Instead, significant government support and funding is required. The Boston Consulting Group reported similar reactions among other U.S. companies. Typical comments were:

- "Margins are too low, and investment is too high."
- "It takes too long to pay off."
- "U.S. interest rates are too high to put money in consumer electronics."
- "A commodity business—constant cut-throat competition."
- "Vulnerable to dumping."
- "We've been there and gotten out; we're not going back."[11]

Compounding the problems for the United States in the HDTV industry is that American companies are far behind those in Japan and Europe in providing the quality engineering/manufacturing infrastructure needed to support a HDTV business. These qualities include rapid and innovative product design tightly linked to a flexible, low-cost production system. Component infrastructure for HDTV is weak in the United States, such as VCR heads and some semiconductors. Some key technologies required for HDTV are also American weaknesses, such as high-resolution cathode-ray tubes (CRTs), flat panel displays, and random-access memory processes. Thus, BCG concluded that the United States must implement the following policies if the country is to compete successfully in HDTV:

- Select and administer standards in a way that fosters U.S.-based ATV industry.
- Make lower-cost capital available to the ATV industry for infrastructure development.
- "Pump-priming" investments to boost programming availability and receiver base.[12]

Echoing this view, Stephen Fields, director of strategic planning at National Semiconductor, insisted that the United States cannot compete in HDTV unless the country adopts an industrial policy along the lines of Japan. "They wrote the book," he observes. "We have to be willing to do what they did as a nation and as an industry."[13]

The AEA's proposal for $1.35 billion from the U.S. government is consistent with these viewpoints. The association, which includes not only consumer electronics firms, but also computer, telecommunication, and semiconductor companies like IBM, DEC, AT&T, Hewlett-Packard, Apple, Intel, Motorola, and National Semiconductor, has a broad representation. Thus, AEA contains big, profitable and technologically advanced corporations, which leads some to doubt its need for massive U.S. government help. As *Fortune* magazine observed, "By pooling their efforts, in a single year IBM, AT&T, Digital, Hewlett-Packard, Motorola, Intel, and Apple could match the $500 million Japan has already spent on HDTV research and development by adding just 5.2 percent to their combined 1987 research budgets of nearly $10 billion."[14]

Business Week reflected additional concerns by cautioning that:

> Boosters of industrial policy would do well to look before they leap. . . . The current enthusiasm for winning the United States a piece of the HDTV market may be well placed. But Congress and the Administration should be careful that their search for a better TV screen doesn't turn into another raid on the Treasury.[15]

HDTV TECHNOLOGY AND INDUSTRY LINKAGES

The concerns of the American computer and semiconductor companies in pushing for U.S. government support in HDTV was rooted not so much in a desire to produce and market HDTV products themselves, but was motivated more out of fear that foreign domination of HDTV would further erode their positions in computers and semiconductors. In fact, the growing Japanese presence in consumer electronics had contributed to the declining U.S. position in semiconductors, which is reflected in Exhibits 5 and 6.

The linkage between the VCR and semiconductor industries is symbolic of this relationship. The VCR industry, which uses a high number of random-access memory (RAM) chips, is totally dominated by the Japanese. Of the 13.3 million VCRs sold in the United States in 1987, only 230 thousand were made in the United States, and all of these were assembled from imported parts. The United States's total import bill for VCRs was thus $3 billion in 1987. At the same time, an estimated 12 percent of all semiconductors produced in Japan were used in VCRs.

More generally, over 40 percent of Japanese chip production went into consumer applications, versus the United States's 6 percent. As a result, Japan produced an estimated 7.2 billion semiconductors for consumer products in 1987, while the U.S. produced only 0.9 billion. Since standardized semiconductors like RAMs are such a volume-sensitive industry, with per-unit costs declining rapidly with large production runs, U.S. semiconductor companies have faced increasing competitive disadvantages vis-a-vis the Japanese. As Jeffrey Hart and Laura Tyson observed, "The abandonment of consumer chip production made it difficult for U.S. semiconductor firms to produce certain kinds of generic circuitry at commercial volumes."[16] Such generic circuitry included RAMs, charge-coupled devices (CCD), composite metallic oxide on silicon (CMOS), and liquid crystal displays (LCD). Consequently, U.S. firms were either shut out of or faced competitive disadvantages in the VCR, video camera, laptop computer, and personal TV markets.

The strong Japanese position in both the production and innovation of generic circuitry has given them a headstart in the upcoming battle for the HDTV market, which becomes particularly evident when one looks at the basic technologies involved in HDTV. What makes this product so attractive is that HDTV can produce a picture as sharp as a photograph enlarged from 35mm film, whereas the picture on conventional TVs is only 25 percent as sharp. One factor to explain this difference is that much of the information carried by TV signals on the present National Television Standards Committee (NTSC) system is not seen by the viewer because of the physiological characteristics of human vision; HDTV will have the capability of delaying the delivery of key data, thereby packing more useful information into the same video signal. This is accomplished by two types of semiconductors, namely digital-processing chips to massage the signal and RAM-like memory devices to store the delayed information.

Digital-processing is particularly important in enhancing the quality of HDTV. One must remember that most electronic systems still rely on analog technology, which produces signals in the form of waves, rather than digital technology or the zero-or-one coding of computers. Digital techniques improve picture quality because they can address each tiny spot of light on a screen, called pixels. Initial HDTV broadcasts, however, will be analog signals, which are converted to digital information inside the TV set in order to repair imperfections in the data. Then the TV set will reconvert the signal back to analog waves required for displays on a conventional CRT. Of course, eventually all digital techniques will replace this hybrid approach.

Picture quality on HDTV is also enhanced by an increase in the number of horizontal lines from the top to the bottom of the screen. In the United States, conventional TVs have 525 lines, which become annoyingly visible as the screen gets bigger. For HDTV pictures, however, there will be over 1000 lines, making possible vividly detailed images on very large screens. In addition, HDTV sets will be wider. Instead of conventional tubes which have a squarelike 4 to 3 width-to-height ratio, HDTV will have a more movie-screenlike ratio of 5.33 to 3, which will enhance the visual impact of many widescreen movies and sporting events.

Given the size of HDTV sets, there will be huge incentives for the development of large displays that best utilize space, such as flat panel displays which depend on LCD and semiconductor-based projection technologies. Flat panel displays are particularly attractive because, as HDTV screens get larger, CRTs become prohibitively expensive. In addition, space becomes a problem since CRTs are at least as deep as they are wide. Unfortunately for U.S. competitors, many of these component needs are areas of distinct competitive advantage for the Japanese, largely because of the earlier and large-scale withdrawal of American companies from consumer electronics.

The fear of U.S. computer, telecommunications, and semiconductor firms is that a similar absence of American companies from the HDTV market will give the Japanese tremendous competitive advantages in the development of new, more sophisticated technologies that have significant applications to other industries. For example, the image and digital-processing systems that will be used in HDTV will also be needed for the fast displays of color images on advanced computer workstations. Thus, firms that produce large, high-resolution displays for HDTV will have the capability to produce cheaper and more competitive displays for computer workstations. In addition, the networking of advanced computer workstations and the use of HDTVs as interactive terminals face similar network architecture design problems. Advances or technological breakthroughs in HDTV will contribute to networking solutions in other industries. If future demand for interactive or two-way television is high, then the linkages between HDTV and telecommunications will be even greater.

Perhaps more important than these basic technological linkages, the HDTV and telecommunications industries have a common tie to the upcoming telecommunications infrastructure based on optical fibers. Without a doubt, U.S. homes will be receiving HDTV signals long before the optical fiber system is in place, but since optical fibers deliver such a clean signal, the demand for an optical fiber system will increase once HDTV broadcasting starts. Of course, the reverse is even more true—demand for HDTVs will probably skyrocket once an optical fiber system is operational.

HDTV thus has many linkages to other industries, which can be characterized as upstream, downstream, and manufacturing effects. Upstream effects are mainly related to the large demand consumer electronics has for semiconductor components. Downstream effects are instead related to the impact of consumer electronics on other industries that use semiconductors, like computers and telecommunications equipment. Lastly, manufacturing effects refer to the loss of competitiveness in generic production skills and technologies that flow from the deterioration of the U.S. consumer electronics industry. For these reasons, the stakes in HDTV are viewed by AEA members to be much larger than consumer electronics alone. Hart and Tyson have perhaps summarized these linkages the best.

> TV sets, even HDTV sets, will never be major items driving total semiconductor demand. It is much more likely that HDTV will become an important factor in the development of integrated circuit technology because of new types of circuitry it requires. There is an opportunity to use HDTV-related integrated circuits to promote the U.S. semiconductor industry because of the greater sophistication of circuitry in HDTV as compared with NTSC receivers. HDTV receivers will require more video memory, faster digital signal and video image processors, and more complex analog/digital hybrid circuits than NTSC receivers. Some of these circuit techniques will have uses outside consumer electronics. Video memories and video image processors will be important components in computers and computer workstations. Faster digital signal processors and analog/digital converters will be used in telecommunications equipment. To the extent that HDTV circuit technology has applications outside consumer electronics, there will be major spinoffs from its development.[17]

PUBLIC POLICY QUESTIONS

Numerous issues for public policy have emerged in the HDTV debate. The first and most basic issue is how, when, and what kind of HDTV transmission standard should be developed in the United States. The resolution of this issue is shaped by underlying HDTV technologies. As stated earlier, the HDTV produces a picture of tremendous quality and clarity. To accomplish this feat, the circuitry of the HDTV receiver is not only more complex and sophisticated, but the HDTV broadcast signal and bandwidth also need to be substantially bigger than conventional TV signals. For instance, HDTV's bandwidth will probably range between 9 and 12 megahertz (MH_Z), compared to the present standard of 6 MH_Z. Such differences create significant problems in implementing a new HDTV standard, for existing TV channels simply do not have the room to carry all the information a HDTV signal contains. By implication, HDTV transmissions may require the reassignment of all TV channels. The development of HDTV could also interfere with other communication systems. Namely, if TV broadcasters transmit HDTV signals with a wider MH_Z bandwidth, then other industries using the electromagnetic spectrum could be affected. Specifically, broadcasters have stated a desire to send HDTV on UHF frequencies designated but not yet used for television; however, operators of two-way mobile radios, which are used by big-city police, fire departments, and ambulance services, have also applied for those channels.

The FCC thus faces unavoidable tradeoffs if a transmission standard and broadcasting system for HDTV are chosen today. In short, the spectrum problem is the key constraint on the development of a HDTV transmission standard. Of course, the problem would be more manageable if a HDTV signal of six MH_Z could be developed. Japan's NHK has in fact accomplished this, but the transmitted signal does not deliver a picture of high quality. Zenith has also designed a system that can pack a HDTV picture into a 6 MH_Z signal, but broadcasters would need two 6-MH_Z channels—one to transmit signals to current TVs and the other to new HDTVs. Given these and other problems, some observers have recommended a delay in setting an HDTV transmission standard until U.S. firms develop HDTV technology further. Other analysts, however, stress the need for a transmission standard to be in place in order to guide and accelerate research and development. In addition, it has been argued that "any effort to delay the adoption of HDTV standards until some specific group of U.S.-owned systems firms can catch up to the international state of the art in HDTV technology will only result in the building of a 'hot house' industry that is unlikely to be internationally competitive."[18]

A second public-policy issue in the HDTV debate is raised by both AEA's proposal for $1.35 billion and DARPA's decision to grant $30 million on research for HDTV displays. The issue, simply stated, is whether the government should target financial support to a particular industry and set of companies. Certainly the precedent to target public funds to a high-technology industry under intense competitive pressures from abroad, particularly from the Japanese, has already been established.

Sematech, a nonprofit research consortium, was created in 1987 under antitrust exemptions to develop manufacturing techniques and testing equipment for semiconductors. With a projected annual budget exceeding $200 million, the semiconductor industry asked for and received an annual government subsidy of $100 million, which is dispersed through the Department of Defense. As Bruce Scott observed, "Sematech is unique in recent peacetime history in representing a U.S. commitment to provide special support to a targeted industry."[19]

Sematech was initially proposed by the Semiconductor Industry Association (SIA), which includes many of the same companies that are members of AEA, such as IBM, Hewlett-Packard, Digital, Motorola, Intel, and AT&T. The successful creation of Sematech with substantial government support was due to many factors. As David Yoffie argued:

The semiconductor industry's experiences illuminate four general principles for making things happen in Washington:

1. *Companies need a united front. . . .*
2. *Government allies are essential.* Friends inside the government are as important as corporate allies. An industry should identify and cultivate executive branch agencies and members of Congress with a stake in its agenda. This means crafting positions that will appeal to targeted officials and factoring their interests and agendas into the industry's own political calculations. An industry should also identify potential adversaries in government and take steps to minimize their impact.
3. *CEOs have a special role to play. . . .*
4. *Political action by company executives is more effective than trade association efforts.*[20]

With AEA's proposal, however, it was not clear if the impact of potential adversaries could be easily minimized since they had direct access to the president as leading members of his White House staff. Richard Darman in particular was a powerful opponent, given his position as director of the Office of Management and Budget. Final spending proposals went to Congress from his office. Given his opposition, in principle, to targeted industrial policies, AEA's proposal had to overcome a powerful and determined obstacle.

A related issue for public policy is the definition of qualified recipients of government funding, if and when it is approved. In particular, should such funding be open or closed to subsidiaries of foreign companies with manufacturing and research operations in the United States? As the *Wall Street Journal* reported in regard to DARPA's $30 million research grant:

> Although the Pentagon agency in charge of the research, known as DARPA, hasn't yet excluded non-American companies, it has come under strong pressure to do so from U.S. industry and government leaders, including Commerce Secretary Robert Mosbacher. The U.S. units of two European companies—N. V. Philips of the Netherlands and France's Thomson S. A.—have submitted research proposals to the agency. The only other non-U.S. application has come from Sony Corp. of Japan.[21]

Of course, the argument for an exclusionary policy is that U.S. government support is meant to make American companies more competitive, not foreign firms. A variant of the exclusionary policy is to target the exclusion. In fact, some West German officials have proposed a joint U.S.-European effort to fight the Japanese in HDTV.

Arguments against any exclusion of foreign firms are varied, starting with the possibility of retaliation, particularly from the European Community (EC), which has allowed American subsidiaries to participate in a host of Eureka projects. Such projects are collaborative research efforts partially funded by EC governments. In addition, U.S. companies could benefit from the knowledge and technology of foreign companies that are further along the learning curve in HDTV. Moreover, as Hart and Tyson argued, "Because foreign firms already possess such an important stake in U.S. research-and-development and manufacturing of consumer electronics, they should be included in efforts to promote the HDTV industry."[22] In effect, this position asks the following question: If research-and-development expenditures and manufacturing of HDTV equipment take place within the United States, does it really matter who conducts the research and produces the product as long as the U.S. consumer benefits, American jobs are created, and the country's balance of trade is positively affected?

These issues loomed large in the HDTV debate, which could spill over into other industries and affect existing research consortiums. Presumably, even the Sematech decision could be revisited. Thus the stakes seemed immense. Certainly AEA, like SIA, argued that concerted, collaborative efforts in partnership with the U.S. government were needed to address the competitive problems of their respective industries.

Darman, Boskin, and others, however, rejected these arguments and stressed the need for corporations to change their attitudes, values, and spending habits in order to become more competitive. Darman, in particular, was highly critical of American managers, with his most vocal and stinging criticism coming in a speech in late 1986; he attacked "corpocracy," which was defined as: "An inefficient, unimaginative, risk-averse corporate management that has acquired the worst characteristics of the government bureaucracy."[23] Although his attacks on American managers were less vocal and stinging in 1989, Darman had not changed his mind. As *Business Week* reported:

> Darman has muted his rhetoric a bit. But his fundamental criticism is just as harsh. "We have a societywide value problem," he says. "The energy of our best people is going into financial papershuffling." That tendency, Darman complains, results in a focus on short-term profits at the expense of such long-term concerns as improved quality and manufacturing prowess. . . . Darman's list of suggested solutions includes tax breaks for [all] research and development and new incentives to encourage business to use equity financing rather than debt. . . . Don't look for gobs of money from Uncle Sam, though: Darman believes that subsidies and the like "can only help marginally." The key, he argues, is a fundamental shift in national thinking. "We've got to change the system so that society attends more to the future," Darman insists. "It's more a moral matter than one of financial incentives."[24]

A more free-market approach to HDTV would be to encourage U.S. electronic, computer, telecommunications, and semiconductor companies to form a research consortium, as is allowed under the 1984 National Cooperative Research Act. Under this law, 70 research-and-development consortiums have been established in areas as diverse as steelmaking, semiconductors, and supercomputers. Perhaps the most successful example of these consortiums is the Microelectronics and Computer Technology Corporation, which was created to counter Japan's Fifth Generation intelligent-computer effort; without government funding, member companies in the consortium are now individually marketing products based on technology developed there.

A key difference between these consortiums and that proposed by AEA is that the joint effort in HDTV would be a research *and* marketing consortium. In other words, the consortium would produce and market a common product, which required a special antitrust exemption. In addition, the U.S. government would finance nearly half of the budget. Such a proposal, however, had little support in the Bush administration, although the precedent for substantial government funding of a particular consortium had already been established with Sematech. Had AEA overplayed its hand or was their proposal a legitimate and understandable request given both conditions in the electronics industry and prospects for HDTV?

NOTES

1. *The Wall Street Journal,* May 10, 1989.
2. *Ibid.*
3. *The Washington Post,* May 7, 1989.
4. *Ibid.*
5. *Ibid.*
6. *Ibid.*
7. *Business Week,* January 30, 1989.
8. *Ibid.*
9. Todd L. Hixon, vice president, Boston Consulting Group, presentation at the Ninth Annual Strategic Management Society Conference, October 13, 1989.
10. *Forbes,* May 30, 1988.
11. Hixon, *op. cit.*
12. *Ibid.*
13. *Fortune,* October 24, 1988.
14. *Ibid.*
15. *Business Week,* May 29, 1989.
16. Jeffrey A. Hart and Laura Tyson, "Responding to the Challenge of HDTV," *California Management Review,* Summer 1989.
17. *Ibid.*
18. *Ibid.*
19. Bruce R. Scott, "Competitiveness: Self-Help for a Worsening Problem," *Harvard Business Review,* July–August 1989.
20. David B. Yoffie, "How an Industry Builds Political Advantage," *Harvard Business Review,* May–June 1988.
21. *The Wall Street Journal,* May 31, 1989.
22. Hart and Tyson, *op. cit.*
23. *Business Week,* March 13, 1989.
24. *Ibid.*

Exhibit 1 HDTV Receiver Prices Remain High

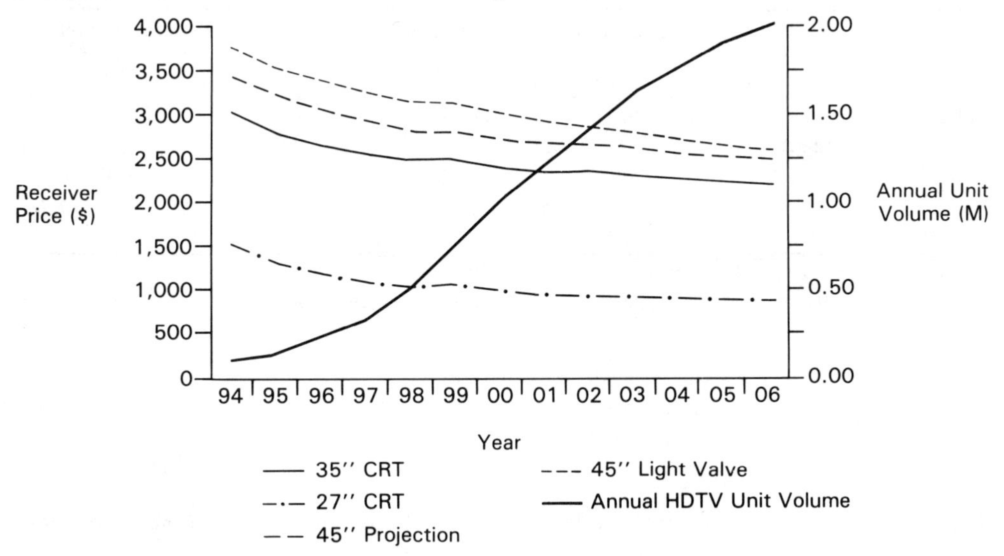

Source: Field Interviews; BCG Analysis

Exhibit 2 Color TV Penetration, Programming and Real Prices

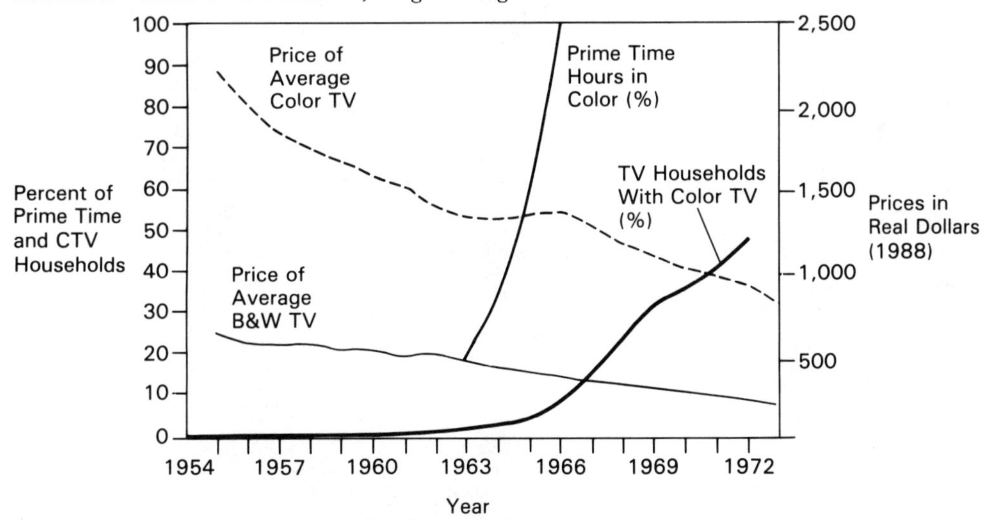

Sources: NBC Research; CBS Research; BCG Analysis

Exhibit 3 Market Development Scenario

		Annual Market in mid-90s		Annual Market ~2000	
		Units (K)	($M)	Units (K)	($M)
ATV	-projection	75K	$500M	500K	$2,000M
	-direct view	75K		500K	
AVCR		115K	$125M	850K	$800M
Broadcast Equipment			$1000M–$3000M		$500M–$1500M

*Total market of $12–15 billion between 1993 and ~2005 for first time conversions

Source: BCG rough estimates based on interviews and a range of industry statistical sources; dollars are current dollars

Exhibit 4 Fixed Assets Committed and Returns Earned, Major Consumer Electronics Companies, 1988

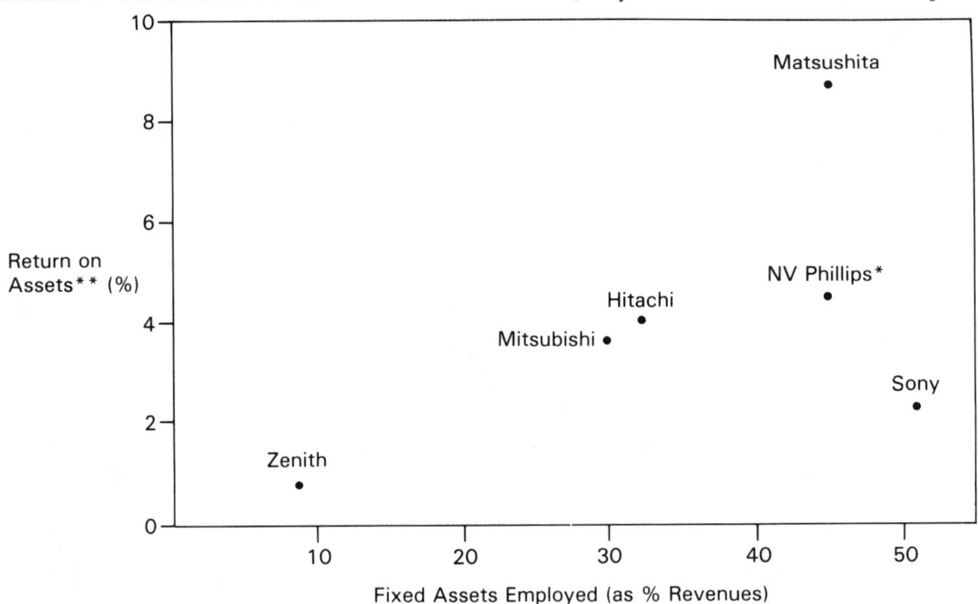

*1987

**Operating profit as percent of assets

Sources: Annual Reports; Goldman Sachs Investment Research

Exhibit 5 Percent Share of World DRAM Shipments in Units

	U.S.	Japan	Europe
1980	57	41	2
1982	53	43	4
1984	38	56	6
1986	18	75	3
1987	22	65	3

Source: Dataquest Inc., February 1988.

Exhibit 6 Semiconductor Consumption in Millions of U.S. Dollars

	North America	Japan	Europe
1980	6,053	3,383	3,686
1982	6,970	4,082	3,167
1984	13,139	8,845	4,805
1986	10,201	12,356	5,532
1987*	11,743	14,239	6,780

*Estimated

Source: Dataquest Inc., August 1987.

9

MANAGING COUNTRY RISK

International banks have followed a pattern of experience and adaptation to the external environment that is quite similar to multinational, industrial firms. Of course, bankers tend to discuss external environmental issues in terms of country risk. For them, political risk is a subset of country risk. Whereas political risk is tied directly to a political event, country risk is the probability that financial returns will be lower than expected because of the inherent risks in conducting business in the economic, social, and political environment of a foreign country. However, since sociopolitical and economic phenomena are highly interrelated and often inseparable, this book views these two terms as conceptually interchangeable.

Like nonfinancial companies, banks began to formalize their approach to country risk after the first oil shock. What had been a fairly stable and certain external environment was now a very volatile and unpredictable one. As William Butcher, chief executive officer for Chase Manhattan, observed, "The world prior to 1973 was somewhat simpler economically and politically. Since that time the risks have escalated."[1] Another banker reported, "We always did country evaluations on a more or less informal basis, but after the first oil shock, it became clear we had to evaluate things more carefully."[2]

The first major U.S. bank to formalize an approach to country risk was Citibank in 1974. By 1976, an Export-Import Bank study authored by Jerome Blask revealed that thirty-two of thirty-seven major U.S. banks interviewed had a systematic approach to country risk. Therefore, the spread of formal approaches to country risk was quite rapid after 1973.

The Iranian revolution had a major impact on how country risks were assessed. In particular, banks reacted to the Iran shock by changing the predominant method of analyzing country risk. Sociopolitical factors were now considered as perhaps equally important to macroeconomic considerations. As a result, assessing country risk became increasingly difficult and complex.

The Iranian revolution also stimulated more resources going to the country risk function in major U.S. banks. International bankers had the same reaction after the explosion of the debt crisis in 1982. After each major crisis, the perceived need among international bankers for an improved approach to country risk has grown stronger. As Irving S. Friedman, the Citibank manager who established the first formal approach to country risk, recently commented, "More and more bankers believe that a practical, efficient country risk system is essential."[3]

The need for better methods and more resources going to country risk, moreover, transcends different sizes of international banks and types of loans. For example, even trade financing can be adversely affected by country risk. In fact, Gerald J. Alifano, a former executive vice president at Pittsburgh National, noted that one of the "lessons for the future" that grew out of the debt crisis of the 1980s was that "short-term lending, including deposit placements, have become an integral part of country debt renegotiation."[4] Daniel R. Denison, a vice president at First Interstate Bank of California, reinforced these comments; he observed, "When a country approaches default, its currency becomes nonconvertible. Short-term creditors (even overnight creditors) can suffer along with long-term creditors."[5]

Thus all kinds of banks and financial transactions can be affected by country risk. More importance is being placed on the function as a result. As Alifano recommended, "If the cost of maintaining an on-the-spot presence in a country, or at least, a full-time political-economist, cannot be justified, you're better off staying out."[6]

Given both the recent experiences with country risk during the debt crisis and the continued presence of attractive international lending opportunities, the decision by most banks to upgrade their capabilities to assess country risk seems appropriate. Even if sovereign lending is avoided, banks must still serve their corporate clients abroad, and the extent and method in which this strategic, competitive imperative is followed varies by one's assessment of country risk. In addition, the management of old loans to debt-crisis countries is increasingly affected by country risk. Such assessments impact various decisions, such as whether to swap the debt of one country for another country, to sell debt in the secondary market, to engage in debt-for-equity swaps, or to choose from various options that are presented to banks in recent restructuring packages, such as that for Mexico in 1989.[7] Thus, improving a bank's capabilities to assess country risk is necessary in many respects.

NOTES

1. "Meet the New Breed of Bankers: The Political Risk Expert," *Euromoney*, (July 1980), p. 9.
2. *Ibid.*, p. 12.
3. Irving S. Friedman, *The World Debt Dilemma: Managing Country Risk* (Philadelphia: Council for International Banking Studies, 1983), p. 281.

4. Gerald J. Alifano, "A Reassessment of International Banking: A Regional Bank Point of View," *The Journal of Commercial Bank Lending* (January 1984), p. 12.
5. Daniel R. Denison, "A Pragmatic Model for Country Risk Analysis," *The Journal of Commercial Bank Lending* (March 1984), p. 30.
6. Alifano, "Reassessment of International Banking," p. 13.
7. *Wall Street Journal,* July 25, 1989, and *Wall Street Journal,* December 6, 1989.

Rabat Portland Cement Company Evaluating International Loans

In December 1976, Robert X. Shiflett of the First National Bank of Richmond, Virginia, was evaluating a proposed $8.36 million international loan (Exhibit 1) being syndicated and managed by the Project Finance and Syndication Group of the Manhattan National Bank, (MNB). The borrower was a new Moroccan company, the Rabat Portland Cement Company (RPC), chartered to produce cement and other building materials. RPC had ordered its cement processing equipment from an American company and sought American financing for it. The equipment would not be built or shipped until financing was in place. In addition to background information on Morocco's economy and cement industry supplied by MNB (summarized in the text below), Mr. Shiflett gathered information on Moroccan politics and social conditions from published sources. On the basis of this information, he wanted (1) to know how to analyze the risks associated with the loan and if the loan proposal adequately covered these risks, (2) to know what additional information he might need, and (3) to decide whether First National should join the syndication.

MANHATTAN NATIONAL BANK

MNB had total assets of $20.0 billion, deposits of $16.3 billion, and total loans of $11.4 billion as of December 31, 1975. Its international loans at the end of 1975 were $3.8 billion, comprising 33.1 percent of total loans. International assets had increased from $2.7 billion (12/31/71) to $7.4 billion (12/31/75), and annual international income (before securities, gains, and losses) had grown from $10.3 million to $37.4 million between 1971 and 1975. For 1975, international assets were 36.9 percent of total assets, and international income was 45.1 percent of total income before securities, gains, and losses.

MNB's international business was handled by domestic headquarters offices and by foreign branches and subsidiaries. Foreign branches and subsidiaries carried $2.7 billion in loans at the end of 1975, equal to 71.1 percent of total international loans. The international division had nine overseas branches, fifteen representative offices, correspondent banks in 174 countries, and thirty subsidiaries and affiliates. Its financial services included short- and medium-term lending,

This case was prepared by James P. Marshall, under the supervision of Leslie E. Grayson, Professor of International Business Economics, The Colgate Darden Graduate School of Business Administration of the University of Virginia. Case is disguised, with cooperation of the bank, which wishes to remain anonymous.

Table 1 ***Manhattan National Bank* Summary Financial Data (December 31, 1975)**

Total Assets and Resources	$20.0		billion	100 %
Domestic		12.6	billion	63.1%
International		7.4	billion	36.9%
Total Loans	$11.4		billion	100 %
Domestic		7.6	billion	66.9%
International		3.8	billion	33.1%
Total International Loans	$ 3.8		billion	100 %
Domestic Headquarters		1.1	billion	28.9%
Foreign Branches and Subsidiaries		2.7	billion	71.1%
Net (After Tax) Income Before Securities gains and losses	$82.9		million	100 %
Domestic		45.5	million	54.9%
International		37.4	million	45.1%

project financing and syndication, letters of credit, acceptances, and foreign exchange transactions.

FIRST NATIONAL BANK OF RICHMOND, VIRGINIA

First National was a regional bank, concentrating its activities in Virginia and other Southeastern states. It divided its services into the areas of consumer banking, corporate banking, and mortgage banking. Its total assets at the end of 1975 were $1.6 billion, of which $0.9 billion were loans. Of these loans, $34.7 million or 3.9 percent were classified as international loans. In 1970, in contrast, only $2.4 million of $492 million in total loans were international.

First National's international banking activities were basically an extension of its domestic activities. It primarily served the international financial needs of its domestic customers. It had representative offices in London and Tokyo and correspondent banks in other countries.

Table 2 ***First National Bank* Summary Financial Data December 31, 1975**

	($ millions)
Total Assets	1,649
Total Earning Assets	1,320
Total Loans	894
Foreign Loans	35

MOROCCO'S POLITICAL AND SOCIAL ENVIRONMENT

From 1912 to 1956 France ruled Morocco as a protectorate. Moroccan nationalist agitation continued throughout the period of occupation, culminating between 1953 and 1956 with militant opposition to French rule and the ruling sultan Sidi Mohammed ben Youssef. In 1956, Morocco declared its independence and Ben Youssef became King Mohammed V in 1957. Internal political dissension continued with leftist groups demanding constitutional government, economic reform, and more militant anticolonialist policy. The king died in 1961 and was succeeded by his son, Hassan II, who assumed personal rule and who dismissed parliament in 1962. The king suppressed the opposition parties, which had been poorly organized and coordinated. Party members faced an indifferent and disillusioned populace and were under the threat of arrest and imprisonment.

As of 1975, King Hassan seemed firmly in control of Morocco, but undercurrents of dissatisfaction had the potential for major change. Political unrest was pointedly expressed in unsuccessful military coups in 1971 and 1972. These attempts lacked popular support, and military rule was said to be generally feared. There had been several incidents of militant popular rebellion, the most notable of which took place in November 1970, when peasants gave unprecedented though unsuccessful armed resistance to the sale of a state-owned farm to absentee landlords. Corruption and the spoils system continued. Both the king and government officials were said to be accumulating personal wealth through their positions. The military was neutralized by implicit threats and explicit benefits and would not support opposition.

Significant economic inequalities remained. Average income was less than $190 a year, and over 14 million people earned less than $90 a year. GNP growth was offset by population growth. Unemployment was 20 percent to 30 percent in cities and 40 percent in the country. The population was young: 57 percent was younger than 20 years old (1972) and 72 percent was younger than 30. The educated youth were politicized and alienated from the government. Youth generally were unhappy with the job outlook, repression, educational opportunities, and governmental corruption. Foreign investment in Morocco fell to nothing from mid-1971 to September 1973. Investment laws had to be changed to guarantee foreign investments. Nationalization laws were weak, and major industries were exempt.

The international situation was not calm either. Spain gave up control of the Spanish Sahara, in February 1976, splitting the area between Morocco and Mauritania. However, guerrilla forces, called the Polisario, backed by Algeria, contested the division, claimed that the inhabitants had a right to self-government, and set up a Sahara Arab Democratic Republic. Morocco was able to maintain military control of its share of the area, but Mauritania, with its limited resources and manpower, was not. Hence, sporadic fighting continued, and the desert remained a source of controversy between Algeria and Morocco, although the likelihood of open war had diminished by the end of 1976. United States interests in this North African area included Algerian petroleum and natural gas supplies as well as military and business interests in Morocco. It thus tried to maintain peace between the two countries.

MNB'S STUDY OF THE LOAN

RPC was founded in October 1975, following the Moroccan government's decision to build a cement plant near Rabat, the capital, as part of its economic development plans. After a site with limestone deposits sufficient for one hundred years of production was found, the New Water Pipe Company (NWP) took over the project and formed RPC for the purposes of "extraction, fabrication, sales, import, and export of all materials of construction." NWP (17 percent government-owned) made prestressed concrete irrigation pipe and would be an RPC customer. Taking competitive bids, RPC selected American Mineral Processing, Incorporated (AMPI), a subsidiary of a United States *Fortune* 500 firm, to supply the cement-processing equipment.

Nine closely related parties owned RPC (see Table 3). The National Irrigation Company (NIC), a subsidiary of NWP, was a manufacturer of irrigation equipment. The Government Development Corporation (GDC) was a government holding company that provided debt and equity capital to government-sponsored projects. Messrs. Yamini and Nazer owned all of Oasis Construction Company and most of Ash Shabb Leasing Company, a leasing and real-estate development company. Mr. Yamini, an engineer and former officer of NWP, owned or directed a number of real-estate, construction, and other companies, including the country's newest cement plant which came on-line in 1976; he was also once a highly placed government official. Mr. Nazer was a former cabinet member and was related by marriage to the king. Mr. Qusaibi was an industrialist and contractor. Mr. Khalil was the director general of NWP.

Equity was to be increased from $2.2 million to $11.6 million before the loan was made. Sources for the new equity would include, in addition to Messrs. Yamini and Nazer, the National Association for Investments (a private investment company), the National Bank for Economic Development (NBED), the International Finance Corporation (IFC) (a subsidiary of the World Bank), a Saudi Arabian road-building contractor, and a Belgian cement company.

Table 3 Ownership of RPC

	Share	
Owner	%	$ (000)
1. National Water Pipe Company (NWP)	10	220
2. Government Development Corporation (GDC)	15	330
3. National Irrigation Company (NIC)	5	110
4. Oasis Construction Company (OCC)	5	110
5. Ash Shabb Leasing Company (ASL)	15	330
6. Mr. Hisham Yamini	15	330
7. Mr. Ghazial Nazer	15	330
8. Mr. Zaki Qusaibi	15	330
9. Mr. Mohamed Khalil	5	110
	100	2,220

PURPOSE, AMOUNT, AND TIMING OF LOAN

The selection of an American contractor was a break with precedent; such contracts had in the past been made with French companies. RPC provided the bank an itemized list of the equipment to be purchased.

RPC wanted to borrow $26.2 million from the United States banks. Of this amount, $2.5 million was for insurance and the rest for the equipment itself. Since an American company was exporting the equipment, RPC qualified for financing by the Export-Import Bank of the United States (Ex-Im). Ex-Im's participation was not necessary for international lending. However, as a government agency it could have had access to more detailed confidential information on foreign countries than private banks; it was able to lend at subsidized rates and to provide insurance on the loan package. Hence, it was sometimes asked to participate in loans—as it was in this case—if a private bank wanted Ex-Im's tacit evaluation of a country's risk. Thus, Ex-Im and the syndicate would each lend $11,050,000, and MNB by itself would lend $3,900,000. As a condition of lending, the Export-Import Bank required a cash down payment of 15 percent of the total loan, so RPC planned to borrow in two parts, one for MNB for the down payment and one for the balance, of which the Export-Import Bank would lend half.

FINANCIAL PERFORMANCE AND PROJECTIONS

RPC's final capital structure would consist of equity, local debt, and foreign debt. Equity, originally conceived at $15.6 million, was lowered to $11.6 million after it was decided to finance the down payment with foreign debt. Locally raised debt would be $16.4 million, and foreign debt would be $26.2 million, for a total of $54.2 million. Sources and uses are shown in Exhibit 2.

Projections based on expected volumes and costs were the data available on RPC's future financial performance. MNB assembled these in November 1976, using the assumptions described in Exhibit 3. Projected cash flows were shown in Exhibit 4 and estimated import savings (to the Moroccan economy) in Exhibit 4A.

BUSINESS AND ECONOMIC CONDITIONS

Moroccan Cement Industry

A report by the Manhattan National Bank indicated that RPC could market its full capacity from the beginning and that almost immediately a doubling of capacity might be justified. A nationwide shortage of capacity was predicted because of the government's desire to meet demand with domestic production.

Between 1970 and 1975 Morocco had cement production capacity shortages annually. Imports ranged from 12,000 metric tons to 224,000 metric tons per year in that period, as Exhibit 5 shows. In 1975 Morocco had five plants with

Table 4 Projected Cement Production, 1976–1985 (000 Metric Tons)

	1976	1980	1985
Existing Plants	2,160	2,790	3,220
New Plants	—	1,420	2,610
Total Production	2,160	4,210	5,830

Source: Private communication from the World Bank

Projected Demand 1976–1985

	1976	1980	1985
	2,900	5,071	10,195

Source: Government Study provided to MNB

capacity of 2,057,000 metric tons. Two plants already under construction would bring capacity to 2,761,000 metric tons. Two existing plants were to be expanded and two new plants built before 1980, and another six additional plants before 1985 were planned. Growth in production and demand were projected through 1985 in Table 4.

REPORTS ON THE ECONOMY

Mr. Shiflett had available to him an assortment of analyses of the Moroccan economy. Excerpts from the most important of these are reproduced in this section.

1. Manhattan National Bank

Morocco's land area is 172,415 square miles—about 14,000 more than California. Its population, estimated at 17.4 million (1975), was growing at 2.7 percent per year. The economy was basically agricultural. However, King Hassan was trying to build an industrial base, an economic infrastructure, and centralized development of mineral resources.

Economic growth was stimulated by direct public investment and governmentally encouraged private investment. Since 1970 there had been three development plans; a fourth would run from 1978 to 1982. The 1972–1977 plan stressed public investment and had four major objectives:

1. Annual growth in real terms of 7.5 percent in Gross Domestic product (GDP),
2. Industrial growth rate of 11 percent per year,
3. Yearly rates of growth in exports of 10 percent and in imports of 8 percent per year, and
4. Agricultural rates of growth of 3.6 percent per year.

Gross investment between 1971 and 1975 averaged 18.9 percent of GDP, and 1975 was 29.6 percent of GDP. Of this amount, 42 percent was from public and

58 percent from private sources (Exhibit 6). Since 1972, poor harvests, shortages of raw materials, and rising oil prices had caused high inflation (see Table 5 below).

MNB's study discussed three major sectors of the economy: agriculture, manufacturing, and mining, fuel and power. In 1975, agriculture employed 65 percent of the labor force, provided 70 percent to 80 percent of domestic food requirements, and contributed 27 percent to 57 percent of exports (depending on the weather). Its share of GDP was about 25 percent.

Manufacturing accounted for 15 percent of GDP. It had grown at 5.8 percent per year between 1971 and 1975. Food processing and textiles were important light industries. The government planned to develop the chemical industry, particularly phosphate byproducts.

The mining industry produced phosphate, iron, cobalt, coal, manganese, lead, zinc, copper, and petroleum. The government owned all phosphate production. Phosphates were the major export, accounting for 55 percent of the total dollar value of exports in 1975. Morocco was the world's third largest producer of phosphate rock, exceeded only by the United States and the U.S.S.R., and was the largest exporter. Petroleum production did not equal needs, and 75 percent of the country's energy was imported. Electric power was generated from both hydroelectric and fuel-burning plants.

The dollar had been losing value against Morocco dirham over the last five years. In 1971 the dirham was worth $0.20; its current worth was almost $0.24 (see Table 6 below).

Morocco had a large foreign trade sector. In the period 1971 to 1975, exports equaled 21.4 percent of GDP, and imports 28.3 percent. Exports increased 98.6 percent in 1973 when the price of phosphates rose sharply. The foreign exchange thus earned was used to finance imports, mostly the higher price of oil, which rose 77 percent. However, in 1975 the worldwide recession and a European drought led to declining demand for phosphates, and the value of exports declined 16.2 percent from 1974. The value of imports continued to rise as demand grew for energy, imported food, and capital goods. Therefore, the trade deficit grew. The 1976 outlook for food exports looked good, however, because Europe was again experiencing drought, while Morocco's own harvest looked favorable. Exhibit 7 gives the Moroccan balance of payments.

MNB's report made the following observations:

> The government has indirect obligations primarily in the form of guarantees for the semipublic financial institutions such as the NBED, the GDC, and the National

Table 5 Price Indexes

Year	WPI	CPI
1970	100.0	100.0
1971	104.2	104.1
1972	106.3	108.0
1973	124.8	112.5
1974	153.7	132.4
1975	159.6	142.9

Source: MNB Bank Study

Table 6 Exchange Rate

Year	Dollars/Dirham
1971	0.2001
1972	0.2143
1973	0.2331
1974	0.2407
1975	0.2390

Source: MNB Study

Farmers' Credit Bank (NFCB). The total foreign obligation of these obligations [sic] amount to $291 million.

In May 1976, the country was able to successfully place a $300 million five-year loan syndicated by a major bank group. The country's credit worthiness is further evidenced by loans and assistance from other sources, such as Saudi Arabia, Kuwait, the United Arab Emirates, Qatar, and the Arab Fund for Economic Development. Also, the World Bank and a direct government-to-government loan from the United States, France, and West Germany [sic]. Since independence on March 2, 1956, all foreign borrowings and guarantees have been paid in full by the government.

2. U.S. Department of State

A study by the U.S. Department of State stressed that Morocco was undertaking long-term, heavy industrial investment that provided sales opportunities for U.S. companies:

> Morocco's continuing ambitious investment plans, combined with rapidly expanding contracting authorization for future projects, offer U.S. firms attractive opportunities for increased sales of capital goods and related services. Planned projects range from a steel mill to roads, rail lines, chemical plants, an oil refinery, dams, and irrigated lands plus a spectrum of other industrial and agricultural undertakings. During the past year the Embassy has forwarded 41 government tenders to the Department of Commerce. Private trade opportunities were submitted for a wide variety of projects on behalf of more than 150 firms.

The State Department noted that this business also meant opportunities for American banks "to manage or participate in medium-term project and government loans."

The Department of State thought that the rate of growth in foreign borrowing could not continue, although Moroccan officials considered these problems transitory and it was their judgment that the country could carry more foreign debt than it did. The Department of State felt, however, that the growth of the economy must be slowed in the near future to bring finances under control.

3. The World Bank

John Browning, an economist for the World Bank who did an economic study of the country in 1975, shared the Department of State's view. He had predicted the decline in phosphate prices and the subsequent constraints on the national budget. In an interview with a MNB officer, he concluded that, "Given the unfavorable turn in the trade balance, and the probable continuation of depressed phosphate prices, the current high rate of investment is untenable." He expected a financial crisis by the end of 1977 if public sector investments were not reduced. For instance, the International Monetary Fund (IMF) had already required, as a condition of lending to the Moroccan government, that it submit to a three-year IMF stabilization plan. Browning thought that government officials would prefer a lower rate of growth to these constraints. He also thought that more control of consumer demand was needed. Morocco seemed to be implementing more control by at least two measures, one, a Central Bank ceiling on borrowing, and the other, consultation with the IMF on the 1978–1982 Economic Plan.

Browning did see cause for optimism, however. Agriculture was expected to recover in the coming year. Expatriate workers continued to repatriate their earnings, and these were expected to increase 2 percent to 3 percent. Foreign debt services as a percentage of exports was expected to remain stable at about 10 "beyond 1982, the relative price of phosphates will rise, and Morocco will have a virtual monopoly on the market." Exhibits 8, 9, 10, and 11 give further data on Morocco's economy and foreign sector.

Toward the end of 1976, however, the economy presented a mixed picture. Two IMF loans indicated Morocco was suffering from lower export prices and higher fuel costs. These loans, announced in April 1976, for $20.8 million and $113 million, were to help pay for oil imports and to offset declining exports. The European Economic Community, of which Morocco was an associate member, was also preparing to extend aid. Thus, Morocco was apparently having trouble generating the foreign exchange necessary for imports.

Exhibit 1 Loan Proposal from Manhattan National Bank

PROPOSAL FOR A 4 1/2 YEAR TERM LOAN TO RPC

1. *Amount:* U.S. Dollars 22,100,000 as follows:

Export-Import Bank Direct Loan	$ 11,050,000
Commercial Banks — Eurodollar Loan	
Agent Bank	2,690,000
Syndicate members	8,360,000
Total	$ 22,100,000

2. *Purpose:* In conjunction with the Export-Import Bank of the United States (Ex-Im Bank), to assist in the financing of cement plant equipment export by American Mineral Processing Incorporated to the borrower and the erection of a 625,000 metric ton cement plant. The proposed financing of the U.S. sourced equipment is as follows:

(000's)	
Export-Import Bank — Direct Loan	$ 11,050 (42.5%)
Eurodollar Loan —Commercial Banks	11,050 (42.5%)
Downpayment Loan — Agent Bank	3,900 (15.0%)
Total for U.S. Equipment and Services	$ 26,000

3. *Guarantor:* Central Bank of Guarantee, an agency of the Government of Morocco, pledging the full faith and credit of that government.

4. *Term:* Approximately 4 1/2 years from the date of the signing of the loan agreement.

5. *Availability Period:* From the date of satisfaction of Conditions Precedent until July 31, 1978.

6. *Repayment:* Commercial Banks: In seven (7) equal, consecutive, semi-annual installments beginning December 31, 1978. Final maturity no later than December 31, 1981.

   Export-Import Bank: In seven (7) equal, consecutive, semi-annual installments beginning June 30, 1982, with a final maturity of June 30, 1985.

7. *Interest:* Commercial Banks: 1.5% per annum over the 3 or 6 month London Interbank Offered Rate (LIBOR), 360-day basis, payable on the last day of each interest period. LIBOR + 2.5% for penalty interest.

   Export-Import Bank: 8 3/4% fixed rate.

8. *Interest Period:* Commercial Banks: Six (6) month periods ending June 30 and December 31. Upon five business days notice, the borrower may choose either two 3-month periods or one 6-month period.

9. *Commitment Fee:* 1/2 of 1% p.a. calculated on the daily undrawn portion computed from February 7, 1977 and paid quarterly beginning September 30, 1977.

10. *Management Fee:* Commercial Banks: 5/8% of the total amount of the loan broken down as follows:

    For a participation of:

Dlrs. 1MM	.125% flat
Dlrs. 2MM	.250% flat
Dlrs. 3MM	.375% flat

11. *Agency Fees:* $20,000 for ongoing costs of administration payable to the Agent.

12. *Disbursement Procedure:* The Agent will make payments of six (6) days drafts drawn under Letters of Credit issued and confirmed by the Agent in favor of U.S. suppliers.

Exhibit 1 (*Continued*)

PROPOSAL FOR A 4 1/2 YEAR TERM LOAN TO RPC

13. *Letters of Credit Fees*:	1/10 of 1% negotiation fee on letters of credits issued by Agent.
14. *Alternate Interest Rate*:	If it is not possible to fairly ascertain the rates to prime banks in the London Interbank Market for offering U.S. Dlrs., the Borrower and the Agent shall negotiate to find an alternate Interest Rate. If none is determined within 30 days, the Rate shall be 1.5% over the Agent bank's cost of funds.
15. *Prepayments*:	Details in the original loan proposal. Omitted from the case.
16. *Taxes*:	Ditto.
17. *Conditions of Lending*:	Ditto.
18. *Representations and Warranties*:	Ditto.
19. *Affirmative Covenants*:	Ditto.
20. *Negative Covenants*:	Ditto.
21. *Guarantee*:	Ditto.
22. *Events of Default*:	Ditto.
23. *Miscellaneous*:	Ditto.

Source: Manhattan National Bank.

Exhibit 2 Project Cost and Investment ($000)

	Foreign Debt	Local Debt	Equity
Engineering Studies			$ 1,711
Organization Expense			222
Land			
Site Preparation			667[1]
Civil Construction		$11,111	
Mechanical Equipment	$19,722 4,000[2]		
Electrical Equipment		2,222	
Erection		3,111	
Ocean Freight and Insurance	2,500		
Inland Freight			280
Contingency			2,222
Working Capital and Interest During Construction			6,444
Total	$26,222	$16,444	$11,556
TOTAL PROJECT COST			$54,222
Debt/Equity Ratio			79:21

[1]Government grant, valued at $2.2 million. (400 hectares, at D 25,000/II. = D 10 million, at D 4.5:$1, – $2.2 million).

[2]Temara plans to borrow about $4 million "cash payment" abroad, which is assumed to reduce equity investment from $15.6 million to $11.6 million, and increase debt/equity ratio from 71:29 to 79:21.

Source: Revised investment projection, 10-20-76, adjusted to reflect information received 11-8-76 from Manhattan National Bank.

Exhibit 3 Financial Projections ($000)

	1978	1980	1986
Production (thousand tons)	231	625	625
Sales Volume[1]	$7,000	19,163	19,163
Cost of Production	3,832	8,256	10,475
Gross Profit	3,358	10,907	8,688
Interest expense[2]	3,374	2,640	540
Depreciation	5,849	5,872	4,360
Profit before taxes	(5,965)	2,394	3,787
Taxes	—	—	947
Net profit	(5,965)	2,394	2,840
Net profit as % of sales	(84.1%)	12.5%	14.8%
Net profit/original equity	(51.6%)	20.7%	24.6%
Production cost per ton	16.57	13.21	16.76

[1]At cement prices of $30.66/ton (constant).

[2]Assumes (A) larger foreign loan of $22.1 million, 7 years at 8-3/4%; (B) Development Bank Loan of $14.2 million, 12 years at 8%; (C) local bank loan of $2.3 million, 5 years at 8%; and (D) foreign bank loan of $4.0 million, 4SA beginning Dec. 1977 at 8%.

Source: Company projections received 10-27-76, adjusted to reflect information received 11-8-76 from Manhattan National Bank.

First, the Moroccan government sponsored this project both through the donation of the site and through specific incentives, including:

1. A five-year tax holiday,
2. Concessionary interest rates on local debt from the National Bank for Economic Development (NBED),
3. A refund of energy costs,
4. Construction of infrastructure (e.g., roads, electricity, water facilities),
5. An investment subsidy up to $12.4 million over the first two years,
6. Controlled prices of $30.66 per metric ton (in 1976 dollars), and
7. Government-guaranteed profit after the first year of 6 percent in the second and third years, and 12 percent thereafter.

Second, the project was scheduled to come on line in 1978, producing 231,000 metric tons (mt) the first year, 500,000 mt the second, and 625,000 mt (full capacity) the third. Costs were expected to start at $16.57 per ton, fall to $13.21 per ton in 1980, and then rise gradually to $17.53 per ton in 1987. No change in selling price was projected.

Third, MNB made assumptions about the costs and schedules of RPC's loans. The larger foreign loan of 22.1 million would be for seven years at 8.75%. The smaller foreign loan of 3.9 million for the down payment would be for two years at 8 percent. The local loans, one of $14.2 million for 12 years and one of $2.3 million for 5 years, would be at 8 percent. Projected income statements and cash flow are in Exhibits 3 and 4.

Exhibit 4 Projected Cash Flow ($000)

	1978	1980	1986
Net profit	($5,965)	$2,394	$2,840
Depreciation	5,849	5,872	4,360
Interest	3,374	2,640	416
Cash available for Debt Service (A)	3,258	10,906	7,616
Principal (B)	3,410	4,820	1,200
Interest (C)	3,374	2,640	416
	6,784	7,460	1,616
Cash Surplus (deficit)	($3,526)	$3,446	$6,000
Interest Coverage (A ÷ B)	0.97	4.13	18.31
Debt service coverage (A ÷ (B+C))	0.48	1.46	4.71

Source: Company projections received 10-27-76, adjusted to reflect information received 11-8-76 from Manhattan National Bank.

Exhibit 4A RPC-Projected Import Savings

	1978	1980	1984
Production (thousand tons)	231	625	625
Import cost (at $45/ton)	$10,395	$28,125	$28,125
Foreign exchange cost	7,763	12,581	11,606
Principal	2,580	3,160	3,160
Interest	2,054	1,519	413
Materials and supplies	234	282	413
Fuel (at $12/ton)	2,775	7,500	7,500
Technical assistance	120	120	120
Net import savings	$ 2,632	$15,544	$16,519

Source: Company projections received 10/27/76.
Source: Manhattan National Bank.

Exhibit 5 Production, Consumption, and Import of Cement, 1970–75 (000 metric tons)

Year	1970	1975
Domestically produced	1,391	2,230
Domestically consumed	1,402	2,254
Shortfall	11	224
Imports	35	224
Percent growth in consumption (over previous year)	20.1	17

Source: Manhattan National Bank.

Exhibit 6 Level of Gross Investment, Morocco (millions of dirhams at current prices)

Investment	1971	1975
Private	1,577	3,256
Public	1,123	4,454
TOTAL	2,700	7,710
GDP (current prices)	16,440	26,040
Percent of GDP	16.4	29.6

Source: Manhattan National Bank Study

Exhibit 7 Balance of Payments, Morocco (in millions of dollars at current prices)

	Year Ended December 31	
	1971	1975
CURRENT ACCOUNT		
Goods and Services		
TOTAL	(178.7)	(1,011.0)
Transfer Payments		
TOTAL	115.4	481.9
Balance on Current Account	(63.3)	(529.1)
CAPITAL ACCOUNT		
Private		
TOTAL	33.3	121.7
Public		
TOTAL	92.7	391.1
BALANCE ON CAPITAL ACCOUNT	126.0	512.8
I.M.F. SPECIAL DRAWING RIGHTS (ALLOCATIONS)	12.8	—
OVERALL BALANCE OF PAYMENTS	$ 75.5	$ (16.3)

Source: Office des Changes from Manhattan National Bank Study.

Exhibit 8 The Moroccan Economy: Trend of Exchange Reserves ($ millions at year end)

	1971	1975
Gold	23	25
SDRs	3	17
IMF Reserve Position	—	33
Foreign exchange	148	302
Total	174	377

Source: QER, Annual Supplement, 1976.

Exhibit 9 Total Debt of Moroccan Treasury (millions of dirhams)

December 31	Domestic	Foreign	Total Total
1971	2,056	3,964	6,020
1972	2,349	4,257	6,606
1973	2,632	4,178	6,810
1974	3,174	4,341	7,515
1975	3,770	5,536	9,306

Source: Ministere des Finances from Manhattan National Bank Study

Exhibit 10 Projected Debt Service Schedule, Morocco

Payment Periods	Principal	Interest	Total Debt Service
		(millions of dirhams)	
Due 1976	308.5	406.2	714.7
Due 1977	325.6	355.9	681.5
Due 1978	537.2	323.9	861.1
Due 1979	576.4	396.5	872.9
Due 1980	609.7	270.8	880.5
Due 1981	632.3	253.5	885.8

Source: Banque du Maroc from Manhattan National Bank Study.

Exhibit 11 Estimated Budget of Morocco (millions of dirhams at current prices)

	Year Ended December 31	
	1971	1976
Ordinary Revenues: TOTAL	3,571	8,930
Ordinary Expenses: TOTAL	3,258	8,630
Current Balance	+ 313	+ 300
Capital Expenses	−1,123	−6,500
Special Accounts of Treasury and Annexed budgets	—	−100
Financial deficit	− 810	−6,300
Financed by; Total	+ 810	+6,300
OF WHICH FOREIGN BORROWING	441	4,370

Source: Office des Changes from Manhattan National Bank Study.

The Debt Crisis in Zaire (A)

In October 1979, Zaire's major commercial bank creditors received a memorandum from the country's central bank requesting their support for a private debt rescheduling. Such rescheduling would set a major precedent; it was the first major renegotiation case faced by private banks in the developing world during the 1970s. The outcome of the Zairian negotiations would thus establish significant ground rules for future relations between private banks and developing countries.

The Zairian debt crisis began in 1975 (see Exhibit 1 for a chronology of events). The world price of copper, a major export for Zaire, had fallen from a record high annual average price of $0.9319 per pound in 1974 to $0.5595 in 1975. In the following years, the price fluctuated around 60 cents per pound. Around that same time, Zaire's oil bill went from $36 million (1972) to $140 million (1974). These international economic conditions caused severe balance-of-payment problems. To finance this balance-of-payment deficit and the overspending of the Zairian government, Zaire accumulated $1.6 billion in debt by 1975 ($400 million of which was privately held, outstanding loans). In 1975, both interest and principal payments went into arrears.

The memorandum requesting rescheduling came after four years of effort by bankers, governments, and the International Monetary Fund (IMF)* to come up with an effective way to resolve the debt crisis faced by Zaire. One of the prominent figures in these efforts was Dr. Irving Friedman of Citibank. Dr. Friedman, who had worked in the U.S. Treasury Department, the IMF, and the World Bank, was the senior vice president and senior advisor for international operations at Citibank during the years of the Zairian debt crisis. Dr. Friedman was concerned that the solution to Zaire's debt crisis be such that it corrected the problems which initially caused the crisis. He was even more concerned with the precedent the solution would set.

Dr. Friedman's concerns led him to oppose the initial suggestion of some within Citibank to declare default on Zaire's loans. He feared the ripple effect the

This case was written by Associate Professor Charles R. Kennedy, Jr., of the Colgate Darden Graduate School of Business Administration, The University of Virginia. The collaboration of Dr. Irving S. Friedman is gratefully acknowledged. The case was prepared as a basis for class discussion rather than to illustrate either effective or ineffective handling of an administrative situation.

*The IMF was created at Bretton Woods in 1945 to promote exchange-rate stability, international monetary cooperation, and expansion of world trade. Member countries, which number well over one hundred, can borrow from the IMF for balance-of-payment assistance, and in return, the IMF may prescribe appropriate means of adjustment to help ensure that countries can overcome their deficit problems.

action would have on other third-world countries. A general debt moratorium, in fact, had been discussed at the Nairobi meeting of the United Nations Conference on Trade and Development (UNCTAD) in April 1976. As *Euromoney* noted, "At the time, bankers and politicians in the industrial world were at one in their fear of the precedent that might be set by Zaire if it were to declare a moratorium on its debt."[1]

Declaring default was a valid consideration due to the fact that the action would establish the banks' intentions to adhere to commercial lending principles to the letter: Everyone agreed that Zaire was technically in default for payment arrears. By declaring default early a bank would also have the advantage of seizing Zaire's assets before they were claimed by any other bank. Zaire, however, had few assets outside the country to seize.

The primary alternative to default initially pursued by most creditors was rescheduling. This alternative gained considerable momentum after the summer of 1976 when the Paris Club* of twelve government creditors rescheduled Zaire's public debt. In return, the Zairian government promised to adjust commercial debt "on a comparable basis." During the fall of 1976, Governor Sambwa Pida Nbagui, the head of Zaire's central bank, demanded that all private debt be rescheduled over 15 years. Most of the 13 agent banks** were swayed by the rescheduling argument. As one European banker observed, "Everyone was resigned to a rescheduling or refinancing.*** We felt we had to agree to the Paris Club's approach because we could see no way of avoiding it."[2]

Dr. Friedman was not caught up in the movement to support the Paris Club's rescheduling approach. He insisted that rescheduling was unacceptable without more data on Zaire's external debt and economy. He noted that even with existing adverse circumstances in the international environment (oil and copper prices), much of Zaire's problems could be resolved by an efficient administration of the country's foreign exchange budget. For example, Dr. Friedman surmised that if all of Zaire's foreign exchange earnings were collected by the Central Bank, instead of being siphoned off by smuggling, Zaire's balance-of-payments crisis would probably disappear. Simply rescheduling the debt would not solve the basic economic problems that cause debt crises for Zaire, or for any other debt-ridden country such as Peru, Turkey, Pakistan, and Sudan. Dr. Friedman observed, "We don't really like to make loans on the assumption that in the end we shall reschedule them."[3] His intent was to evaluate Zaire's situation and restore the country's creditworthiness so that further financing of economic development in Zaire by commercial banks would be possible. Thus, in order to understand the approach taken by Dr. Friedman and Citibank toward the debt problem in Zaire, which lead

*An informal group of government officials from major lending nations who would meet at the French Foreign Ministry whenever a developing country had trouble paying its public debt.

**An agent bank was the lending institution that headed and formed a syndicated loan. The 13 agent banks involved with Zaire were Bankers Trust, Banque de Paris es des Pays Bas, Banque Nationale de Paris, Chase, Citibank, Citicorp International, Commerce Union Bank (Nashville), Credit Commercial de France, Grindlays Brandts, Morgan Grenfell, Morgan Guaranty, Societe Generale de Banque (Brussels), and the Tokai Bank.

***Refinancing replaces current debt with a new loan, whereas rescheduling stretches out maturities on existing debt.

to the October 1979 rescheduling memorandum, some background information on Zaire is required.

ZAIRE'S RECENT POLITICAL AND ECONOMIC SITUATION

In June 1960, Zaire (then the Belgian Congo) received its independence and was called the Republic of Congo. Joseph Kasavubu became the head of state, with Patrice Lumumba as the prime minister. Five days after the granting of independence, the armed forces mutinied. The mineral-rich province of Katanga (now Shaba) seceded. Upon request the United Nations (U.N.) sent a peacekeeping force to Congo to aid in maintaining order and preserving the country's territorial integrity.

Disagreements between Lumumba and Kasavubu concerning the involvement of the peacekeeping forces and the handling of the secession of Katanga led to the dismissal of Lumumba in September. The government was then taken over temporarily by then Col. Joseph-Desire Mobutu (Mobutu eventually became a general and later changed his name to Mobutu Sese Seko). Lumumba was imprisoned, but his supporters set up a rival government in Stanleyville (now Kisangani) and controlled most of the eastern portion of the country. Mobutu returned power to President Kasavubu in February of 1961. Only a few days after Kasavubu returned to office, the murder of Lumumba was announced.

The strong reaction within Africa and the U.N. to Lumumba's murder led to negotiations between Kasavubu and the followers of Lumumbu. Eventually a new government was established in August of 1961 with Cyrille Adoula as prime minister. Eventually, the Katangan secession ended with the Katangan leader Moise Tshombe going into exile in January of 1963. The rebels who followed Tshombe formed the Congolese Liberation Front (FNLC), which later fought with the Marxist groups in the civil war of neighboring Angola. The FNLC remained in Angola and participated in the 1977 and 1978 rebel attacks on the province of Shaba. Though the rebels were repelled on both attempts, they were successful in disrupting the Zairian economy on each occasion.

After assuming full powers, Kasavubu closed the legislature and arrested opposition elements. In early 1964, Kasavubu faced yet another rebellion in the Kwilu region, near the capital city of Kinshasa. In July of 1964, Kasavubu appointed Tshombe as an interim prime minister pending elections. Early in 1965 the Kwilu rebellion crumbled. In the aftermath of the revolt, Kasavubu and Tshombe struggled with one another for control of the newly created office of president. In the midst of the struggle, Mobutu, once again, seized control of the government. He continues to serve as president, with the next elections scheduled for 1991.

Mobutu abolished all political parties shortly after taking office. He created his own party, the Movement Populaire de la Revolution (MPR). Mobutu appointed Colonel Leonard Mulamba Prime Minister and gave him the charge to form a government with representatives from each of Zaire's twenty-one provinces and the capital city of Kinshasa. Once the government was in place, Mobutu began to consolidate the executive and administrative functions, with political power being increasingly centralized in the office of the president.

In the following years, Mobutu eliminated the position of prime minister with all the powers of that office being turned over to the president. Because Mobutu saw the provincial government as costly and unwieldy, he reduced the number of provinces first to twelve and then to eight. The provincial assemblies became consultative rather than legislative bodies. The provincial governors became subject to supervision from central authorities. Eventually the governors were appointed by Mobutu and were assigned to provinces other than their regions of origin. Mobutu had the power to annul any decision of the governors if he felt it did not fit with government policy. Mobutu would shift the appointed leaders of both the provincial and central governments around so that no one was able to establish any sort of powerbase. All the political leaders in Zaire were dependent upon Mobutu for their survival.

In July 1974, Mobutu further enhanced his dominance in Zaire by announcing several measures he labeled "Mobutuism." These measures called for a new doctrine and constitution, reorganization of the Political Bureau, and the creation of a party school. He also attempted to integrate the military into the MPR. Mobutu eventually maintained direct control of the military. With the military behind him, a coup against Mobutu was squashed in 1976. Following the attempted coup, the U.S. ambassador was expelled from Zaire as he and the CIA were accused as supporting the plot against Mobutu.

A centerpiece of Mobutu's economic policy was Zairianization, which was introduced in November 1973. Zairianization took 1,500 to 2,000 enterprises (mostly plantations, retail houses, and wholesale trading houses, which were owned, for the most part, by Europeans) and assigned ownership of them to selected Zairians. The effect of the program was public resentment of the new "acquirers," a decline in agricultural output, and the demolishing of a major portion of Zaire's distribution system. These effects were the result of liquidation of businesses due to lack of interest on the part of the new acquirers and poor management of the remaining businesses due to lack of management experience.

Mobutu was forced to nationalize the larger Zairianized enterprises in December of 1974. This put a tremendous strain on the banking system since the newly nationalized enterprises were experiencing liquidity problems and required credit. At this time Mobutu also banned all foreign bank accounts and property holdings and dismantled the effective but foreign-dominated religious educational system.

In 1975 as the balance-of-payments crisis worsened, imports of goods and services were restricted. The crisis made foreign exchange scarce, which led to a lack of spare parts and raw materials. The lack of spare parts combined with the rising cost of motor fuel and the falling price of copper caused revenues from copper exports to fall. Copper production fell from 471,000 tons in 1974 to 410,000 tons in 1976. Real GNP stagnated.

In 1975 and 1976, neighboring Angola was fighting a civil war. The war made Zaire's use of the Benguela railway impossible. The Benguela railway was Zaire's means of transporting over 56 percent of its copper to the coast and to eventual markets. Alternative routes were costly, slow, and had limited capacity. As the war progressed, Mobutu supported the Frente Nacional de Libertacao de Angola (FNLA) along with the U.S. The Soviet- and Cuban-backed Movimento Popular de Libertacao de Angola (MPLA) eventually won the war after the United States discontinued aid but not before embarrassing Mobutu by severely defeating his armies.

Contributing to Zaire's debt crisis was the overspending on the government's ambitious development programs. There were several huge construction projects. Phase two of the Inga Dam, estimated at $250 million, had doubled in cost; the Inga-Shaba high-tension power line experienced massive overruns on a $350 million estimate. The government also financed twelve multimillion-dollar cargo ships for the Zairian shipping line, DC-10s for Air Zaire, an ambitious airport construction and improvement program, and a steel mill of dubious profitability. As revenues failed to cover these capital expenditures plus the government's current expenditures, Zaire increasingly turned to external financing from governments and private creditors.

As the debt crisis erupted, but before the Paris Club rescheduling, Zaire contacted Dr. Friedman to request that he arrange a meeting between the government and all private creditors. Dr. Friedman, however, feared that such a meeting would lead to a declaration of default by the creditors, so instead he persuaded President Mobutu to invite an IMF mission to negotiate a stabilization program and standby credit arrangement. From the beginning, Dr. Friedman urged Zaire's financial authorities to adopt a realistic foreign exchange budget, and to stop the immense loss of foreign exchange through the smuggling of coffee and diamonds.

By March 1976, Zaire had adopted an IMF program and purchased $48 million in foreign exchange from the IMF under an enlarged first-credit tranche. Only economic monitoring by the IMF accompanied a first-tranche drawing, and compliance with the IMF program was voluntary. Subsequent tranche drawings, however, were accompanied by mandatory compliance with IMF guidelines. In early 1977, Zaire began further negotiations with the IMF for the right to draw the higher credit tranches. By March, President Mobutu had formally presented an economic and financial program that met IMF guidelines. This move led to a $52 million second- and third-tranche borrowing authorization and a $33 million disbursement by July.*

The Friedman Plan

As Zaire worked with the IMF mission and other banks to solve the debt crisis, Dr. Friedman and Citibank colleagues Hamilton Meserve and Allen Goldie privately sought an alternative to rescheduling. By the end of October 1976, Dr. Friedman had persuaded Zaire to drop the private debt rescheduling demand (announced

*The IMF acquired the resources for lending primarily through member subscriptions. Each IMF member was assigned a quota, which determined the size of the subscription. Each member, moreover, had automatic drawing rights only up to 25 percent of its quota—the first, or so-called reserve, tranche. For higher credit tranches, each member was required to comply with an IMF stabilization program.

after the Paris Club rescheduling of public debt in 1976) and accept an alternate plan instead. As outlined by Dr. Friedman, a syndication headed by Citibank would make its "best efforts" to raise a new loan of about $250 million if Zaire paid its arrears, continued to be current on interest payments, and reached a loan agreement with the IMF on a possible second and third tranche draw-down.

The payment of arrears of principal would go into a special, blocked Bank for International Settlements (BIS)* account. The amount would be released to commercial banks when total arrears were paid into the BIS account and after Citibank produced a written commitment for the new loan. The new loan, however, could only be used for essential imports and as open-dollar letters of credit. Friedman viewed the Citibank proposed loan not as a refinancing but as an effort to make funds available to the Zairian government for investment in the growth and improvement of the Zairian economy.

The Citibank plan was accepted by the other agent banks, and a Memo of Understanding to that effect was signed with Zaire in November 1976. Citibank would begin to solicit the necessary funds as Zaire met its obligations. The most crucial obligation in the eyes of the bankers was an IMF agreement. The agreement would require Zaire to allow IMF intervention in the central bank, customs, and treasury department. This intervention would entail placing IMF representatives in positions of authority within the Zairian government. It was hoped that this would enable Zaire to actually correct the problems which originally caused the debt crisis.

Several unexpected events, however, delayed the implementation of Citibank's loan proposal. The invasion of mineral-rich Shaba province by rebels based in Angola in March 1977, the appointment of a new central bank governor in August 1977, and snags in reaching the IMF agreement were all cited by Citibank as causes for the delay in putting together a loan in accordance with the Memo of Understanding. Nevertheless, in February 1978, a $220 million loan commitment to Zaire (the $250 million figure cited earlier was only an upper-level target), was finally ready. Many banks which had no previous exposure in Zaire were included in the more than 50 banks in the syndicate. Before the loan could be implemented, however, Zaire would still be required to pay the principal in arrears (about $40 million) and come up with an IMF agreement. All interest arrears had been paid.

Progress toward overcoming the key obstacle to the new loan, the IMF agreement, was apparently made by the end of March 1978. President Mobutu Sese Seko declared that an IMF agreement for a standby second- and third-tranche loan of $150 million had been reached in principle. For his part, President Mobutu pledged to cut public spending by two-thirds and to improve the balance of payments and public-sector efficiency by allowing IMF and other international officials to administer key foreign exchange and customs functions within the Zairian government. The plan, dubbed the "Mobutu Plan," called for over $1 billion in foreign assistance through 1980 in exchange for the IMF intervention. The banks felt enough progress toward an IMF agreement had been made to send the loan docu-

*The BIS was a consortium of European central bankers formed in 1930 and joined by the head of the Federal Reserve Bank of New York in 1960. The primary purpose of the group was information sharing and ad hoc crisis management.

ments to the central bank in early May for Zaire's approval, which had been given orally.

Any hope of a quick formal agreement evaporated, however, with a new and more serious invasion of mineral-rich Shaba province by Katangan rebels in mid-May 1978 (see Exhibit 3). Unlike the 1977 invasion, which had no significant effect on mineral production, the rebels in 1978 sabotaged enough mining installations to reduce total copper production by 25 percent and nearly eliminate all cobalt production. Because these two products accounted for as much as 60 percent of Zaire's foreign exchange earnings, the existing balance-of-payments crisis quickly deepened. In addition to the balance-of-payments crisis, Zaire had to finance a war and invest in the rebuilding of many of the mining operations. By August 1978, Zaire had become so strained for foreign exchange that it raided the BIS account for $18 million. *Business Week* called this action "the fatal blow to the Friedman Plan."[4]

ROAD TO RESCHEDULING

In June 1978, the first meeting of the Zaire Group took place in Brussels. Under the chairmanship of the World Bank, the Zaire Group included eleven countries (United States, France, Belgium, United Kingdom, West Germany, Canada, Italy, Saudi Arabia, Iran, Japan, and Zaire) and the IMF. The conference approved a plan jointly submitted by Zaire and the IMF which was based on the "Mobutu Plan." The $1 billion in aid would not be forthcoming, however, until Zaire adopted an IMF plan and policies. After that the Citibank-led loan was still expected to follow.

The BIS withdrawal by Zaire in August 1978, however, ended most expectations that the Citibank-sponsored loan was possible. Instead, the incident was quickly followed by the arrival of Erwin Blumenthal to Zaire as the IMF representative at Banque du Zaire, the central bank. Blumenthal had formal responsibility for all monetary and foreign exchange policy and for bank inspection. His authority to make decisions on these matters was completely independent of the Banque du Zaire governor. Blumenthal's most important monetary measure was implemented in early September 1978, two weeks after his arrival. The measure, called circulaire 156, was designed to funnel all available foreign exchange to the central bank and to minimize further leaks of foreign exchange abroad. Progress towards these goals, however, was slow.

Momentum toward effecting greater IMF management in Zaire was evident after the second meeting of the Zaire Club in November 1978. At this meeting Zaire's request for a new aid package was refused until it agreed to stringent economic measures negotiated with the IMF. Shortly thereafter, in March 1979, Zaire and the IMF reached and initialed an agreement for a $150 million standby loan, the second such loan since July 1977. A loan of $142 million was formally approved in August 1979. At the same time, the IMF gained greater authority in Zaire's economic management: Ismail Beatik, assistant to the undersecretary of finance in Turkey, was put in charge at the Finance Ministry in Kinshasa to administer budget expenditures. In addition, Belgium Customs officials were now present at various key position in Zaire's Customs Service.

An integral part of the 1979 IMF initiative was the rescheduling of all private and public debt. In fact, in late 1978, the Zairian government informed the commercial banks that it was putting talks on the Citibank-led loan into abeyance—largely because payments in arrears now equaled or exceeded the amount of the Citibank-sponsored loan; thus Zaire had little incentive to pay the banks an equal or greater amount in order to receive a loan of lesser value. By March 1979, Zaire had publicly rejected the Citibank plan and was now in favor of rescheduling. Informal talks to that effect started shortly thereafter between Zaire, the IMF, the Paris Club of public creditors, and the London Club of commercial banks. By November 1979 the various groups were ready for formal meetings, but unlike 1976, public creditors preferred not to reschedule until a decision was reached by commercial bankers.

Before the meetings, private creditors were sent a packet of economic projections and arguments in favor of rescheduling (see Exhibit 4). The packet was jointly prepared by Banque du Zaire and the IMF. At the November meeting, Zaire and the IMF hoped a private-debt rescheduling agreement could be reached.

NOTES

1. *Euromoney,* February 1979, p. 14.
2. *Institutional Investor,* March 23, 1977, p. 22.
3. *Euromoney,* July 1980, p. 13.
4. *Business Week,* April 9, 1979, p. 106.

Exhibit 1 Chronology of Important Events

1974	Friedman arrives at Citibank.
1975	Debt crisis in Zaire begins when interest and principal payments go into arrears; Friedman contacted by Zaire.
March 1976	IMF-Zaire reach agreement on loan and economic program.
June 1976	Paris Club accords reschedule public debt.
September 1976	Secret meetings between 13 agent banks and Zaire.
October 1976	Friedman meets Sambwa in Manila; agreement reached between agent banks on Citibank plan.
November 1976	Memorandum of Understanding signed by banks and Zaire.
March 1977	First Shaba invasion; IMF-Zaire reach stabilization agreement.
August 1977	Sambwa replaced as Central Bank Governor.
November 1977	Mobutu Plan announced.
February 1978	Citibank raises $220 million to support its plan.
March 1978	Mobutu announces new IMF agreement.
May 1978	Loan papers sent to Zaire a few days before second Shaba invasion.
June 1978	Zaire Group holds first meeting in Brussels and endorses Mobutu Plan.
August 1978	Zaire draws down on BIS account; Blumenthal arrives in Zaire as IMF representative to Central Bank.
November 1978	Zaire Group holds second meeting and refuses Zaire's aid request until new IMF agreement is reached.
March 1979	Zaire initials new IMF agreement and publicly rejects Citibank plan in favor of rescheduling.
October 1979	Bank of Zaire sends "Information memorandum" to agent banks asking for a private-debt rescheduling agreement to be reached the following month.

Exhibit 2 Zaire: International Transactions, Money and Inflation

	1974	1975	1976	1977	1978	1979
Exports[a]	690.5	432.5	747.3	846.9	778.2	2342.2
Copper	429.6	216.5	316.5	344.3	322.7	853.6
Cobalt	35.7	48.4	98.6	93.0	180.7	1067.0
Diamonds	31.1	27.6	47.4	55.2	103.2	171.2
Coffee	30.2	27.1	103.1	165.5	138.2	243.4
Imports, cif	525.5	452.4	546.6	522.7	490.7	1046.9
Imports, fob	455.8	392.0	471.2	450.6	423.0	902.5
Money, Seasonally Adjusted	394.3	458.9	670.6	1042.1	1628.6	1630.7
Volume of Exports[b]						
Copper	79	100	91	71	76	53
Coffee	133	100	179	109	140	107
Export Prices						
Copper	167	100	184	182	185	557
Consumer Prices	77.5	100	188.2	307.0	486.2	961.0
Exchange Rate[c]	.500	.500	.861	.831	1.007	2.025
Total Reserves minus gold[d]	118.79	47.91	50.28	133.87	125.75	206.69
SDRs	7.82	23.37	31.49	.04	5.72	.16
Reserve Position in the Fund	34.61	—	—	—	—	—
Foreign Exchange	76.36	24.54	18.79	133.83	120.03	206.53
Gold (Million Fine Troy Oz.)	.500	.260	.260	.260	.308	.252
Gold (National Valuation)	17.50	9.10	10.98	10.98	58.52	91.44

[a]In millions of Zaires

[b]With 1975 volume indexed at 100

[c]Zaires per U.S. Dollar

[d]Millions of U.S. Dollars

Source: IMF, *International Financial Statistics*

Exhibit 3 Zaire: Chronology of Events in Shaba Province

1977	Former Katanganese gendarmeries, who had once tried to create a separate Katangan state in Shaba, raided and pillaged the key mining center of Kolwezi.
1978	A major invasion, compared to the 1977 incursion by Katanganese rebels, led to the killing of 93 whites and a thousand Africans. French paratroopers were required to end the invasion.
1979	Fears of a third Shaba invasion mount, but the presence of French and Belgium advisors to the Zairian army has made Shaba a more difficult target. Nevertheless, the Katanganese insurgents have substantial East German and Cuban support in their bases in Angola, which is adjacent to Shaba province. Many feel a third invasion is only a matter of time.

Exhibit 4

CONFIDENTIAL

The Republic of Zaïre

SUMMARY OF INFORMATION

OCTOBER 1979

BANQUE DU ZAÏRE

LE GOUVERNEUR

29th October, 1979

Dear Sirs,

I refer to the recent meeting which has taken place between members of your esteemed Bank and representatives of Kuhn Loeb Lehman Brothers International, Lazard Freres Paris/New York and S.G. Warburg & Co. Ltd., in their capacity as financial advisers to the Government of the Republic of Zaire and have pleasure in enclosing with this letter the following information:

1. An information memorandum providing general information on the Republic of Zaire, including economic and financial developments since 1974, the country's present economic situation and principal measures recently taken by the Government, particularly as regards external debt.

2. A memorandum giving balance of payments projections and a forecast of the external resources position of the Republic of Zaire for the period 1980/1985.

3. A summary of the external debt position of the Republic of Zaire as at 30th June, 1979, including a debt service profile from the second half of 1979 to 1985.

As discussed between you and representatives of the Advisory Group, it is proposed to hold a meeting with the agent banks concerned in New York on Thursday, 8th November, 1979. You will shortly receive a formal invitation for this meeting. The purpose of this meeting will be to discuss the conclusions which can be drawn from the information provided in the enclosed set of documents as to the necessity of a rescheduling of the Republic of Zaire's non-insured bank debt in a form which is not only acceptable to all parties concerned, but which also provides a realistic long term solution.

I hope that it will be possible to reach a broad consensus of opinion at the meeting on the outline of a rescheduling programme which you feel you would be able to recommend to your syndicate members.

EMONY MONDANGA

Republic of Zaïre

BALANCE OF PAYMENTS PROJECTIONS FOR 1980-1985
AND ANALYSIS OF EXTERNAL RESOURCE GAP

OCTOBER 1979

Introduction

This Memorandum presents in summary form a set of calculations which describe the outlook for the Republic of Zaïre's ("Zaïre") balance of payments position for the period 1980–1985.

The basic assumptions underlying this analysis have been developed after consultation with the International Monetary Fund ("IMF") and the International Bank for Reconstruction and Development ("IBRD") staffs and are summarized at the end of this Memorandum.

From the current account projections, an external resource gap analysis for the years 1980–1985 has been derived. The principal conclusion which can be drawn from this analysis is that large inflows of resources are required in the near future in the form of emergency aid, balance of payments support, project assistance and debt rescheduling so as to meet Zaïre's humanitarian, development and finance requirements.

I Balance of Payments—Summary

Two balance of payments scenarios—a "base" case and a "high" case—have been calculated to show Zaïre's net foreign exchange position for each of the years 1980–1985. Contractual debt service obligations in respect of principal and interest are not included in this summary. The effect of contractual debt service on the country's net foreign exchange position is shown in Section II of this Memorandum and this illustrates Zaïre's resource gap for 1980, 1981 and 1982.

(a) The "base" case scenario is shown below.

	1980	1981	1982	1983	1984	1985
	(in millions of US dollars)					
Trade Balance	383	345	501	541	627	723
Exports	1,954	2,242	2,654	3,019	3,428	3,936
Imports	-1,571	-1,897	-2,153	-2,478	-2,801	-3,213
+Services (net) (excluding interest payments on external debt)	-719	-689	-793	-786	-808	-912
+Transfers (net)	46	51	56	62	68	75
=Current Account (excluding interest payments on external debt)	-290	-293	-236	-183	-113	-114
+Capital	125	100	100	100	75	—
=Net Foreign Exchange Position (excluding debt service and servicing of total arrears, representing an aggregate amount of US$2,280 million in 1980)	-165	-193	-136	-83	-38	-114

The balance of trade for 1980–1985 shows a significant recovery from its position in the years 1974–1976 when Zaïre experienced large trade deficits. Exports in the "base" case represent a projected annual average growth rate of 3 percent in real terms as from 1979. However, this scenario is not the most pessimistic case since it envisages neither any major upheaval in the economy caused by external factors nor any further deterioration in domestic conditions. The "base" case scenario, in fact, assumes a slow but steady improvement in all sectors of Zaïre's economy. The annual capital inflows included in the above table have been calculated on the basis of assumptions as to the drawdown of existing external loan commitments. Under reasonable assumptions regarding future new capital inflow commitments and resulting disbursements, the net foreign exchange position during the latter part of the 1980–1985 period should show an improvement over the net projected foreign exchange positions set out above.

(b) The "high" case scenario is shown below.

	1980	1981	1982	1983	1984	1985
	(in millions of US dollars)					
Trade Balance	693	603	879	998	1,068	1,257
Exports	2,214	2,500	3,032	3,476	3,869	4,470
Imports	1,571	1,897	2,153	2,478	2,801	3,213
+Services (net)	-757	-726	-847	-829	-836	-946
+Transfers (net)	46	51	56	62	68	75
=Current Account (excluding interest payments on external debt)	-68	-72	88	231	300	386
+Capital	125	100	100	100	75	—
=Net Foreign Exchange Position (excluding debt service and servicing of total arrears, representing an aggregate amount of US$2,280 million in 1980)	57	28	188	331	375	386

The "high" case scenario assumes a more rapid rehabilitation of Générale des Carrières et des Mines' ("GECAMINES") mining operations, which constitute Zaïre's main source of foreign exchange income. Without any increase in the international unit price of copper used in the "base" case, the completion on schedule by GECAMINES of a number of specific investment projects would generate between $70 and $120 million additional foreign exchange in each of the 5 years shown above (see *Table 5*). In addition, in the "high" case scenario, it has been assumed that the international cobalt price is higher and agriculture policies are more effective than in the "base" case. In this scenario, the projected annual average export growth rate in real terms is forecast to reach 6 percent. The "high" case is, however, very optimistic and no policy conclusions as to its effect on Zaïre's net foreign exchange position should, therefore, be drawn from it.

II. External Resource Gap

In the table below for each of the years 1980-1985 the external resource gap has been calculated by adding to the annual projected current account deficits shown in the "base" case (which exclude contractual interest payments on external debt) the contractual debt service payments. No payments on total arrears (amounting to approximately $1.76 billion) on debt outstanding as of June 30, 1979 are included in this table.

	1980	1981	1982	1983	1984	1985
	(in millions of US dollars)					
Deficit on Current Account (excluding interest payments on external debt)	-290	-293	-236	-183	-113	-114
Debt Service	-516	-515	-477	-428	-351	-316
Of which:						
Principal	-355	-368	-349	-325	-267	-252
Interest	-161	-147	-128	-103	-84	-64
External Resource Gap	-806	-808	-713	-611	-464	-430

The external resource gaps shown above can be financed by a combination of :

—disbursements on existing external loan commitments;

—emergency aid within the framework of the Brussels meeting;

—balance of payments support and project-related assistance within the context of the forthcoming Consultative Group meeting on Zaïre;

—external debt rescheduling;

—net transfers of IMF resources;

—private foreign lending;

—private foreign direct investment.

It is important that efforts to finance the external resource gap should be concentrated in the years 1980, 1981 and 1982 as these three years constitute the period of the recovery program developed in the "Mobutu Plan".

For the years 1980–1982, it has been assumed that:

—disbursements on existing external loan commitments will amount to respectively $125 million, $100 million and $100 million;

—net transfers of IMF resources will represent approximately $75 million in each of the three years;

—there will be no significant inflows of foreign private lending or direct investment.

The conclusion which may be drawn from the foregoing is that the remaining external resource gap excluding payment of arrears in each of the years 1980, 1981 and 1982 amounts to respectively $606 million, $633 million and $537 million. These gaps will have to be financed by a combination of emergency aid, other official aid (primarily balance of payments support), project assistance and debt rescheduling.

III. Key Assumptions Underlying the Balance of Payments Projections

1. Exports

(a) *Volume*

The main difference in the export volume assumptions underlying the "base" and "high" case scenarios is constituted by the respective levels of GECAMINES' copper and cobalt production. The differing production levels assumed under each of these two scenarios are caused by varying the assumptions as to the speed with which the GECAMINES' rehabilitation and expansion programme is implemented. This in turn depends on factors such as the availability of raw materials, adequate energy supply, the availability of expatriate management, transportation, etc.

(b) *Prices*

For most export commodities, the IBRD price projections have been used, although there are some exceptions.

For copper, the IBRD projected a price of $0.85/lb. in 1980. However, this analysis assumes a price of $0.91/lb. in 1980 which assumption is based on a different assessment of the impact of a possible world recession and of the degree of speculative activity. For the period 1981–1985 the IBRD copper price projections have been used.

The IBRD does not make official projections for international cobalt prices. It has been assumed in this analysis that in the "base" case prices will remain at the level of $20.0/lb. in real terms during the entire period of 1980–1985. In the "high" case a price in real terms of $23.0/lb. during the same period has been assumed.

2. Imports

Using the level of 1979 as a base, an increase in the value of imports of 10 percent in real terms has been projected for 1980 and 1981. For each of the subsequent 4 years an annual increase of 5 percent in real terms has been projected.

The 1979 imports forecast is the level which has been assumed in the stabilization program agreed with the IMF. The projected 10 percent increases in the import levels for each of the years 1980 and 1981 represent the minimum import requirement to avoid a further decline in Gross Domestic Product during these two years. The 10 percent increase in real terms projected for 1980 can be compared with the 15 percent increase in real terms of 1979 imports over the preceding year which has been incorporated in the IMF stabilization program.

3. Parallel Market

It has been assumed that the value of unrecorded exports of diamonds and coffee as shown in Tables 8 and 10 represent the minimum levels of parallel market exports. The value of parallel market imports is assumed to be equivalent to the value of unrecorded diamonds and coffee exports and the effect of this on imports for the period 1980-1985 has been calculated by reducing import levels accordingly. It is acknowledged that over and above the unrecorded diamond and coffee export levels taken into account in this presentation, there are additional unrecorded exports, the proceeds of which are not repatriated. It is not possible to estimate the level of these additional unrecorded exports and its effect on the balance of payments projections shown in this Memorandum has therefore not been assessed.

4. Services Account

The services account is based on Bank of Zaïre calculations and those of the IMF. The amounts shown for the period 1980-1985 include refining and merchandising fees payable by GECAMINES and Société Minière de Bakwanga ("MIBA"). The amount of services payable by GECAMINES has been progressively reduced as from 1983 as it has been assumed that the coming on stream of a flash-smelter and electro-refinery will result in a reduction in foreign refining charges. The services account also includes cash payments for the reduction in arrears on external debt in 1979 and 1980 agreed under the IMF stabilization program.

5. Transfer Account

This account represents net public and private transfers as recorded by the Bank of Zaïre. Projections are direct extrapolations from past data and do not take into account the effect of emergency aid requested by Zaïre for 1980.

6. Capital Account

This account incorporates assumptions on annual disbursements of multi-lateral and bi-lateral foreign loan commitments as of June 30, 1979. These disbursements amount to $50 million during the second half of 1979 and $500 million during the period 1980-1985. No assumptions have been made in the capital account projections on inflows of new capital.

7. Inflation Factor

An 8 percent inflation factor has been assumed throughout the analysis, except for calculating projected import levels as a percent of past years' levels. In the latter case, IMF/IBRD import deflators have been used.

Projected Total External Debt Service Payments (thousands US $)

Principal	182,271	354,644	367,817	
Interest	93,813	161,165	147,121	
Total	276,084	515,809	514,938	
Principal	349,465	325,041	267,009	252,145
Interest	127,756	103,241	84,205	64,338
Total	477,221	428,282	351,214	316,483

Exhibit 4 (*Continued*)

Sovereign Lending In Turkey

Bob Stout, the chief credit officer at Midwest Regional Bank (MRB), was reviewing a proposal from the international lending department to join a $300 million syndicated loan* to Turkey's Central Bank in February 1984. Jim Clancey, the recommending loan officer, was very enthusiastic about joining the syndicate, headed by Manufacturers Hanover Trust (MHT). Jim's country risk evaluation, which was required of any loan officer submitting such a proposal, painted an optimistic picture about Turkey under the new leadership of Prime Minister Turgut Ozal. The spread on the loan, moreover, was very attractive at 1 1/2 points above LIBOR,** which was well above returns on the average domestic loan. The loan maturity was for six years, and MRB was invited to participate in the area of $10 million.

At MRB, the chief credit officer chaired a Country Risk Review Committee (CRRC), which gave final approval for all country exposure limits.*** At this time, the bank had no exposure in Turkey, and the syndicated loan proposal was routed to the CRRC for a quick decision. MHT wanted to conclude the loan agreement within thirty days.

MIDWEST REGIONAL BANK

MRB was a well-respected regional bank located in a large midwestern city. In terms of total deposits, MRB was the thirtieth largest bank in the United States, with total assets nearing $8 billion; this was up from forty-fifth place in 1977. As with many regional banks, MRB had been an active participant in the international lending "frenzy" of the 1970s. In 1975, foreign loans accounted for less than 6 percent of the bank's total loan portfolio, but by 1978, this percentage had climbed to 12 percent. By 1984, foreign loans constituted 14 percent of total loans, after reaching a peak of 16 percent in 1981. Selected financial data for the bank are provided in Exhibits 1–3.

*Syndicated loans are commonly used in sovereign lending and are put together by a lead bank, usually one of the largest U.S. or European banks, which receives a fee for managing the syndicate and for inviting other banks to participate in the loan. Syndicates are formed because the size and/or risk of the loan is too large for one bank to handle alone.

**LIBOR is the London interbank offer rate or the interest charged for bank loans to other banks.

***The country exposure limit is the maximum amount of aggregate loan exposure allowed by a bank, including its branches and subsidiaries, in a given country.

MRB's international exposure was concentrated in the debtor countries of Latin America. Mexico and Brazil headed the list, with loans outstanding to those two countries equaling $152 and $121 million respectively. The bank also had outstanding loans to Chile ($50 million), Argentina ($43 million), and Venezuela ($37 million). These five countries constituted about two-thirds of foreign exposure.

The motivations behind MRB's international lending were common to other regional banks. Most apparent was the profit motive. In 1982, for example, the average yield or rate of interest on the bank's total loan portfolio was 14 percent, versus 17 percent on foreign loans. Another important motive, however, was the competitive need to serve corporate customers or clients in foreign countries. About 40 percent of MRB's foreign loans was to firms in the private sector, and it was perhaps no coincidence that the bank's only two representative offices* in the developing world were located in Mexico City and Sao Paulo, Brazil. On the sovereign lending side, MRB's loans to foreign governments were always made within syndicated loan packages, which were put together by a lead bank, usually one of the major money center banks. The object of a syndicated loan was to diversify the risks; it can also give a regional bank a "safety-in-numbers" illusion.

In the aftermath of the international debt crisis, MRB and many other banks were introduced to the concept of "involuntary lending," when virtually all of a country's creditors are required (or strongly persuaded) to loan new money to a debtor that is simultaneously rescheduling old debt. In Mexico, for example, MRB had agreed to reschedule $50 million of loans and to lend another $13 million at market rates for eight years. Without considerable pressure from money center banks, the Federal Reserve Board, the U.S. Department of the Treasury and the International Monetary Fund (IMF), the bank would not have lent the Mexican government such a sum of money in the post-1982 period.

COUNTRY RISK MANAGEMENT AT MRB

During the 1970s, the country risk management system at MRB could be characterized as line-driven. For instance, country managers or loan officers in Mexico and Brazil would initiate country risk reports and recommend country exposure limits during the annual budget process. At corporate headquarters, an executive vice president for international affairs gave final approval for country exposure limits.

After the international debt crisis exploded in 1982, however, the bank changed the way country exposure limits were decided because top management felt the old system was too line-driven and loan-biased. Although country managers and loan officers were still required to submit country risk evaluations and exposure limit recommendations, the new country risk management system contained two major changes. First, a country risk analyst was hired and attached to the

*Representative offices have the primary function of helping the bank's clients when they conduct business in the country, but they cannot accept deposits, make loans, or deal in drafts or letters of credit. Such offices simply provide information, advice, and contacts.

Credit Department; he was responsible for submitting country risk evaluations to the CRRC. Second, final approval of country exposure limits was shifted to the CRRC, which was newly created and headed by the chief credit officer; this committee had two other members, executive vice presidents involved in international business. Although disputes that arose in the committee were formally settled by majority vote, the final decision never ran counter to the chief credit officer's wishes. In fact, the chief credit officer can alone approve loans above exposure limits when the committee is not meeting.

The new country risk management system had not been really tested. During 1983, no major loan involving a decision to raise the exposure limit of a developing country had been proposed, and Turkey, although a member of the North Atlantic Treaty Organization (NATO), was economically and politically more a developing than a developed country. Turkey had also been one of the first countries to reschedule outstanding debt in the 1970s. Now the bank was considering a $10 million loan to the country's central bank in early 1984.

THE DECISION

Bob Stout knew the decision he made on the Turkey loan would be, in all likelihood, the final decision. One of the executive vice presidents on the CRRC had already informally voiced his inclination to approve the loan; he also related rumors that MHT was close to finding the needed participants for the entire $300 million syndication. Jim Clancey, the international loan officer in charge of the Middle East and Africa, had made a compelling case for approving the loan in his memorandum to the committee. (Exhibit 4) Jim Bucknell, however, the vice president in charge of country risk analysis at the Credit Department, had written a country evaluation which concluded that "Turkey continues to be an unacceptable risk for credits of any maturity." (Exhibit 5) Bob had to decide for himself what the level of risk was and how it related to both the return the loan would bring and the bank's overall portfolio.

Exhibit 1 Consolidated Financial Data, Midwest Regional Bank (in millions)

Summary of Operations	1979	1980	1981	1982	1983
Net interest income	$135	$151	$180	$225	$287
Provision for credit losses	10	11	17	22	28
Noninterest income	49	58	63	72	79
Noninterest expenses	118	129	150	186	192
Applicable income taxes	7	8	15	28	34
Income before security transactions	48	54	63	72	74
Net Income	45	48	56	60	62
Balance Sheet Highlights					
Total assets	$ 5,650	$ 6,110	$ 6,840	$ 7,321	$ 7,963
Loans and lease financing, net of unearned income	2,631	2,985	3,350	3,550	3,873
Deposits	3,798	4,087	4,321	4,595	4,863
Other borrowings	40	49	73	124	132
Shareholders' equity	319	348	379	420	474

Exhibit 2 Loan Maturities, Midwest Regional Bank

Loans as of December 31, 1983 (in thousands)	One year or Less	1–5 Years	Over 5 Years
Commercial	$1,020,978	$713,463	$296,480
Real estate—construction	134,860	8,760	—
Real estate mortgage	1,930	7,041	6,248
Money Market	158,930	—	—
Foreign	306,371	147,096	88,753

Exhibit 3 Allowance for Credit Losses, Midwest Regional Bank (in thousands)

Amounts Charged Off	1979	1980	1981	1982	1983
Commercial	$6,878	$6,148	$8,089	$11,368	$13,598
Real estate mortgage	—	—	14	73	57
Installment	1,567	2,383	1,829	1,557	1,379
Foreign	—	1,241	1,878	2,264	2,794
Recoveries on Amounts Charged Off					
Commercial	1,103	1,111	1,823	1,598	1,467
Real estate mortgage	—	—	—	19	21
Installment	283	410	350	257	243
Foreign	419	964	2	242	301

Exhibit 4 Memorandum

TO: CRRC
From: Jim Clancey, International Loan Officer, Middle East and Africa
Re: Syndicated loan to Turkey
Date: February 1, 1984

I recommend that MRB participate in the syndicated loan to Turkey. The invitation to join the syndication by Manufacturers Hanover Trust is at attractive rates, and a $10 million dollar commitment is an affordable and reasonable risk given the return and following country analysis of Turkey.

HISTORICAL OVERVIEW

As commonly known, Turkey experienced difficult economic and political times for many years. From 1959 to 1980, there have been five multilateral debt renegotiations between the Turkish government and the country's official public creditors. In terms of private debt rescheduling with commercial banks, Turkey was the third major such rescheduling in the 1970s, following Zaire and Peru. The August 1979 rescheduling agreement gave Turkey a five-year grace period on debt payments, with the first payment of $2.3 billion being due this year, as Table 1 shows.

Table 1 Total Debt Service Requirements of Medium- and Long-Term External Debt as of December 31, 1983 (millions of dollars)

	1984	1985	1986	1987	1988	1989
Principal	1,356	1,862	1,767	1,783	1,827	1,518
Interest	894	809	732	656	527	389
Total debt service	2,250	2,671	2,499	2,439	2,354	1,907

In spite of these problems, Turkey has made tremendous progress in managing the economy since the 1979 rescheduling agreement. Under a 1980 IMF stabilization program, the following economic advances have been made:

1. Real GNP growth has reached an annual average of 4 percent the last three years.
2. Inflation has subsided significantly at the same time.
3. The balance on trade and current account have shown steady improvements.

As the *IMF Survey* commented in the August 23, 1983 issue.

> Since the beginning of 1980, the Turkish authorities have been implementing a far-reaching stabilization program, with bilateral and multilateral financial support from abroad. The efforts made have met with considerable success in strengthening the balance of payments, reducing inflation, and restoring the basis for sustainable growth.

I have attached to this memo a copy of economic data on Turkey found in the IMF's *International Financial Statistics* for your review.

What is most encouraging is not these positive economic trends but the fact that the principal architect of Turkey's economic reforms has just been elected prime minister. In December 1983, Turgut Ozal became the new prime minister after his Anavatan (Motherland) Party won 45 percent of the popular vote and a majority of seats in the Grand National Assembly. Ozal's victory came as a surprise to most analysts, including the Turkish military, who openly supported a rival candidate and party. Subsequently, Ozal and the military reached an understanding that would allow the new prime minister a free rein in economic policy, while internal security, defense, and foreign policy remained in the hands of the military's National Security Council, headed by Chief of Staff and President Kenan Evren, who has six years remaining on his seven-year term. Ozal's election was applauded by prominent international bankers, the World Bank, and the IMF because of his background as the architect of Turkey's 1980 austerity program.

Since being elected prime minister, Ozal has made the most sweeping reforms of Turkey's government since the Kemalist Republic was created in the aftermath of the fall of the Ottoman Empire. Ozal has centralized economic decision-making into his hands. He has streamlined an unwieldy bureaucracy by eliminating six ministries and dozens of government agencies. The cabinet now has only twenty-two members. The previous civilian cabinet had thirty members. Ten of the cabinet members are, like Mr. Ozal, businessmen trained as engineers.

There is no doubt in anyone's mind that Ozal is fully committed to the continued economic liberalization of Turkey. Ozal, however, tempers this commitment with a healthy dose of realism; he clearly understands that sacrifices will have to be made and progress judged on a long-term basis. Ozal, moreover, has been quite candid with the Turkish electorate concerning his program. Significantly, not only did the Turkish people freely opt for a "blood, sweat, and sacrifice" approach (Ozal's words), but the military seems willing to support the liberalization program as well. Perhaps, Ozal has the perfect political base from which to implement far-reaching reforms. The program has popular consent, and the military, operating under martial law regulations in many parts of Turkey, gives the civilian government even more leeway in implementing fundamental changes in the economic system.

In short, Turkey appears to be headed in the right direction both economically and politically. An attractive economic program is in place, and a strong government is fully committed to the liberalization of the economy. Strategically speaking, the goals of the government are reasonable and laudable, and economic performance measures are beginning to show real payoffs. Turkey thus presents a good opportunity for the bank to participate in the continued development of the Turkish economy and make a handsome profit at the same time.

BALANCE OF PAYMENTS ANALYSIS

Prime Minister Ozal clearly has the will to meet the country's external debt obligations, so the key question is will the Turkish government have the ability to service the debt? This requires an extensive analysis of Turkey's balance of payments and debt-servicing structure.

As already mentioned, Turkey's balances on trade and current account have improved since 1980. Although the country still had deficits, the trend was positive. Improvement in the trade position was due to the rate of change in exports exceeding increases in imports. Notice that under Ozal's liberalization program, the volume and real value of imports rose; therefore, any improvement in the trade balance required an export-promotion strategy.

Turkey was able to promote exports through diversification of both markets and products. By 1983, the direction of trade was as follows.

Table 2 Direction of Trade with Major Partners, 1983

	Exports	Imports
EEC	35.1%	28.1%
Iran	19.0%	13.2%
Saudi Arabia	6.3%	5.1%
Iraq	5.6%	10.3%

Substantial export penetration of Middle Eastern markets took place in the 1980s, particularly in the above three countries.

Mr. Ozal has selected Turkey's ambassador to Moscow, Vahit Halefoglu, to now serve as foreign minister. Mr. Halefoglu speaks fluent Arabic and will be a key figure in the continued development of the export markets in the Middle East. Mr. Halefoglu also served in Bonn as an ambassador for ten years. This experience will enable him to handle the arguments which the West Germans make concerning Turkish workers in Germany.

Turkey was also diversifying the export base into higher value-added manufactured goods, as Table 3 shows.

Table 3 Percentage Composition of Exports

	1979	1980	1981	1982	1983
Manufactured Goods	28.0	28.8	39.9	49.8	52.2
Processed Agricultural Products	6.7	7.2	8.8	9.9	11.7
Fruits and Vegetables	28.7	25.9	16.9	11.3	10.3
Industrial Crops and Forestry Products	24.7	20.8	17.3	12.9	9.3
Cereals	7.5	6.2	6.9	5.9	6.6
Other	4.4	11.1	10.2	10.2	9.0
	100.0	100.0	100.0	100.0	100.0

Given this diversification, Turkey's export drive should be sustainable, and further reductions in the trade deficit can be expected.

Under this assumption, a baseline scenario for the 1984–89 period yields the following projections for Turkey's balance of payments and debt-servicing capabilities.

Table 4 Baseline Scenario for Turkey's BOP, 1984–89 (in billions)

	1984	1985	1986	1987	1988	1989
Trade Balance	(3.0)	(2.5)	(2.1)	(1.8)	(1.5)	(1.3)
Unilateral Transfers	1.8	1.8	1.8	1.9	1.9	1.9
Current Account	(1.2)	(0.7)	(0.3)	0.1	0.4	0.6
FDI, net	0.1	0.2	0.4	0.5	0.5	0.5
Other Long-Term Capital, net	(0.6)	(0.3)	(0.2)	(0.2)	(0.3)	0.0
Basic Balance	(1.7)	(0.8)	(0.1)	0.4	0.6	1.1
Short-Term Capital, net (including E & O)	0.5	0.5	0.5	0.5	0.5	0.5
Overall Balance	(1.2)	(0.3)	0.4	0.9	1.1	1.6
Official Reserves at year end (including gold)	1.52	1.22	1.62	2.52	3.62	5.22

As one can see, the trade balance on goods and services, which includes interest payments on the external debt, will improve but remain in deficit during the period. Unilateral transfers to Turkey, both from private and public sources, will increase slightly from the 1983 level of $1.6 billion but will never reach the 1979–82 annual average of over $2 billion. Small increases will be recorded because of a rise in foreign aid grants and worker remittances as economic recovery in Western Europe proceeds. As a result, the current account will be virtually balanced by 1986 and show slight surpluses from 1987 to 1989.

In terms of capital flows, foreign direct investment in Turkey will increase as international businesses are attracted to the new economic liberalization climate after many years of strict controls. In the 1973 to 1983 period, for example, net annual FDI inflows have averaged only around $80 million, so the baseline scenario projects some large percentage increases. Recently, most FDI activity has been focused in the financial services sector. As Business International's issue of *Investing, Licensing, and Trading Conditions Abroad* observed about Turkey in August 1983, the largest net capital inflows in the early 1980s have been in the banking sector. In fact, eleven foreign banks are now licensed to have branches* in Turkey, and Manufacturers Hanover Trust plans to establish a Turkish branch this year.

*A branch bank is a legal and operational extension of the parent bank and conducts the full range of banking services under the name and legal obligation of the parent. Thus unlike representative offices, branch banks can accept deposits, make loans, and deal in drafts or letters of credit.

Other long-term capital, net, on the other hand, will show small deficits for most years as principal payments on the external term debt slightly exceed the amount of new term loans** acquired. For example, principal payments in 1984 total nearly $1.4 billion, so the baseline scenario projects new term loans of around $800 million. The level of new term loans is assumed to increase to around $1.5 billion annually for the remainder of the period. These projections, moreover, are probably conservative, for it is not unreasonable to assume that new term loans will exceed amoritization of long-term external debt in the next few years. Regardless, even under a conservative estimate, the basic balance turns positive in 1987, with these surpluses increasing in 1988 to 1989.

Short-term capital, net, projections are also conservative. The "Dresdner Scheme," a program whereby that bank offers special savings accounts to Turkish expatriates, encouraged Turks abroad to make deposits in these special accounts rather than sending the money home. From around $20 million involved in this program in 1980, the amount has climbed to nearly $450 million in 1983. These deposits, moreover, are available to the Turkish central bank and are recorded as short-term capital flows. In 1983, Turkey registered nearly a $900 million surplus in short-term capital movements, versus deficits in three of the previous four years. Errors and omissions (E&O), on the other hand, showed positive entries in four of the past five years; Turkey averaged about $450 million in annual surpluses in the E&O category for the 1979 to 1983 period, after big deficits in earlier years.

Since the use of the Dresdner Bank accounts is expected to increase further and there will be no changes in the E&O pattern under continued economic liberalization, the projection of $500 million annual surpluses for the 1984 to 1989 period is indeed very conservative. Nevertheless, the resulting overall balance turns positive as early as 1986, and the surplus increases each successive year. Official reserves consequently rise at the same time. Thus Turkey appears to be an attractive lending opportunity from both a strategic and balance-of-payments perspective.

CONCLUSION

I am aware that this loan proposal, if approved, would be the bank's first major decision since 1982 to raise a developing country's exposure limit. The bank should not allow the bad experiences of the international debt crisis, which adversely affected our loan portfolio in Latin America, to cloud our thinking about new and profitable business opportunities elsewhere. Turkey in 1984 seems to be such an opportunity. The risk relative the return is quite attractive.

On a more cosmic plane, the bank should also consider the possibil-

**Term loans are usually loans with a maturity of more than one year, repayable according to a specified schedule that is detailed in a legal document between the bank and borrower.

ity of Turkey being a model for the resolution of the debt crisis in Latin America. If Turkey can successfully manage the transition from debt rescheduling to a return to creditworthiness and access to international capital markets, then surely the more resource-rich, industrialized countries of Latin America can make the transition as well.

Sovereign Lending in Turkey
Turkey: International Transactions, Money, and Inflation

	1979	1980	1981	1982	1983
Exports[a]	75.74	221.50	530.72	937.31	1298.96
Cotton	6.44	24.66	48.51	48.15	48.48
Hazelnuts	10.93	17.35	33.76	38.74	55.62
Tobacco	5.09	17.25	33.72	56.31	52.71
Imports, cif	178.51	613.27	1002.36	1461.42	2127.09
Imports, fob	156.45	537.96	879.26	1287.95	1865.87
Money, Seasonally Adjusted	423.10	665.20	892.50	1234.10	1782.60
Volume of Exports[b]					
Cotton	85	100	153	129	86
Tobacco	83	100	156	125	83
Volume of Imports	87.2	100.0	120.7	123.8	140.6
Unit Value of Exports	36.7	100.0	131.7	178.4	219.6
Consumer Prices	51.48	100.00	137.61	182.57	235.22
Exchange Rate[c]	35.35	90.15	133.62	186.75	282.80
Total Reserves minus gold[d]	767	1274	1285	923	1270
SDRs	—	—	—	—	1
Reserve Position in the Fund	—	—	—	—	34
Foreign Exchange	767	1274	1285	923	1235
Gold (million fine troy ounces)	3765	3768	3768	3769	3775
Gold (National Valuation)	159	159	159	159	159

[a]In billions of Lira.

[b]With 1975 volume indexed at 100.

[c]Liras per US Dollar.

[d]Millions of US Dollars.

Source: IMF, *International Financial Statistics*

Exhibit 5 Memorandum

To: CRRC
From: Jim Bucknell, Vice President
Re: Turkey Loan Proposal
Date: February 16, 1984

The following analysis will support a recommendation to not participate in the syndicated loan. Turkey continues to be an unacceptable risk for credits of any maturity. In essence, the fundamental weaknesses of the Turkish economy far outweigh the country's strengths. These fundamental weaknesses, in order of importance, are:

1. A debt-service profile which presents potential rescheduling problems in the 1985 to 1988 period.
2. Both the agricultural and industrial sectors need modernization.
3. Domestic energy sources are inadequate and present a barrier to sustained economic growth.
4. High unemployment.

The strengths of the Turkish economy are as follows:

1. Substantial worker remittances which have helped offset trade deficits.
2. Ability to cultivate new export markets.
3. Reasonably adaptive economic programs have been implemented.
4. Strategic position in NATO has resulted in substantial multilateral and bilateral aid.

Each of these weaknesses and strengths can be discussed prior to reaching an overall conclusion.

DEBT-SERVICE PROFILE

An analysis of Turkey's debt-service profile yields some positive developments, but as a whole, major problems appear in the country's ability to service the external debt. Although Turkey is now able to raise funds in international capital markets, it seems that the new credit facilities were utilized quickly since undisbursed credit commitments from commercial banks rose only $100 million in 1983 (see Table 1).

Table 1 Turkey's External Debt from Commercial Banks (in billions of U.S. dollars)

	12/80	12/81	12/82	12/83
Undisbursed Credit Commitments	0.6	0.5	0.5	0.6
Maturities of One Year or less	1.3	1.0	1.0	1.2
Months of imports covered by short-term debt	1.7	1.2	0.9	1.5

Short-term debt, however, rose from 0.9 months of imports to 1.5 months during 1983. This trend, plus new term loans from commercial banks, suggests some improvement in foreign bank confidence, albeit cautious given the small increases in undisbursed credit commitments.

Of great concern is the decline in the macroeconomic financing ratio (MEFR), which measures a country's ability to service the external debt in the near term. The MEFR is a ratio calculated by adding four variables measuring financial resources (gross official reserves, banks' net foreign assets, available credit lines with private-sector creditors and exports of goods and services,) and by then dividing that number by the country's total financing requirements, measured by imports of goods and services and debt service payments. For a developing country that is not newly industrializing (a non-NIC LDC), the acceptable minimum standard for the MEFR is 1.00, and a change in any given year of 0.05 triggers substantial concern. As one can see in Table 2, the 0.09 decline in 1983 for Turkey's MEFR suggests rising debt service problems, caused by a decline in international reserves and banks' net foreign assets and by an increase in imports of goods and services. In addition, principal amoritization of term debt grew as well, which sharply boosted debt service obligations.

Table 2 Selected External Debt Statistics

	1979	1980	1981	1982	1983
% of public loans with variable interest rates	29.4	25.5	24.6	N.A.	N.A.
Total External Debt to GNP	16.5	24.1	24.5	29.0	N.A.
MEFR	0.75	0.60	0.75	0.90	0.81

Since international liquidity remains inadequate and the decline of the MEFR is unsatisfactory, Turkey continues to be an unacceptable risk for credits of all maturities.

AGRICULTURAL AND INDUSTRIAL MODERNIZATION

Turkey is still a developing country, with 60 percent of the economically active population located in the primary sector. Consequently, the urbanization rate is only 44 percent. Little is being done in the investment area to modernize agriculture or industry. In fact, gross fixed investment as a percentage of GNP has declined almost every year since 1979, as Table 3 shows.

Table 3 Gross Fixed Investment (Percent/GNP)

1979	1980	1981	1982	1983
21.6	19.4	19.6	18.9	18.7

Given the low capacity utilization rate in manufacturing, it is unlikely investment will be strong in the near term.

DOMESTIC ENERGY SOURCES

Domestic energy production continues to be inadequate. Turkey's oil fields are past their prime, and there is little promise of any large new fields. Electricity production is also a problem, with the recent drought slowing the output of hydroelectricity. Power imports from the USSR and Bulgaria consequently increased 23.4 percent in 1983. The Ataturk hydroelectric project in Eastern Turkey will lessen the problem, but the first generator is not scheduled to be on-line until 1991. Thus, the inadequacy of sufficient power will continue to be a serious constraint on industrial expansion and sustained economic growth.

In spite of these constraints, however, one has to admit that real growth in the Turkish economy has improved during the last three years, as Table 4 shows.

Table 4 Real GNP Growth (in percent)

	73–78 (avg.)	1979	1980	1981	1982	1983
GNP	6.5	(0.4)	(1.1)	4.2	4.4	3.4
Consumption	6.7	(2.5)	(3.4)	3.0	4.2	2.9
Fixed Investment	14.1	(3.6)	(10.0)	1.7	2.6	2.1
GNP Price Deflator	21.6	71.1	103.8	41.9	26.5	27.6

Nevertheless, the 1981 to 1983 growth rate is far below the level achieved in the 1973 to 1978 period and is fragile because of volatile export markets and energy/infrastructure constraints.

UNEMPLOYMENT

Total unemployment, which includes disguised agricultural unemployment, increased from 18.1 percent in 1982 to 19.4 percent in 1983. Turkey's strong population growth rate of 2.3 percent is simply increasing the workforce faster than jobs are being created. In 1983, only 10 percent of the 450,000 new entrants into the labor force found jobs.

WORKER REMITTANCES

Remittances from expatriate workers continued the decline started in 1982, as shown in Table 5.

Table 5 Selected Expatriate Worker Statistics

	1979	1980	1981	1982	1983
Remittances (millions of US$)	1,694	2,071	2,490	2,187	1,544
Number of Workers (thousands)	802	888	953	1,086	N.A.

The decline has been caused by the appreciation of the U.S. dollar against the worker's host country currency, increased unemployment among expatriate workers, and more use of Dresdner Bank accounts by workers in West Germany. Nevertheless, remittances continue to help offset chronic trade deficits, as shown in Table 6.

Table 6 Merchandise Trade and Current Account Balances (in millions $)

	1979	1980	1981	1982	1983
Exports, f.o.b.	2,261	2,910	4,703	5,746	5,728
Imports, f.o.b.	4,435	6,920	7,816	7,737	8,081
Trade Balance	(2,174)	(4,010)	(3,113)	(1,991)	(2,353)
Current Account	(1,356)	(3,233)	(1,908)	(790)	(1,747)

NEW EXPORT MARKETS

Beginning in 1979, Turkey actively sought new export markets in the Middle East. In particular, three countries stood out. Iran, Iraq and Saudi Arabia received less than 3, 5 and 2 percent of total Turkish exports in 1979, respectively. By 1983, Iran and Saudi Arabia bought 19 and 5 percent of total Turkish, respectively. Iraq, on the other hand, climbed to over 10 percent of Turkish exports in 1982, but this dropped to 5½ percent in 1983. In fact, sales to the Middle East and North Africa declined in general, from 47 percent in 1982 to 45 percent of exports last year. This indicates how fragile these new export markets might be.

Table 7 shows the commodity composition of Turkey's major exports. The growth that can be observed is due, for the most part, to the Middle Eastern markets.

Table 7 Composition of exports in millions of US Dollars

	1980	1981	1982	1983
Agricultural Products	1,672	2,219	2,141	1,881
(percent of total)	(57.5)	(47.2)	(37.3)	(32.8)
Cereals and pulses	181	326	337	376
Fruits and Vegetables	754	795	649	591
Cotton	323	348	297	197
Tobacco	234	395	348	238
Other Crops	49	70	96	97
Livestock	131	285	414	382
Mining Products	191	194	175	189
(percent of total)	(6.6)	(4.1)	(3.1)	(3.3)
Industrial Products	1,047	2,290	3,430	3,558
(percent of total)	(36.0)	(48.7)	(59.7)	(63.9)
Processed Agricultural products	190	412	568	670

(continued)

Table 7 (Continued)

	1980	1981	1982	1983
Textiles and Clothing	440	803	1,056	1,299
Hides and Leather	50	82	111	192
Forestry Products	8	20	333	15
Chemicals	76	94	148	120
Rubber and Plastics	16	72	61	77
Petroleum Products	39	107	344	232
Glass and Ceramics	36	102	102	108
Cement	40	198	207	81
Iron and Steel	34	100	362	407
Nonferrous Metals	18	30	45	79
Machinery and Metal	30	85	143	123
Electrical Equipment	12	26	75	69
Motor Vehicles	50	117	110	126
Other	8	42	63	60
TOTAL	2,910	4,703	5,746	5,728

Source: *Structural Reform, Stabilization, and Growth in Turkey*, Occasional Paper No. 52, International Monetary Fund, May 1987, p. 43.

ECONOMIC PROGRAMS

A number of economic reforms have been implemented under the influence of Prime Minister Turgut Ozal, who was formerly the deputy prime minister under the previous military government. Most importantly, the Turkish lira has been devalued daily since May 1, 1981. These adjustments are primarily based on the U.S. dollar, and this policy, together with the maxidevaluation of 33 percent in January 1980, has largely corrected the problem of an overvalued currency, which was a major cause of the country's chronic balance-of-payments deficits.

Fiscal policy has become more responsible as well, with the central government's budget deficit having declined from 1.2 percent of GNP in 1982 to 0.4 percent in 1983. The Public Sector Borrowing Requirement, which includes the country's many and large state-owned enterprises, also declined from 6.0 percent of GNP in 1982 to 5.2 percent in 1983.

Monetary policy, however, was eased last year after a domestic bank crisis in 1982. As Table 8 indicates, the M_1 growth rate, after moderating in 1981 to 1982, surged in 1983 and remains too high for stable, noninflationary growth.

Table 8 M_1 **Growth Rates and the Consumer Price Index**

	1979	1980	1981	1982	1983
Annual percentage increase in M_1	59	58	35	39	45
Annual percentage increase in CPI	64	94	38	33	29

Because of this surge, the recent success in lowering the inflation rate will be only temporary.

Besides these concerns about inflation, the political foundation upon which these reforms are based is shaky and uncertain. Although Ozal enjoys a clear majority in the 400-member unicameral National Assembly, with 212 seats controlled by his Motherland Party, he still faces important local elections late next month. The structure of the government, moreover, is similar to the Gaullist system in France, in that there is a strong president, General Kenan Evren, with a term of office separate from the legislature. Given that the Turkish military supported a rival candidate and was reportedly surprised by Ozal's election, it is unclear how much freedom the prime minister will have over economic policy. In 1982, Ozal and the military had a falling out over economic policies, and Ozal resigned from his post as deputy prime minister instead of easing on his tight monetary policy. This relationship certainly clouds the future.

FOREIGN AID

Turkey is the recipient of significant unilateral transfers in the form of grants from foreign governments. These inflows have averaged around $30 million per year in the 1979 to 1983 period and have risen to over $40 million the last two years. In comparison to other balance-of-payment problems, however, these figures are too meager to really have much of an impact on Turkey's ultimate ability to meet debt-servicing obligations.

OVERVIEW AND SUMMARY

The preceeding analysis strongly indicates that the fundamental weaknesses of the Turkish economy far outweigh the strengths. The most important indicator of a country's creditworthiness, debt service capacity, is weak in Turkey, with the deteriorating MEFR being most disturbing. Even the country's strengths have underlying weaknesses or uncertainties. Worker remittances are declining, new export markets in the Middle East are volatile and unreliable, economic reforms are incomplete and rest on an uncertain political base, and large foreign grants are small relative to the problems of an underdeveloped and weak economy. Under any reasonable definition, Turkey is not a creditworthy country because it faces fundamental debt servicing and economic structural problems. A loan to Turkey's central bank, moreover, will unlikely be used for productive investments but for balance-of-payment purposes instead. This bank should not participate in the syndication in order to fund the repayment of old debt, especially when the firm has no previous exposure in the country.

10

SCENARIO DEVELOPMENT

Scenario development has become a widely used technique in corporate planning. The popularity of scenario planning increased dramatically in the 1970s. The trend toward scenario development was particularly evident in capital-intensive, international-oriented industries like petroleum, which invested in projects with very long lead times. Greater uncertainty and an extremely long time perspective made scenario planning very attractive to top oil executives. By the 1980s, however, the use of the scenario technique had spread to more and more industries, with approximately one quarter of major U.S. industrial firms now employing scenario development.[1] Banks are also big users of scenarios, with a 1981 study of eleven major banks showing that over half employed scenario development.[2] Planning based on scenarios is expected to remain a prominent feature of political risk management for some time. Some scholars of business strategy, in fact, strongly associate scenario development with strategic management. As Lawrence Jauch and William Glueck stated:

> Today's approach is called strategic planning or more frequently strategic management. . . . Strategic management focuses on "second-generation planning," that is, analysis of the business and the preparation of several scenarios for the future. Contingency strategies are then prepared for each of these likely future scenarios.[3]

Given the prevalence of scenario development and its importance to strategic management, a suggested approach to scenario planning might be useful. The following recommendation has five discrete steps.[4] First, scenarios or alternative futures should be anchored on a specific problem or issue that impacts the firm. In this way, the development of scenarios will be decision-oriented. To a large extent, the issue chosen will be shaped by temporal and location considerations. For instance, a medium- or long-term perspective on international banking may lead to a focus on prospects for the international debt crisis. Conversely, a specific loan proposal might dictate a shorter-term perspective that focuses on a certain country or project. The interaction between such global and country scenarios is important as well.

After the focal point of analysis has been identified, the second step is the selection of key environmental variables that have the greatest impact on business-specific interests. Assumptions are made about variables whose future outcome is relatively certain, whereas drivers may have several plausible futures.

This step is perhaps the most crucial in scenario development. If assumptions and drivers are not carefully chosen, scenarios will not accurately represent or encapsulate the future and will not be of much value. Obviously, this step largely dictates the scope and direction of subsequent analysis.

Before assumptions and drivers are chosen, one should study the issue or problem extensively. As a Bankers Trust executive who headed the bank's Political Assessment Group observed:

> The first phase [of scenario development] is a period of careful study of the history of the situation and of present relationships. No projection into the future can aspire to validity unless it is rooted in an understanding of the past as well as the present.[5]

Once this extensive assessment is made, only a manageable number of drivers should be selected, perhaps four or five at most.

The third step in scenario development is the projection of driver outcomes. Each driver should have two to three contending projections. The possible outcomes should be plausible and represent all significant possibilities for the future.

Step four entails the combining of drivers into scenarios, which naturally flows from the process of projecting driver outcomes. A key consideration here is to combine outcomes so that subsequent scenarios are reasonable and internally consistent. For instance, it would be unreasonable and inconsistent to have a scenario that contained the two driver outcomes of rapidly rising oil prices and strong, long-term global expansion of GNP. Lastly, this step is a good point to ask if the scenarios so developed provide a satisfactory range of possible futures. Typically, three scenarios will do the job, with the most likely scenario being the base case. Best- and worst-case scenarios are commonly projected as well.

The fifth step is the strategic assessment of scenarios, which requires the projection of the consequences each scenario has on business-specific interests. The relative probabilities of the different scenarios can be made explicit as well. Managers then have certain options for integrating scenarios into strategic planning. Optimally, one strategy can be formulated that is best for all scenarios, but usually different strategies will be attractive under different scenarios. Under these conditions, strategies can be formulated that maximize gain under most scenarios, while risk is minimized at the same time. Alternatively, a strategy that gambles on the development of a certain scenario can be followed, particularly if one scenario is highly probable or if the benefits of guessing right far outweigh the costs of guessing wrong. Of course, management values will shape which approach is taken, but in general, prudent and wise managers will not gamble. Instead, managers should maximize their options through contingency planning. Even if a single scenario is highly probable, trigger events or leading indicators can still be developed and monitored. Strategy can then be sequenced to fit various contingencies. In other words, strategic flexibility is preferred over rigidity.

NOTES

1. Stephen J. Kobrin, John Basek, Stephen Blank and Joseph La Palombara, "The Assessment and Evaluation of Noneconomic Environments by American Firms: A Preliminary Report," *Journal of International Banking Studies,* 11 (Spring–Summer 1980), p. 40.
2. Robert Grosse and John Stock, "Noneconomic Risk Evaluation in Multinational Banks," *Management International Review,* 24 (1984), p. 46.
3. Lawrence Jauch and William Glueck, *Strategic Management and Business Policy,* 3rd Edition (New York: McGraw-Hill, 1988), p. 5.
4. These recommendations are adapted from W. P. Rossiter, R. S. Karplus and N. Jones, "Managing for the Future: The Scenario Technique," Conoco internal memorandum, Wilmington, Delaware, 1984, which is cited by Leslie E. Grayson, *How and Who in Planning for Large Companies* (London: Macmillan, 1986), pp. 27–28.
5. William H. Overholt, "The Scenario Technique," in *Political Risks in International Business: New Directions for Research Management and Public Policy,* ed. Thomas L. Brewer (New York: Praeger, 1985), p. 153.

Axy and Oil Scenarios

Gary Weber, vice president of exploration and a member of the Strategic Planning Committee of Axy Oil Company, a large independent oil company based in Houston, Texas, considered the upcoming joint meeting of the committee and the board of directors in late 1988. Among the subjects to be discussed would be the expectations of future oil prices—particularly the intermediate and longer-term outlook over the next five to ten years. As a key member of the committee, he would be expected not only to present possible scenarios but also to propose potential strategies to achieve the longer-term objectives of the board. Gary knew from past experience that the assumptions and other factors comprising the scenarios would be subject to detailed scrutiny. His staff had gathered a tremendous amount of data, much of which he was already familiar with, and he intended to spend the next few days formulating several scenarios from which to begin the strategic planning process.

STRUCTURE OF THE OIL INDUSTRY

Companies in the petroleum industry can be characterized in three different categories:

1. international versus domestic,
2. by size, or
3. by function.

These categories, of course, overlap with one another forming a matrix of companies with varying degrees of similarity. In the arena of operations, a company can be multinational—operating in several countries with globally integrated operations—or domestic, when operations are primarily restricted to one country. Obviously, companies working within these two spheres face different risks and are concerned with distinctly different problems. Companies range in size from giant corporations with hundreds of thousands of employees and budgets that dwarf those of moderate-sized countries to one-person operations with an annual budget of a few hundred thousand dollars.

Functionally, companies can participate in a wide range of activities. The cycle of operations starts with exploration and development of reserves—a low-labor, high-capital intensive activity. It takes from six months to five or more years to find and develop an oil or gas field. Next, the reserves must be extracted, or produced—again, a low-labor, high-capital intensive activity. Production of reserves ranges from three years to forty years or more, with the life of gas reservoirs being approximately half that of oil. These segments of the cycle are called the "upstream" operations. Once the oil or gas is out of the ground, the operations become

This case was prepared by John B. Bristow, Darden MBA '89 and Associate Professor Charles R. Kennedy, Jr., Babcock Graduate School of Management, Wake Forest University, 1989.

"downstream." The oil or gas is then transported, refined, and marketed. Transportation can take place by trucks, ships, or pipeline. Transportation is generally more labor intensive and less capital intensive than the upstream operations. Refining is the process by which crude oil and natural gas are converted into the products demanded by consumers. Products range from gasoline, fuel oil, asphalt, and heating gases, which are called the direct products, to fertilizers, plastics, and drugs, the indirect products. Refining, after the initial cost of the refinery, is a low-labor and low-capital segment of the business relative to other operational segments. Marketing and distributing the products to the consumer is the highest labor- and lowest capital-intensive segment of the operation. It is usually the low-risk, low-margin segment of the business.

Companies can participate in the full range of operations or can specialize in one or two segments. As the risks and opportunities are different for various companies, it is useful to use the above categories as descriptive terms for three primary groups of firms within the industry:

1. major integrated oil companies,
2. major independent oil companies, and
3. small independents and consultants.

Major Integrated Oil Companies

This group consists of very large, global and fully integrated companies. The familiar names of Exxon, Mobil, Texaco, Chevron, BP, and Royal Dutch Group (Shell) have historically been associated with this group. Several newer entrants into this field would be Aramco and the Kuwait National Oil Company (KNOC), as they have greatly expanded their scope of operations in the last ten years.

These companies operate in all phases of the industry and could be making the majority of their profits from any given segment. Historically, as prices have risen, the upstream operations have been more profitable, while during price declines the downstream operations become more profitable.[1] They take proportionally higher risks since they possess vast resources. Their budgets tend to shift 25 percent to 33 percent up or down as major shifts in industry trends occur.

Major Independent Oil Companies

This group consists of very large companies operating in one or more phases of the oil business. Firms such as Tenneco, Amerada Hess, Pennzoil, Axy, Mitchell Energy, and Mesa Petroleum are typical of major independents. These companies usually do not market to consumers (although a few do). Many of the companies specialize in the upstream operations and sell crude oil to either the major integrated companies or to major independents who specialize in downstream operations.

Major independents often have a shorter-term outlook relative to big integrated firms. Because of their fewer sources of income, they are more susceptible to cash-flow problems that result from margin erosion during price swings. They often plan in terms of three to ten years instead of the longer time horizons common in the integrated companies. The companies in this group compete aggressively with the major integrated companies in the segments in which they operate. Because of fewer resources, their budgets shift significantly upward and downward in line with swings in prices—and consequently their staffing needs often change over two-to-three-year time horizons.

Small Independents and Consultants

This group consists of companies which are not well known by the public or even within the petroleum industry. Companies often have regional reputations and, although some are publicly traded companies, many are privately held. These companies are concentrated in the upstream operations, although a few independents operate in the downstream segment. Such firms are generally undercapitalized and are cash-flow driven. They concentrate on niches seeking areas or markets passed over by the larger firms. They do not have the resources to compete head on with the large companies.

Because of sparse capital, these companies have extremely short planning horizons—on the order of six months to two years. They are very price-sensitive since revenues from today's production provides today's capital investment funds. This vulnerability to price swings means their budget and staffing needs vary radically from year to year or even month to month. The investments these firms make are very high risk in proportion to their size: they are, in effect, "betting the farm."

THE OIL ECONOMY

In 1988, the world consumed 21 billion barrels of oil worth over $350 billion dollars (U.S. dollars). During the span of the last ten years, worldwide annual consumption volumes of crude petroleum have varied less than 20 percent, shown in Figure 1,

Figure 1 Historical World Oil Consumption Volumes

Year	Volume (MMBO)	Year	Volume (MMBO)
1972	18,601	1981	20,377
1973	20,368	1982	19,347
1974	20,538	1983	19,197
1975	19,502	1984	19,753
1976	21,191	1985	19,488
1977	21,901	1986	20,329
1978	22,158	1987	20,143
1979	22,877	1988	21,013
1980	21,760		

Source: U.S. Department of Energy, Energy Information Agency, Petroleum Supply Annuals, Washington, D.C.

Figure 2 Historical World Oil Prices

Year	Price (US$/B)	Year	Price (US$/B)
1972	3.75	1981	35.75
1973	5.25	1982	33.00
1974	10.50	1983	30.00
1975	12.00	1984	29.50
1976	13.10	1985	27.50
1977	12.50	1986	14.75
1978	13.25	1987	18.25
1979	27.50	1988	16.75
1980	38.75		

Source: Courtesy of Permian Corporation, Midland, Texas.

while per-barrel oil prices have varied over 350 percent, as shown in Figure 2. With these significant variations in prices for such a strategic commodity, it is understandable that many companies, including Axy, spend considerable time and effort attempting to forecast future price movements. But in light of the price volatility present in the market, particularly since 1978, the value of straight-line forecasting techniques is questionable.

The changes in the price of oil for 1988, shown in Figure 3, bore very little similarity to the forecasts put forth by many knowledgeable and prominent individuals and institutions. The reasons lie in the level of understanding of the interrelatedness of the world economic system and the diverse nature of the independent factors affecting oil prices. The Strategic Planning Committee of Axy Oil believed that the future price of oil is not simply dependent on economics alone or the future supply and demand for oil. Nor is the reverse true: that supply and demand are dependent on the future price. Rather, they believed that the future

Figure 3 1988 Oil Price Volatility

Date	Price ($/B)	Date	Price (S/B)
Jan 4	16.70	Jul 5	14.94
Jan 18	16.95	Jul 18	14.86
Feb 1	16.94	Aug 1	16.31
Feb 15	16.25	Aug 15	15.52
Feb 29	15.78	Aug 29	15.34
Mar 14	16.29	Sep 12	14.18
Mar 28	17.03	Sep 26	14.18
Apr 11	16.88	Oct 10	12.94
Apr 25	18.30	Oct 24	14.37
May 9	17.74	Nov 7	14.04
May 23	17.17	Nov 17	12.40
Jun 6	17.50		
Jun 20	16.45		

Source: Courtesy of Permian Corporation, Midland, Texas.

price is driven by a number of distinct situational characteristics that are both political and economic in nature. These characteristics include the following factors: the producers' willingness to produce; inflation and currency fluctuations; trade deficits and balance-of-payments difficulties; maturity of supplies; tax laws; economic growth; technology change; the propensity of the consumer to switch to alternative fuels; environmental concerns; and the geopolitical stability of producing regions of the world. Moreover, prices change when buyers' and sellers' perceptions of these characteristics change. Gary knew he needed to consider all of these factors when projecting scenarios for oil prices in the future.

PAST PRICING MOVEMENTS

From 1946 to 1973, oil prices were relatively stable. Demand for crude grew at a compound annual rate of 7.6 percent, but supply, measured by sustainable daily production rates, grew at a faster rate, at least through 1966. Prices were effectively controlled by the power of the multinational oil companies (MNOCs) over the marketplace, sanctioned by the U.S. government, in conjunction with the Texas Railroad Commission's (RRC) prorated production schedules. The RRC, the arm of the Texas state government charged with regulating the oil industry in Texas, worked to restrict oil production below actual production capacity in an effort to provide economic stability both within the industry and without. The RRC was a direct response to the wild swings in prices and volumes characteristic of the early days of the developing industry. Large discoveries and predatory pricing policies made price swings of several thousand percent commonplace over periods as brief as several months. For the most part, the RRC was successful in bringing price stability to the marketplace because of the dominant position of Texas among the world's producers: during the late 1950s and early 1960s, Texas possessed nearly 25 percent of the world's oil production capacity.

In the period from 1966 to 1973, a number of events occurred which changed the factors controlling oil prices. The excess capacity to produce shifted to the Middle East and several other developing areas and away from the control of the RRC since the oil reservoirs in Texas began their inevitable decline. Demand for crude oil began to grow faster than supply. Demand was stimulated by both the increased economic power of Japan and Western Europe and the increased economic development of the lesser developed countries (LDCs). Finally, the member countries of the Organization of Petroleum Exporting Countries (OPEC)[2] began to perceive a change in their power over oil policies relative to the MNOC's power. These perceptions were strengthened by the 1971 Teheran and Tripoli negotiations. This shift in bargaining power culminated in the embargo of oil exports to the United States and the unilateral quadrupling of the selling price of oil by OPEC in 1973 to 1974.

The period following the 1973 to 1974 oil price shock was a period of tremendous adjustment and response by oil importers, companies, and OPEC. As the cost of energy increased, OECD economies slowed, and the world demand for crude oil grew at less than 2 percent annually through 1979. Demand then declined to 20.3 billion barrels in 1981, the same level it stood at in 1973. Improved efficiency measures and conservation practices contributed to this drop in demand. At the same time, the oil industry, reacting to the improved profitability of upstream operations, greatly enlarged its efforts to locate new sources of crude. In addition, many existing sources of oil deemed to be uneconomic at pre-1973 prices became profitably exploitable at the higher price levels. The industry was so successful in this effort—an effort which included rapid production increases in Alaska, Canada, Mexico, Indonesia, the North Sea, the Soviet Union, the Middle East, and parts of Africa—that by 1981 the demand for OPEC oil was falling, and OPEC members were unable to control the price of crude oil. At a time when OPEC cohesiveness was most needed to retain their control over prices, OPEC discovered that the transfer of wealth which had taken place during the 1970s had divided the organization into two groups: a group of high capital absorbers—those countries needing and able to absorb high volumes of capital into developing infrastructures[3]—and low absorbers—those countries with more developed economies in which the high volumes of capital became excess investment funds.[4] The motivations of these two factions and the related level of production at which they are willing to produce is one of the bases for the tremendous price volatility present in the oil markets of the 1980s.

During the 1980s, the role of OPEC in general, but specifically that of Saudi Arabia and Kuwait, became that of "swing producers"—producing only enough oil to meet aggregate demand—while non-OPEC-producing countries produced (and exported) at near capacity. As continued development of oil reserves took place, the gap between supply and demand widened, and OPEC's share of the world oil market fell. Efforts of the high absorbers within OPEC to retain their inflow of capital resulted in widespread discounting of prices in an attempt to reclaim market share. Reclaimed market share was primarily at the expense of Saudi Arabia, whose production level had slipped to under 2 million barrels of oil per day (MMBOPD) by 1985, compared to 1978 levels of 5.5 MMBOPD. Current estimates of the Saudis' production capacity range from 8 to 13 MMBOPD. In November 1985, after repeated efforts by the Gulf Cooperative Council (GCC)[5] to reach agreement with producers, both within OPEC and without, on reduced production levels necessary to stabilize the price of oil, Saudi Arabia and Kuwait abandoned their posted prices and dramatically increased their production levels. The resulting change in the supply of crude based on the willingness of the producers with excess producing capacity to sell at a discount produced a free fall in the price of oil, reaching a nadir of less than $10 per barrel in July 1986, a fall of nearly 70 percent in six months. Since that time, several production agreements have been reached, raising the price of oil temporarily, only to have prices fall once again when production-restraint agreements fail. This has produced an environment in which monthly price swings of 15 percent to 20 percent are not uncommon.

FACTORS DRIVING OIL PRICES

Gary's analysis showed that the many factors and circumstances affecting world oil prices can be encompassed by discussion of five primary drivers:

1. capability of producers to extract and sell
2. willingness of the producers to extract and sell
3. OECD[6] economic growth
4. OECD policies
5. OECD inflation

Changes or perceived changes in any or all of these drivers in the future, as in the past, can produce significant movement in the price of oil on the world market.

Physical Production Capacity

Oil is a nonrenewable resource. Without additional exploration and development effort on the part of the producers, ultimate recoverable reserves will decrease each year with production. Because of the physical characteristics of oil reservoirs, oil fields can be exploited at lesser daily rates over the life of the field. In mature areas such as the continental United States, it is not uncommon for the production rate of a well to drop by 80 percent or more in the first five years of its life and then stabilize at a low rate for 25 to 30 years. This characteristic is crucial when analyzing the physical production capacity of the various oil producers. Figure 4 shows the maximum sustainable physical production capacity of a number of countries, given proven reserves.

Figure 4

Country	Maximum Productive Capacity (in MMBOPD)
U.S.S.R.	12.783
Saudi Arabia	10.958
United States	9.012
Iraq	4.059
People's Rep. China	3.078
Iran	2.954
Venezuela	2.728
Mexico	2.664
United Kingdom	2.524
Kuwait	2.503
Libya	2.231
Canada	1.949
Nigeria	1.831
Indonesia	1.617
Norway	1.432
United Arab Emirates	1.352
Total productive Capacity for Major Producers	63.675
Rest of the World	8.310
Total Productive Capacity for the World	71.985

Sources: Various, including U.S. Department of Energy, Energy Information Administration, World Crude Oil Production Annual; Central Intelligence Agency, International Statistical Review; OECD Economic Outlook, June, 1988; and the Oil & Gas Journal Weekly Summary.

Despite the apparently large excess capacity of oil production present in the world today, there are technical factors which make this level of production less desirable. Studies of oil reservoir characteristics have indicated that a higher volume of oil can be recovered over the life of the well by producing at a rate somewhat below the maximum sustainable rate. Reevaluation of Figure 4, in light of this information, would indicate a worldwide maximum efficient rate of 64.27 MMBOPD, or slightly over 112 percent of current demand.

The production capacity rates of several producing regions are rising. This is primarily the result of increased exploration and production expenditures. Iraq has recently indicated its production capacity to be 4.0 MMBOPD, up from an estimated 2.9 MMBOPD only five years ago. This expansion of production capacity has been the result of an extensive development effort. The potential of a number of promising areas in Iraq is still untested, and it is believed that these areas, once drilled, could increase Iraq's production capacity in excess of 50 percent from its current level. Iraq, however, is currently constrained by capacity limitations of both pipelines and export terminals. While current terminal and pipeline capacity is nearly 3.0 MMBOPD, a moderate capital expenditure program could double this within two years' time.[7]

The productive capacity of the USSR is currently estimated at 12.78 MMBOPD. Although some Soviet productive regions are old and rapidly declining, activity in the last ten years has increased Soviet ability to produce by nearly a third. It is expected that additional development efforts already under way will slightly increase the USSR's capacity in the near term.

The People's Republic of China is a newcomer on the world energy scene. Long a small producer, China is now capable of producing over 3.0 MMBOPD, an increase of over 100 percent since 1981. China's potential is unknown. Vast areas of the interior and the coastal plain are unexplored. It is one of the few remaining significant growth areas for production capacity.

Several areas of the world have stable production rates and are expected to expand the capital necessary to retain that rate for the foreseeable future. Saudi Arabia is the most notable producer in this group. With 43 years of reserves at maximum productive capacity, or 106 years of proven reserves at more reasonable production rates, Saudi Arabia has little incentive to expend capital for exploration ventures at this time. It has been adept, however, at production maintenance programs designed to keep its capacity at adequate levels and is expected to continue this trend in the future.

Kuwait and Indonesia have capacities of 2.50 MMBOPD and 1.61 MMBOPD, respectively. Both countries have sufficient undeveloped areas and are currently producing at low enough levels that their production capacity is expected to remain flat through the 1990s.

The remainder of the world's productive capacity is declining. The productive capacity of the United States, currently the world's second-largest producer and possessing the third-highest capacity, has been declining steadily since 1970. That downward trend was interrupted only in 1979 to 1981, when the domestic oil industry spent huge amounts of capital. Since the fall in oil prices in 1986, productive capacity in the United States has declined nearly 1 MMBOPD. Decreased development budgets by the oil industry indicate this decline will continue at about 3 percent to 4 percent per year. Even the huge Prudhoe Bay producing area, which is responsible for more than one-fifth of the total U.S. production capacity, has shown the first signs of decline. Early indications suggest that the field, which did not start to decline as soon as some analysts predicted, might drop at a higher rate than predicted.

Iran, capable of producing 6.0 MMBOPD in 1978, has seen its production capacity decline to below 3.0 MMBOPD. Iran's oil fields are old, and the country is rapidly running out of oil. Since the fall of the Shah, and during the long war with Iraq, there has been little production maintenance and no exploration. In many instances, the opportunity to repair the damage to neglected reservoirs and install maintenance programs is past and cannot be recovered. Iran's capacity to produce is expected to continue its dramatic decline.

Canada, Mexico, Venezuela, Nigeria, and Libya are established producers with the capability to stabilize their productive capacity declines but at costs which are prohibitive given today's economics. The North Sea region has begun to decline, and although some areas remain undeveloped, these high cost areas will probably remain underdeveloped throughout the 1990s. The remainder of the producing regions are declining at various rates and will continue that trend.

The unknown production potentials of a few areas in the world are significant wild cards. These areas include the Alaskan frontier (both the Arctic National Wildlife Refuge and offshore Beaufort Sea), the Canadian arctic, Mexican offshore areas, the Brazilian basin, areas of the Soviet Union, and the interior of China. However, even if plans were currently under way to develop these areas, which they are not, it would be the late 1990s before their effect would be felt in world oil markets.

As a whole, the world's productive capacity can be expected to decline by approximately 1 percent per year until the late 1990s, at which point the rate should increase slightly. This downward trend is inevitable and can only be affected as to the extent and timing of the decline. Significant new development expenditures can slow the decline or even delay it. Increased rates of production will serve to accelerate the decline.

Other physical restraints on productive capacity occur due to external factors, such as war or embargos. An example of this is the reduced level of production brought about by the Iran-Iraq war during the 1980s. This reduction was the result of the seizure of oil fields in battles, destruction of export terminals, and reluctance of tanker owners to allow their vessels to sail into the upper areas of the Gulf. These factors effectively reduced the physical production capacities of the region and significantly affected the world price of oil.

WILLINGNESS OF PRODUCERS TO PRODUCE

Besides the obvious limiting factor of physical production capacity, actual production rates are controlled to some extent by the producers' willingness to produce. Because oil is a nonrenewable resource, a producer must be convinced that the value received for oil produced today will exceed the value that would be received if production occurred at some point in the future. This willingness to produce is affected by many factors, major among them being the producer's need or desire for capital. These needs or desires are driven by internal budget deficits, trade deficits, and balance-of-payments difficulties, political goals, and the geopolitical stability of the area, including threats of war or embargo.

The oil producers of the world can be classified as fitting into one of three broad categories: high absorbers, low absorbers, and developed economies. It is in the interest of high absorbers to have the price as high as possible and to produce as much oil as possible. In an oversupply situation, these two ends are usually mutually exclusive. The usual course of events is that a balance of supply and demand results in a stable price for oil. The high absorber, producing below capacity, believes that producing a little more oil at a slightly lower price will result in the needed revenues. This assumes that either the demand for oil is purely elastic or that other producing countries will correspondingly restrict their production. Both of these assumptions are valid for small volumes of oil over short periods of time. Neither assumption has been true for larger volumes of oil or for longer periods of time.

The high-absorber, high-producer countries are essentially all developing countries, the largest of whom are China, Mexico, Iraq, Iran, United Arab Emirates (U.A.E.), and Libya. Conspicuously absent among this group are Venezuela, Nigeria, and Indonesia, all widely believed to be restraining their production in an attempt to garner higher prices. The long-term restraint of these producers cannot be assured. In fact, their continued restraint is highly unlikely.

Producers categorized as low absorbers want to produce only that amount of oil which will result in adequate capital for current expenditures. In an oversupply situation, these producers normally are content to restrict their production. Given the propensity of high absorbers to produce at higher rates, low absorbers continue to restrict their production levels downward until insufficient revenues are produced to meet current expenditures. Such a situation occurred in 1986 when Saudi Arabia and Kuwait substantially increased their production rates, creating a large glut of oil on the market. Gary knew there were indications that such an event could repeat itself in the current disorder of the marketplace. These occurrences can be seen as attempts by the economically powerful to gain discipline and order in the world markets, thereby stabilizing prices. The general consensus states the price should stabilize between $18 and $20 per barrel, but there is mounting evidence that the low absorbers, Saudi Arabia and Kuwait, and to a lesser extent Bahrain, Oman, and North Yemen, would prefer a lower price: near or below $15 per barrel. The reasoning for this, as stated by William L. Randol and Thomas A. Petrie of First Boston, is:

> . . . they [Saudi Arabia] are content to let prices average in the mid-teens for several more years, with $18 being an upper limit. Interestingly, the difference between an $18 price and a $15 price is very significant in terms of the earnings impact on international oil companies and their enthusiasm, or lack of enthusiasm, about spending meaningful amounts of money on exploration and production. . . . Budgets have been constructed with the belief that if $18 were really realized, the willingness to spend those budgets is quite real. But somewhere in the $14 to $15

> range, genuine revisiting of that subject is on the minds of many capital decision allocators.[8]

What this price level would accomplish for the low absorbers is a more rapid decline of existing worldwide productive capacity, equilibrating supply and demand more quickly. Gary thought it ironic that the Saudis may be attempting to stabilize an oil market whose volatility is at least partly the result of their own increased willingness to produce.

The third category of producers is the developed countries, predominantly the USSR and the United States, but also including Canada, the United Kingdom, and Norway. These countries generally produce at or near capacity for use within their own economies or the economies within their sphere of influence. The USSR is a modest exporter to the West, a primary source of hard currency. The volumes vary somewhat depending on their internal needs. Canada, the United Kingdom, and Norway are exporters at present, but all are experiencing increasing domestic needs and decreasing production capacities. Their effect on the oil production capacity in the future will be greatly diminished.

Changes in a producer's willingness to produce are usually brought about by changes in the internal conditions of the producing country. Changes can also occur by external application of political pressure. The best example of this is the power held by OPEC in the 1970s, which Saudi Arabia is trying to regain at present. Because of their vast supplies of oil, OPEC in general and Saudi Arabia specifically can greatly influence all but the most economically powerful producers to obtain production levels they desire, resulting in the corresponding price they want. Other events affecting a producer's willingness to produce include: threatened economic retribution (embargos); requirements by the IMF; domestic events such as a change in regimes; or a sudden increase in need for capital due to a natural disaster.

The willingness of a producer to produce is a fluid characteristic, which changes under various conditions. However, understanding a producer's domestic economic condition can be a significant step toward the prediction of a country's policies regarding production.

OECD Economic Growth

Economically developed countries, including the OECD countries and some of the Eastern bloc countries, currently consume over 46 MMBOPD, or nearly 80 percent of the oil consumed in the world each day. Over 38 MMBOPD are consumed by the OECD "Group of Seven," the USSR, and the German Democratic Republic. The United States consumed an average of 17.35 MMBOPD in 1988, up 4.04 percent from 1987.[9] The proportion of the world's demand for oil concentrated in just a few countries indicates the importance of considering the economic growth rates and conditions in the major user countries.

Excluding significant change in economic structure, the relationship between GNP and oil demand has been essentially linear for modest growth rates. During times of rapid growth in RGNP, depending on the nature of the growth, countries often find that increased capacity utilization results in slower growth in demand for oil as efficiencies and scale economies result in a lower energy usage per unit of GNP ratio. Correspondingly, the opposite is often true when economies are in recession—despite reductions in RGNP, energy usage, and therefore demand for oil, does not drop as much.

Another factor in the relationship between oil demand and OECD growth is relative growth rates between developed economies. Despite the interrelatedness of the world's economies, they do not always move in parallel. In addition, different developed economies have higher or lower energy-usage rates per unit of GNP depending on the level of development of the economy, the types of products produced, and other sources of energy available to that country. For example, Japan consumes 7.6 percent of the world's oil demand while producing 15 percent of the OECD's real GNP. The United States consumes 30 percent of the world's demand for oil while producing 35 percent of the OECD's real GNP. These differences can be explained by considering the types of products produced by each country given their relative levels of energy dependencies, other forms of energy consumption, energy efficiencies, and habits and lifestyles of their respective populations.

Economic growth in the developed countries, despite the variances from one country to another, is the most important macrovariable in determining worldwide demand for oil. Throughout the 1990s and into the next century, the relationship established over the last decade will hold: For modest percentage changes in RGNP of the economically developed countries, demand for oil will increase or decrease correspondingly.

OECD Economic Policies

Other factors influencing the supply and demand for oil, not completely unrelated to OECD growth, are the policies of the OECD countries directed toward energy supply and consumption. These policies reflect the country administrator's (and sometimes the population's) attitudes regarding oil and can affect the way the population of that country lives, the products it produces, economic relations with other countries, and even political power shifts within countries. These policies usually can be categorized as supply related or demand related. Examples of supply-side policies are favorable tax treatments for exploration and production companies, tightening or easing of restrictions as to areas open for exploration, emphasis or deemphasis of environmental concerns and regulations, direct subsidies of domestic oil industries, price floors, or government control of ownership of the domestic industry. These policies have a longer-term impact on the ability of a producing country to produce, as the primary stimulus is toward increasing available supplies within the specific country. The lead time necessary for changes in these policies to affect supplies is in excess of five years and, depending on the environment and the policy, may be as long as fifteen years. Shorter-term policies which significantly affect supplies of oil available to a country include negotiated trade agreements, barter agreements, military coercion, or embargos. Oil, because of its importance, can and does affect many countries' foreign-policy decisions. Notable examples include the embargo of the United States in 1973, France's decision to disallow U.S. overflight approval when Libya was attacked in 1986, and the reflagging of Kuwaiti tankers during the mid-1980s.

Demand-side policies are much more common and are designed to alter oil consumer behavior. These types of policies are more common because consumers react more quickly and more predictably than industries and external countries. Such policies include subsidized prices to consumers, economic incentives for alternate energy, control of utility rates, consumptive taxes on energy, emphasis on mass transit, environmental restrictions, conservation supports, and direct funding of research-and-development efforts designed to change the technology of oil usage. One or more of these policies have been or are currently in effect in essentially all economically developed countries in attempts to restrict current levels of consumption.

These policies, both on the supply and demand sides, are subject to change. After the first oil shock, many new policies were enacted in an effort to restrict demand worldwide. In the succeeding ten-year period, oil demand fell nearly 10 percent. In the last three years, however, the urgency of conservation measures is not as apparent and consumption has begun to increase without repeal of most of the restrictive policies. These trends are key in understanding and predicting demand for oil into the 1990s.

OECD Inflation Rates

Oil prices around the world, after adjustments for grade[10] and transportation costs, are essentially equal. Because the vast majority of consumption takes place in developed economies, particularly OECD countries, worldwide pricing is normally in terms of one of the major foreign reserve currencies, usually the U.S. dollar. In times of stable pricing, inflation in the developed economies will make the real price of oil decrease in the market without adjustment by the producing countries. Imbalances in the inflation rates of OECD countries has led to shifts in exchange rates amongst the currencies. Because the majority of oil is sold under U.S.-dollar-denominated contracts, oil may be cheaper or more expensive in one developed country or another. However, in times of relatively stable conditions, prices for oil tend to move with inflation, a characteristic common of many commodities. It is only when imbalances occur between supply and demand, either naturally occurring or contrived, that prices move significantly. In those instances, oil prices become the independent variable, affecting the dependent variable, inflation.

THE MEETING

Gary turned his thoughts back to the meeting and quickly traced through his immediate tasks. His staff had identified the primary drivers of oil prices. He knew at this point he needed to project driver outcomes and develop plausible scenarios. These would need to be accomplished prior to addressing the final task of proposing alternate strategies to the board. Regardless of which strategy he recommended, he knew the board would have much to consider. (See Exhibits 1–4 for an overview of Axy's financial and strategic position in the industry.)

As he was about to start placing his thoughts on paper his eyes caught the headline on this morning's *Wall Street Journal.*

> *Oil Ultimatum:* Saudis Plan to Produce Petroleum All Out If OPEC Can't Agree—Specter of $5-a-Barrel Crude.
>
> Saudi Arabia is threatening to sell all the oil it can unless OPEC regains control over production and prices at meetings beginning in Vienna today. Analysts give the group a 50-50 chance of reaching any accord.
>
> Saudi Arabia, faced with widening deficits as oil prices slip, has reached a Draconian decision: Unless OPEC regains control of world petroleum markets at meetings beginning . . . today, the Saudis will produce all the oil they can sell . . . Indonesian oil minister Subroto [has] warned that oil prices could crash to $5 a barrel if the Saudis pumped oil flat out.[11]

Gary wondered how this latest development, as well as others, would affect the future price of oil.

NOTES

1. This is due to resistance of purchasers to pay increasing prices when prices are rising, so the refiner's or marketer's margins are squeezed. Conversely, "price stickiness" prevents product prices from declining substantially when material (crude oil) prices fall, thereby increasing the refiner's and marketer's margin. On the other hand, crude oil and natural gas are essentially commodities, and their prices are controlled by world market conditions and fluctuate due to a different set of factors.
2. OPEC consists of the countries of Algeria, Ecuador, Gabon, Indonesia, Iran, Iraq, Kuwait, Libya, Nigeria, Qatar, Saudi Arabia, United Arab Emirates, and Venezuela.
3. The high absorbers within OPEC consist of those members who possess relatively lower oil reserves, relatively larger populations, and tremendous pressures for economic development. Included in this group are the countries of Algeria, Ecuador, Gabon, Indonesia, Iran, Iraq, Nigeria, United Arab Emirates, and Venezuela.
4. The low absorbers within OPEC are the members who possess relatively large reserves, smaller populations, and less urgent demands for economic development. They include the countries of Kuwait, Libya, Qatar, and Saudi Arabia.
5. The Gulf Cooperation Council is a political, economic, and military pact, seated in Riyadh, consisting of Bahrain, Kuwait, Oman, Qatar, Saudi Arabia, and United Arab Emirates.
6. The members of OECD are: Australia, Austria, Belgium, Canada, Denmark, Finland, France, the Federal Republic of Germany, Greece, Iceland, Ireland, Italy, Japan, Luxembourg, the Netherlands, New Zealand, Norway, Portugal, Spain, Sweden, Switzerland, Turkey, the United Kingdom, and the United States.
7. William L. Randol and Thomas A. Petrie, *Poison Peace,* Barron's (July 25, 1988), p. 7.
8. Barron's, *Poison Peace* (July 25, 1988), p. 16.
9. Personal communication, courtesy of Mr. W. Rigney with The Permian Corporation, Midland, Texas.
10. "Grade" is the term used to describe the physical and chemical properties of the crude oil. Primary considerations are gravity (viscosity), sweet vs. sour (sulphur content), and paraffin content. Price adjustments move downward for low gravity (thick), sour (more sulphur), and high paraffin content.
11. *Wall Street Journal,* "Saudis Plan to Produce Petroleum All Out If OPEC Can't Agree" (Vol. 212, No. 98, November 17, 1988), p. 1.

Exhibit 1 Axy Oil Income Statements 1986–1988 (000,000)

	1988	1987	1986
Revenues	$2,689	$2,546	$2,511
Costs and Expenses			
Operating expenses	1,933	1,858	1,818
S, G, & A	138	132	125
Depreciation	292	269	302
Exploration	61	49	68
Other	132	142	157
Total Expenses	2,556	2,450	3,000
	133	96	(489)
Other Income	24	31	32
Income (Loss) from Discontinued Operations	8	8	(13)
Income (Loss) from Extraordinary Events	—	(3)	—
Net Income	110	81	(292)

Exhibit 2 Axy Oil Balance Sheets 1987–1988 (000,000)

	1988	1987
ASSETS		
Current Assets		
Cash and equivalents	$ 88	$ 173
Accounts receivable	354	290
Inventories	325	432
Prepaid Expenses	37	19
Total Current Assets	844	914
Investments and Other Assets	59	45
Property, Plant, and Equipment—Net	2,203	2,158
Deferred Charges	17	15
	$3,123	$3,132
LIABILITIES AND STOCKHOLDERS' EQUITY		
Current Liabilities		
Short-term debt	52	51
Accounts payable	276	311
Current portion of LTD	42	12
Taxes payable	131	119
Accrued liabilities	113	115
Total current liabilities	614	608
Long-Term Debt	615	638
Deferred Credits	426	474
Minority Interest in Subsidiaries	46	49
Stockholders' Equity		
Common stock	53	53
Capital in excess of par	232	231
Retained earnings	1,277	1,221
Treasury stock	(140)	(142)
Total Stockholders' Equity	1,422	1,363
	$3,123	$3,132

Exhibit 3 Axy Oil 6-Year Historical Data ($ amounts in MM)

	1988	1987	1986	1985	1984	1983
Sales	2,689	2,546	2,511	3,256	3,447	3,395
Net Income (Loss)	110	81	(292)	137	65	118
Current assets	884	914	911	1,184	1,341	1,227
Current liabilities	614	608	572	890	935	801
P, P, & E—Net	2,203	2,158	2,255	2,737	2,628	2,730
Total Assets	3,123	3,132	3,231	4,033	4,050	4,037
Long-term debt	615	638	785	766	765	916
Stockholders' equity	1,422	1,363	1,338	1,722	1,740	1,733
Cashflow—operations	415	466	360	720	504	642
Capital expenditures	323	201	287	366	334	409
Dividends	53	53	53	58	58	58
Stock repurchases	—	4	39	97	—	—
Crude production[2]	38.6	36.6	43.5	47.5	42.5	35.7
Crude reserves[4]	94.0	90.0	98.0	121.0	132.0	146.0
Gas production[3]	261.3	243.4	190.0	183.2	190.0	212.2
Gas reserves[5]	784.0	713.0	766.0	826.0	755.0	820.0
Net exploratory wells drilled	16.99	15.55	14.26	19.58	33.67	14.80
Net development wells drilled	21.08	23.17	19.86	32.76	41.45	24.20
Refining capacity[2]	181.0	181.0	181.0	181.0	181.0	181.0
Refinery runs[2]	141.8	140.9	138.0	121.8	116.0	119.1
Employees	7,771	7,670	7,373	8,351	9,342	9,544
Total wages	325	311	316	340	348	328

[2]Crude oil and refining volumes in thousands of barrels per day

[3]Gas volumes in MMCF per day

[4]Crude reserves in MM barrels

[5]Gas reserves in BCF

Exhibit 4 Axy Oil Summary of Oil Reserves and Production History

Crude Reserves (000,000 Barrels)						
Region	**1988**	**1987**	**1986**	**1985**	**1984**	**1983**
United States	23.2	20.8	25.7	34.1	34.8	38.5
Lain America*	37.1	35.1	35.6	41.5	37.8	26.8
North Sea	12.0	11.6	13.2	16.5	18.1	26.1
Libya	21.7	22.5	23.5	28.9	41.3	54.6
Total	94.0	90.0	98.0	121.0	132.0	146.0

Crude Production (000 Barrels)						
Region	**1988**	**1987**	**1986**	**1985**	**1984**	**1983**
United States	10.4	10.5	11.8	12.0	12.1	9.6
Latin America	9.5	7.8	12.1	15.0	10.0	8.3
North Sea	11.3	11.5	12.4	12.9	12.8	10.2
Libya	7.4	6.8	7.2	7.6	7.6	7.6
Total	38.6	36.6	43.5	47.5	42.5	35.7

*Approximately two-thirds of this was located in Peru.

Assessing the International Debt Crisis at American Regional Bank

In the summer of 1986, Dan Weber was asked to develop scenarios for the international debt crisis by the bank's chief credit officer, Gill McFarlene. Dan was the vice president at American Regional Bank (ARB) in charge of country risk assessment, and he knew that Mr. McFarlene was concerned about the bank's exposure in several Latin American countries, where restructuring or rescheduling packages were likely in the near future, particularly in Mexico. Given the interdependencies among the Latin American debtors and the possibility that the bank would face a wider range of options, including whether to participate in upcoming restructurings, the chief credit officer wanted a fresh look at prospects for the international debt crisis.

AMERICAN REGIONAL BANK

ARB was chartered in Arkansas on September 30, 1968, as the result of the consolidation of American Trust Company (organized in 1839) and Titan Regional Bank (1895). The bank conducted commercial banking business through its sixty-five locations in Arkansas. It was associated with Allied Bank International, a consortium of twelve regional banks with offices in New York, London, Nassau, Hong Kong, and Tokyo. With assets of $3.5 billion, ARB was the largest bank in Arkansas. (See Exhibits 1 and 2 for financial information.)

ARB's international exposure in 1985 was $160 million, $125 million of which were accounted for by Mexico, Brazil, and Argentina. The bulk of these loans was made in the late 1970s by individuals who were no longer with the bank.

BACKGROUND OF THE INTERNATIONAL DEBT CRISIS

Before Dan could formally start the development of scenarios, a clear understanding of how the international debt crisis started and developed was required. The roots of the debt crisis can be traced to the first oil shock, when the problem of recycling petrodollars arose. There was great concern in the international financial community that the global monetary system faced a severe crisis of imbalance and liquidity. Governments that comprised the Organization of Economic Cooperation and Devel-

This case was written by Associate Professor Charles R. Kennedy, Jr., Babcock Graduate School of Management, Wake Forest University, 1989.

opment (OECD) were unwilling and perhaps incapable of managing the needed recycling, so the governments of the industrialized world encouraged commercial banks to do the job instead. At the same time, lending markets in OECD countries were flat and profit margins were squeezed. As a result, commercial banks were generally eager to find more lucrative lending opportunities in the less-developed countries (LDCs). Moreover, major commercial banks received massive deposits of petrodollars from oil-exporting nations, and much of that money needed to be lent to customers who offered the greatest potential return, in large part found in LDCs. In the medium term, at least, this recycling effort was successful, but the international exposure of commercial banks soared as well (see Exhibit 3).

The negative consequences of this large exposure began to be felt in August 1982, when the Mexican government announced it could no longer repay international loans on time. This announcement by Mexico had multiple motives, as explained by Leopolodo Solis, economic advisor to Mexican President de la Madrid.

> In addition to recognizing officially a de facto situation, the announcement was aimed at initiating a process whereby the maturities of the debt—those that remained for 1982, 1983, and 1984—would be restructured. It was also sought to persuade the private banks which were creditors of the public sector to commit themselves to continue lending to Mexico during her period of economic adjustment (1983–1985). The decision to force the negotiation with international banks formed part of a concerted set of acts directed towards a credit agreement with the IMF.[1]

In effect, Solis described a conscious strategy by Mexico to force more money from commercial banks through negotiations with the International Monetary Fund (IMF). Of course, the strategy in terms of these limited, tactical objectives succeeded, and the concept of involuntary lending by commercial banks arose.

Forced lending by creditors became a part of many rescheduling packages after Mexico's was negotiated in the fall of 1982. It should be stressed, however, that the term "involuntary lending" is most relevant for describing pressure applied to the smaller regional banks, instead of large regionals or the nine money-center banks. As Morgan Guaranty Trust Company observed:

> Virtually all large international banks realize that it is in their best interest to continue to work closely with the borrowing countries toward a solution to their debt problem. However, some of the smaller or regional banks—many in the United States as well as some abroad—have a different perspective. They have relatively small exposures and often no interest in continuing to do business with some countries. Even if they can be persuaded to roll over existing loans, they are loath to advance any new money.[2]

Regardless of this reluctance, all creditors in a country were forced to lend new money in initial rescheduling agreements. As a result, the Bank for International Settlements (BIS) reported that bank claims on the ten biggest debtor countries (Argentina, Brazil, Chile, Ecuador, Mexico, Peru, Venezuela, Philippines, Nigeria, and Yugoslavia) increased $9.7 billion between December 1982 to early

1985. This rise in commercial bank exposure largely involved involuntary lending, which was determined in each rescheduling agreement by a pro rata calculation of each existing creditor's exposure in the country. In particular, this procedure resulted in over $24 billion in new money being dispersed between 1983 and 1985, with most of these funds being used to repay old loans or to cover net decreases in trade credits and interbank lines. By March 1985, total outstanding debt in the above ten countries stood at $265 billion. At the same time, total bank claims on all LDCs climbed to $451 billion.

CONTENDING APPROACHES TO THE DEBT CRISIS

Dan also felt he needed to review the debate on how the international debt crisis should be managed. Besides providing insights about future scenarios, this review would also produce factual information about the nature and causes of the debt crisis. In addition, important variables and their interrelationships will be detailed. Lastly, the history of how the debt crisis has been managed in 1982 to 1985 will be described.

Case-by-Case Approach

Several contending approaches to the management of the international debt crisis can be grouped into three camps or schools of thought; they are the case-by-case recovery, systemic write-down, and debtor cartel approaches. The case-by-case recovery group essentially advocated the continuation of the current strategy toward the debt crisis. The approach can be traced back to how the first LDC rescheduling cases were managed, starting most notably with Zaire in the late 1970s. Although the specifics of each rescheduling agreement differed from others, in terms of the exact interest rate charged on old and new money, the amount of service fees, and the length of time the debt is rescheduled, all these agreements were guided by common principles. These principles were: only principal payments were rescheduled; interest payments were kept current and not capitalized; new money was paid in proportion to each creditor's existing exposure; and the agreement was usually accompanied or preceded by a negotiated standby loan program between the country and the IMF.

Vocal proponents of this approach included Paul Volcker, chairman of the U.S. Federal Reserve system, Jacques de Larosiere, managing director of the IMF, Treasury Secretary James Baker, Martin Feldstein, chairman of the Council of Economic Advisers, and William Cline of the Brookings Institution. Although they may disagree on certain specifics, these case-by-case proponents shared a belief that each country's debt problem should be tackled individually. Comparing the perspectives of Cline and the IMF may be particularly instructive in highlighting some differences and similarities in the case-by-case camp.

Cline presented the first theoretical model in support of the case-by-case approach in mid-1983. The model had a number of assumptions, but the most critical one was that the marginal elasticity of LDC export volume with regard to OECD growth rates was three. In other words, for each percentage increase in OECD growth, LDC export volumes rose by 3 percent. Consequently, Cline concluded the following:

> Using this model, my estimates in mid-1983 indicated that the debt problem was indeed one of illiquidity rather than insolvency. Under central expectations for international economic variables (and politically acceptable growth rates in debtor countries), the projections showed that most major countries would show substantial improvements in balance of payments and relative debt burden, and that by the late 1980s, debt-export ratio would be back to levels previously associated with creditworthiness . . . The analysis also indicated that a critical threshold of 2½ to 3 percent was required for OECD growth to avoid stagnation or severe deterioration in external deficits and debt-export ratios for debtor countries.[3]

After two years of managing the debt crisis by the case-by-case approach, Cline declared, "At the end of 1984, it appears that the debtor countries whose debt has systemic consequences are on track for recovery from the debt crisis."[4] Cline was optimistic because "the centerpiece of debt recovery has materialized: recovery in the international economy."[5] Because of this increase in OECD growth rates, the eight major Latin American debtors had increased export earnings by 12 percent in 1984. Based on this performance, Cline predicted that the 1985 to 1987 period would show the following:

> Projections using updated information through mid-1984 reconfirm the broad analysis that the debt problem is manageable. Even assuming some slowdown in OECD growth (2.7 percent in 1985 and 3 percent in 1987), relatively high interest rates (LIBOR at 12.5 percent in 1984, declining to 9.5 percent only by 1987); and assuming a 20 percent decline of the dollar phased over 1985 to 1986 and oil at $29 per barrel, the ratio of net debt to exports of goods and services declines from 200 percent in 1983 to 140 percent by 1987 for the nineteen largest debtor countries. . . . Moreover, these projections provide for debtor-country growth at politically acceptable rates of 4½ percent or more per year. And the projections indicate expansion of nominal export earnings at a faster average rate (14.2 percent, 1984–87) than the level of the interest rate (about 12.5 percent including spread).[6]

Developments in 1985, however, proved Cline's projections to be overly optimistic because LDC export volume grew more slowly than in 1984. Even more significant, the dollar value of LDC exports actually dropped by 6 percentage points. Consequently, the IMF observed that "the precarious medium-term prospects for the more highly indebted capital-importing countries underline the need to further develop the efforts that have been under way since 1982 to strengthen the position of these countries."[7]

The IMF saw this precarious position to be related to various factors: the high dependency of LDCs on OECD growth rates, commodity prices, and OECD interest rates. As Exhibit 4 indicates, IMF projections under their baseline scenario reveal rising debt-service payments for debtor countries into the late 1980s (from 36.9 percent in 1985 to 38.1 percent in 1989), even when assuming average annual OECD growth rates of 3 percent. Factors explaining this trend were the sluggish-to-moderate growth in LDC exports and inadequate adjustment policies within debtor countries.

Cline and the IMF, therefore, disagreed on the relative impact of OECD growth on LDC exports. This disagreement mainly stemmed from their different perspectives of what caused the international debt crisis. Whereas Cline heavily stressed external factors, in that over half the debt was due to the oil shock, 20 percent to the 1981 to 1982 recession, and approximately 10 percent to high interest rates, the IMF placed far more emphasis on factors within debtor countries. As the IMF stated in April 1986:

> The most frequently cited cause of the deteriorating external debt situation of the capital importing countries was the series of external shocks of 1979 to 1983 that to some extent affected all developing countries. But domestic developments prior to that time, as well as earlier external debt management policies, greatly influenced the vulnerability of capital-importing countries to these external shocks.[8]

Eduardo Wiesner, the IMF Director for the Western Hemisphere Department, was even more blunt:

> No other set of factors explains more of the debt crisis than the fiscal deficits incurred by most of the major countries in Latin America. Although there were other factors which were relevant, I have no doubt that the main problem was excessive public (and private) spending . . . The world recession and high real rates of interest in international markets aggravated the crisis, but I do not believe they created it. What actually happened was that previous domestic macroeconomic policies had made economies more vulnerable to exogenous factors.[9]

Because of developments in 1985 and based on its own projections, the IMF was a strong supporter of the Baker plan. Thus, the IMF did not share Cline's optimism and said that the case-by-case approach should not be continued on "automatic pilot" because

> for many heavily indebted countries . . . the adjustment that has occurred has yet to yield a favorable growth performance. It is this weak performance that has led to a set of proposals put forth by the United States Secretary of the Treasury.[10]

The Baker plan, announced at the annual meeting of the IMF and World Bank at Seoul, South Korea, in October 1985, had three major features. As Treasury Secretary Baker stated, the "first and foremost" feature was "the adoption by principal debtor countries of comprehensive macroeconomic and structural policies, supported by the international financial institutions, to promote growth and balance-of-payments adjustments, and to reduce inflation."[11] The policies included privatization, reduction of fiscal deficits, implementation of tax cuts and supply-side incentives, promotion of foreign direct investment, and a liberal trade environment. Baker hoped such policies would discourage or reverse the massive capital flight from debtor countries, estimated at nearly $31 billion in 1983 to 1985 from ten major LDC debtors. Solving the capital flight problem was critical to the Baker plan. As Baker commented:

> As a practical matter, it is unrealistic to call upon the support of voluntary lending from abroad, whether public or private, when domestic funds are moving in the other direction. Capital flight must be reversed if there is to be any real prospect of additional funding, whether debt or equity. If a country's own citizens have no confidence in its economic system, how can others?[12]

The second feature of the Baker plan was the "continued central role for the IMF, in conjunction with increased and more effective structural adjustments lending by the multilateral development banks, both in support of the adoption by principal debtors of market-oriented policies for growth."[13] In addition to the IMF continuing its central role, the World Bank was asked to play a larger part in the management of the debt crisis. In particular, Baker suggested that the bank's Structural Adjustment Loans (SALs), which were policy-oriented loans that started in 1980, should be increased considerably. In fact, Baker proposed that the bank should raise nonproject lending to 20 percent of total credits, up from the current rate of 11 percent. Lastly, Baker encouraged the World Bank and the IMF to increase their collaboration in developing a common strategy toward the debt crisis.

The third feature of the Baker plan was "increased lending by the private banks in support of comprehensive economic adjustment programs."[14] New commercial bank loans would total $20 billion over three years and would be targeted for fifteen countries (see Exhibit 5). This new lending would mean an increase in the total exposure of U.S. banks in Latin America of between 2 and 3 percent per year. New money from multilateral agencies, like the IMF and World Bank, would total about $20 billion over the same three years.

In essence, the Baker plan was a continuation of the case-by-case approach. Adverse developments during 1985 had made a major new initiative seem necessary. Besides macroeconomic setbacks for nearly all major debtors, particularly in the performance of exports, the case of Mexico was particularly disturbing. After being depicted as the model of the case-by-case approach, which led to the first multiyear rescheduling pact in early 1985, Mexico's situation deteriorated in a number of respects. The rate of inflation increased, the fiscal deficit ballooned, capital flight accelerated, oil prices softened, and the country experienced a devastating earthquake in September 1985. For the first time, a high-ranking government official, Mexican Finance Minister Silva Herzog, publicly supported policies that would link debt payments to export earnings; he also suggested the possibility of capitalizing interest payments. President de la Madrid reinforced these comments by suggesting that unless a "new formula" was found, the debt crisis would take a serious turn for the worse.[15] To a great extent, therefore, Mexico was the catalyst behind the Baker plan. In fact, Mexico was prominently mentioned by U.S. officials as the most likely candidate for launching the Baker plan.

It should be noted, however, that supporters of the Baker plan did not consider the initiative to have been born out of the failure of the case-by-case approach. Instead, the Baker plan was the logical extension of earlier efforts to manage the debt crisis. As Martin Feldstein commented, "Although the current strategy has been successful in dealing with the initial stage of the financial crisis, the time has come to shift from crisis management to a policy of promoting Latin American growth."[16] The IMF echoed these comments:

> The debt-servicing difficulties that came to a head in 1982 were handled with a considerable degree of success by strong measures and cooperative efforts of debtor country governments, creditor institutions (and their respective monetary authorities) and the Fund. Nevertheless . . . problems remain . . . . The disappointing growth performance of a number of countries has been due both to relative weakness of the recovery in the industrial world, and to the fact that many indebted countries have given insufficient emphasis to the adjustments needed to stimulate the growth of domestic productive capacity . . . . At the same time, the greater emphasis on growth-oriented adjustment programs, urged in the U.S. initiative, strengthens the efforts of the Fund in promoting policies conducive to economic growth.[17]

Thus the IMF saw the Baker plan, which it liked to call "the U.S. initiative," as a strengthening of a successful case-by-case approach.

Systemic Write-Down Approach

Critics of the case-by-case approach and the Baker plan point out that it makes little sense to increase the debt of LDCs when they cannot repay old loans on time. In effect, all that the Baker plan does is extend new money to LDCs in order to repay old debt, with the end result being that these countries are further indebted. Such a process only postpones the inevitable, which is the write-down of a debt burden that is too excessive for LDCs to service. As *Fortune* magazine observed:

> The main question for the banks is not whether their loans will be written down, but how that will accomplished. The banks seem to have a choice: keeping up the pressure on the debtors or becoming more conciliatory. If the banks keep bearing down, repudiations seem sure to cripple the loan—Peru-style repudiations, if no other. Alternatively, if the bankers were willing to drop the round-tripping charade, they could cap their losses and also begin to bargain with debtors, ratcheting down the debt to levels the countries can more likely handle.[18]

A leading proponent of this view is U.S. Senator Bill Bradley, who spelled out what has been called the Bradley plan in the summer of 1986. The plan is based on three principles.

> First, we have to make clear to Latin America that our objective is a partnership of growth. The idea has to be to address the fundamental problems of poverty and malnutrition that exist there. Second, our proposal has to be seen as bold enough to be a cure, not a palliative, not a marginal assist. And third, we have to say to them, "We will help, but what are you willing to do?" Instead of telling them, "You must do the following before you get help." A shift of emphasis like that makes all the difference in the world in Latin America.[19]

For Bradley, therefore, the successful management of the debt crisis required a systemic write-down of the debt by commercial banks, which would be negotiated at a "Trade Debt Summit," held in conjunction with the General Agreement on Tariffs and Trade (GATT). As a target, Bradley proposed measures that would relieve two-thirds of Latin American debt, which would equal $20 billion worth of debt relief. Such measures would include a reduction in the interest rate of three percentage points over three years, the forgiveness of 3 percent of the loan principal over the same period, and $3 billion a year from the World Bank and other multilateral agencies. These targets, however, were negotiable, for as Senator Bradley stated, "The precise numbers aren't all that important, but the concept of debt relief is."[20]

Bradley saw his proposals as a radical departure from the Baker plan, which he described as "a failure." Bradley argued that the Baker plan was flawed in a number of respects. First, the tone of the Baker initiative made it politically difficult for debtor countries to adopt, for it gave the appearance of the developed world telling LDCs what to do. Second, the Baker plan failed to address the net capital outflow problem for LDCs. For example, around $40 billion in new lending was proposed by Baker over three years, but the annual interest payments of the fifteen targeted countries were nearly $45 billion. Third, the Baker plan encouraged more commercial bank lending to LDCs when the external debt obligations of these countries were already excessive. Thus Bradley insisted that "the Baker plan prolongs the policies that created the debt crisis in the first place."[21]

The Bradley plan had a number of supporters, who believed that a systemic write-down of the debt, facilitated by international organizations and agreements, was necessary. These proponents included Felix Rohotyn, Helmut Schmidt, the Overseas Development Council, the Inter-American Dialogue Group, and Rudiger Dornbusch. Given the debate between Dornbusch and Cline over the last few years, a close look at Dornbusch's arguments will be particularly instructive.

Dornbusch, like Cline, saw that "OECD growth is invariably the central figure of any assessment of the future of the debt crisis." Unlike Cline, however, Dornbusch insisted that the exact "elasticity estimate of LDC export growth with respect to OECD growth cannot be pinned down."[22] In particular, Cline's link of 3:1 is challenged because of data bias, namely Cline's regression analysis used data on total OECD import growth when nonoil LDC exports only account for 17 percent of total OECD imports. Moreover, Dornbusch's attempt to measure the exact impact of OECD growth on nonoil LDC exports produced uncertain results. As Dornbusch concluded, "The instability of the estimates is so large that these [Cline's] high estimates are to a large extent an artifact of the 1974 to 1976 period."[23]

With these differences in mind, Dornbusch projected the following "first-best" scenario, based on the assumption of "a transitory European fiscal expansion, a long-term fiscal tightening in the United States, and an accommodating monetary policy"; the scenario would lead to moderate OECD growth, lower or stable interest rates, and a decline in the exchange rate of the U.S. dollar. Dornbusch sees these outcomes as the most likely scenario because

> [The] outlook makes it clear that neither dollar collapse nor high sustained growth can be expected. Nor, on the other hand, should one expect protracted recession or

> sharp increases in interest rates. In sum the scenario for OECD countries provides a neutral setting for any LDC that does not, as yet, have debt difficulties. Problem debtors should not expect rapid relief. For Latin debtors, most of the relief must come from their domestic adjustment or a rewriting of the debt.[24]

Dornbusch thus reaches macroeconomic conclusions that are quite similar to the IMF's baseline scenario, which was given in the 1986 *World Economic Outlook*. As was shown in Exhibit 4, the IMF's baseline scenario projected around 3 percent annual OECD growth for 1986 to 1991, a slow drop in the dollar of 2.5 percent a year, and slightly declining and stable real interest rates. Dornbusch and the IMF also agree on a more uncertain and perhaps lower elasticity estimate for LDC exports with respect to OECD growth.

Dornbusch and the IMF, however, differed on the proper response to this most likely scenario. Of the two options of solving the debt crisis—domestic adjustment by LDCs or a debt write-down—the IMF clearly favors the former option, whereas Dornbusch prefers the latter. As Dornbusch argued:

> U.S. policy in the debt question has favored the muddling-through strategy of rescheduling loans short-term at considerable spreads . . . Muddling through is poor policy because it does not, in the near term, return the debtor economics to reasonably functioning market economies, poorer but with employment and hope. Muddling through has, for all intents and purposes, created siege economics. The only constructive alternative I see is to work on a double front: in the developed countries, import barriers must be removed and banks must write down some debts (of interest and principal) in exchange for stabilization programs that have as performance criteria not budget cuts but real exchange rates and export growth.[25]

Dornbusch's chief concern is clearly the political stability of debtor countries. In fact, Dornbusch sees LDCs as having reached "debt service fatigue."[26] Of course, Senator Bradley agrees: "If we fail to establish a partnership for growth with the present set of democratic leaders in Latin America, I can imagine repercussions that will put another set of people in power who shares neither our commitment to the present international financial system nor to the market system."[27]

In essence, the difference between the case-by-case advocates, like Baker and the IMF, and those who espouse the need for a systemic debt write-down, like Bradley and Dornbusch, is rooted in their contending views of political risk and instability. For Baker and the IMF, creditor governments and international organizations should continue to facilitate the consummation of freely negotiated rescheduling agreements and then monitor their implementation. For Bradley and Dornbusch, on the other hand, creditor governments and international organizations must act forcibly to prevent a political crisis. Government bodies, therefore, should dictate a systemic write-down of the debt. Although the extent of the debt write-down may vary by country, the mandate to initiate such write-downs should be the result of government-dominated negotiations at a Trade Debt Summit.

The Debtor Cartel Approach

The approach that represents the worst outcome for the international banking community is advocated by those who want a debtor cartel, leading to LDC initiatives to repudiate part or all of their external debt. The best known and most vocal proponent of this approach is Fidel Castro, who recently observed that:

> The political, economic, and social situation of Latin America is such that it can't hold up under any more restrictions and sacrifices . . . . If a solution isn't found for the economic crisis—and above all for the crisis of the debt—South America is going to explode.[28]

Castro thus suggests that the debtor countries "cut out the cancer of debt" via repudiations. This approach to the debt crisis was loudly pronounced at a debt conference in Havana, held mainly for Latin American trade-union leaders in July 1985.

Debt repudiations could be made jointly by LDCs as part of a debtors' cartel or by individual countries acting alone. The most likely organization from which a debtors' cartel could spring is the Cartagena group, which was formed in June 1983 by eleven debtor countries. By mid-1984, the Cartagena group was discussing a coordinated strategy of capping interest rates and putting ceilings on debt-service payments. This strategy received renewed attention in July 1985, when Mexico called and held a secret meeting of the Cartagena group at Oaxtapec. Subsequently, Mexico has insisted on these terms in recent negotiations with commercial banks, the IMF and the United States. In particular, Mexico wants interest-rate relief, or caps, and debt-service payments tied to oil prices. These negotiations have continued into the summer of 1986, but as of yet, there have been no formal joint declarations by the Cartagena group or any other set of debtor countries that unilaterally implements such measures.

At the individual country level, however, such declarations have been made, most notably by President Alan Garcia of Peru. When inaugurated in July 1985, Garcia announced that Peru would limit debt-service payments to 10 percent of export earnings and that official creditors would be paid before commercial banks. In September 1985, Peru then made an almost unprecedented move by missing a payment to the IMF. Garcia even barred the IMF from sending a negotiating team to Lima. By October 1985, U.S. regulators declared Peruvian loans as "value-impaired," which meant commercial banks had to set aside reserves to cover a potential writeoff. Although the country was technically in default, banks have decided not to make that declaration because of the fear that too harsh a reaction against Peru could make Garcia a martyr to be emulated by other debtor countries. Banks had the same fear in the late 1970s when dealing with a technical default in Zaire by the Mobutu government.

Another important factor in explaining the banks' response to Garcia's policies is that the amount of debt owed by Peru is small, especially in comparison to other debtor countries. For example, nearly 60 percent of the total external debt of the fifteen targeted countries of the Baker plan is held by Argentina, Brazil, and Mexico. The international financial community is most concerned with what happens in those three countries. This is largely due to the fact that major banks are heavily exposed in Argentina, Brazil, and Mexico, as revealed in Exhibit 6. As President de la Madrid stated, "Where the debt is concerned, the domino theory must be kept in mind. If a heavy piece falls, the whole game can collapse".[29] Smaller countries, on the other hand, are more easily isolated, preventing them from having a systemic impact on the international debt crisis. Bolivia, for example, was contained and ignored for two years after it stopped debt payments in the early 1980s. Eventually, economic hardships forced the country to reverse course and resume servicing its debt. Banks hope the same fate will be in store for Peru.

SCENARIO DRIVERS

Having undertaken a detailed analysis of the debt crisis in terms of causes, history, and contending approaches to its management, Dan was ready to identify key variables that would drive future outcomes or scenarios. According to nearly all accounts, the single most important driver was OECD growth rates. For example, Cline's model assumed that a change of one percentage point in OECD growth had four times the impact on the debt servicing capabilities of LDCs that a 10 percent change in the U.S. dollar had; the same change in OECD growth, moreover, had five times the effect that an interest rate change of one percentage point had.

Dan thought another important driver would be oil prices. Certainly, the first and second oil shocks were key in causing the debt crisis, when the first led to petrodollar recycling and massive LDC debt and the second to the inability of many debtors to meet their debt obligations. Interestingly, however, the impact of oil prices on the debt crisis is perhaps the opposite of what is commonly believed; that is, falling prices hurt debtors more than rising prices, symbolized by Mexico. Both the Cline and IMF models show this relationship; it is due to the fact that "major debtors as a group are oil exporters on balance."[30] Nevertheless, if the key debtors are Argentina, Brazil, and Mexico, it may matter little if oil prices rapidly and dramatically rise or fall, for any kind of oil shock will severely affect at least one of these major players. The best outcome for the management of the debt crisis would thus be fairly stable oil prices.

A third key driver is interest rates, which directly affect debtor countries since over half their debt is tied to either LIBOR or U.S. interest rates. For Mexico, for example, a drop in interest rates of one percentage point saves the country $800 million a year in debt-service payments. Of course a number of factors influence interest rates, such as GNP trends, inflation, monetary and fiscal policies, and exchange rate developments.

Dan felt the fourth and last driver to be analyzed was the political stability of debtor countries. All economic projections would be meaningless if democratic governments in key LDCs were overthrown and replaced by radical leaders who repudiated external debts. Dan realized this was a difficult driver to assess, but nevertheless it was an important consideration that separated the contending approaches to the debt crisis. Many factors internal to individual debtors would impact the political stability of each country. Dan was not sure he could focus on those country-specific factors at this time. Instead, more systemic variables that have an impact on the stability of all debtors would be analyzed, which included international political and economic trends, including how the debt crisis would be managed by developed countries in the future.

TOWARD SCENARIOS

Now that Dan had identified key drivers, the next step was to project different outcomes for each driver. Two to three outcomes per driver were usually recommended. After that, driver outcomes were combined to produce contending scenarios. Best-, worst- and base-case scenarios are often developed. Relative probabilities for each scenario can also be posited. The last step would be to make strategic recommendations for the bank, which depends on how the scenarios affect the interests of the firm and how the bank can or should influence the development of these alternate futures. Dan knew that Mr. McFarlene was anxious to receive his analysis, for developments in debt negotiations were moving fast, particularly in Mexico during the summer of 1986.

NOTES

1. Leopoldo Solis, "Some thoughts on Mexico's Foreign Indebtedness," *The World Economy,* March 1986, p. 72.
2. Morgan Guaranty Trust Company of New York, "The Baker Initiative: The Perspective of the Banks," *World Financial Markets,* February 1986, p. 7.
3. William R. Cline, "International Debt: From Crisis to Recovery?" *The American Economic Review,* May 1985, p. 186.
4. *Ibid.,* p. 188.
5. *Ibid.,* p. 187.
6. *Ibid.,* p. 187–88.
7. The International Monetary Fund, *World Economic Outlook,* April 1986, p. 99.
8. *World Economic Outlook,* April 1986, p. 89.
9. Eduardo Wiesner, "Latin American Debt: Lessons and Pending Issues," *The American Economic Review,* May 1985, p. 191.
10. *World Economic Outlook,* April 1986, p. 101.
11. James Baker, quoted by Raoul D. Edwards, "The World Debt Crisis and the Baker Plan," *United States Banker,* April 1986, p. 54.
12. Baker, *United States Banker,* pp. 54, 90.
13. *Ibid.,* p. 54.
14. Baker, *United States Banker,* p. 54.
15. *The Wall Street Journal,* September 10, 1985, p. 30; and *The Wall Street Journal,* September 16, 1985, p. 46.
16. Martin Feldstein, "From Crisis to Renewed Growth," *Challenge,* July–August 1984, p. 27.
17. *World Economic Outlook,* April 1986, pp. 100–101.
18. *Fortune,* December 23, 1986, p. 102.
19. Bill Bradley, quoted in *The Washington Post,* July 6, 1986, p. K5.
20. *Ibid.*
21. *Ibid.*
22. Rudiger Dornbusch, "Policy and Performance Links Between LDC Debtors and Industrial Nations," *Brookings Papers on Economic Activity,* no. 2, 1985, p. 336.
23. *Ibid.,* p. 338.
24. *Ibid.,* p. 348.
25. Rudiger Dornbusch, "The Latin American Dimension," *Challenge,* July–August 1984, p. 11.
26. Dornbusch, "Policy and Performance Links," pp. 352–53.
27. Bradley, *The Washington Post,* p. K5.
28. Fidel Castro, quoted in *The Wall Street Journal,* June 12, 1985, p. 30.
29. *The Wall Street Journal,* September 10, 1985, p. 30.
30. William Cline, quoted in *The Wall Street Journal,* May 26, 1983, p. 34; and IMF, *World Economic Outlook,* April 1986, p. 98.

Exhibit 1 Income Accounts (in thousands of dollars) *American Regional Bank*

	1985	1984	1983	1982
Interest Income	282,392	315,890	314,537	263,450
Interest Expense	193,400	230,773	245,925	190,656
Net Interest Margin	88,992	85,117	68,612	72,794
Other Income	37,762	31,858	29,584	29,614
Total Revenue	126,754	116,975	97,196	102,408
Operating Expense	91,396	90,425	82,229	76,033
Provision for Loan Loss	9,224	6,988	3,406	4,555
EBT	26,034	19,362	12,561	21,820
Taxes	3,952	1,296	(2,884)	2,728
Net Income	22,082	18,066	15,445	19,092

Exhibit 2 Comparative Consolidated Statement of Condition, as of December 31 (in thousands of dollars)

	1985	1984	1983	1982
Assets:				
Cash and due from banks	239,045	199,536	283,888	299,228
Due from banks, interest bearing	542,146	583,500	380,851	262,983
Investment securities	283,058	193,811	337,400	391,723
Other short-term investments	238,300	170,000	152,768	54,300
Trading account securities	17,349	3,591	33,803	4,453
Loans	1,831,343	1,606,609	1,506,582	1,418,092
Level allowance for possible losses	22,308	18,769	17,118	18,036
Loans, net	1,809,035	1,587,840	1,489,464	1,400,056
Premises and equipment	50,088	50,721	46,890	47,556
Customers' acceptances	96,363	171,467	149,835	121,846
Other real estate	7,086	18,199	18,981	21,315
Other assets	94,536	59,714	49,078	53,132
Total assets	3,377,006	3,038,369	2,942,958	2,656,592
Liabilities:				
Deposits:				
Demand	493,296	434,898	528,243	544,295
Savings	652,715	492,713	342,453	319,278
Time	1,024,199	929,518	853,088	754,689
Foreign	197,505	217,646	233,582	154,964
Total deposits	2,367,715	2,074,775	1,957,366	1,773,226
Short-term borrowings	651,811	545,986	610,287	542,547
Acceptances	96,363	171,467	149,835	121,846
Accrued taxes, interest and other liabilities	63,809	62,931	54,085	50,245
Long-term debt	4,099	1,832	1,824	8,891
Total liabilities	3,183,797	2,856,991	2,773,397	2,496,755
Stockholders Equity:				
Common stock	23,728	23,394	23,076	23,028
Capital surplus	35,066	34,241	33,552	33,456
Retained earnings	141,415	125,565	113,499	103,994
Equity adjusted from foreign currency transfer	(745)	(284)	243	. . .
Treasury stock	6,255	1,538	809	641
Total stockholders equity	193,209	181,378	169,561	159,837
Total liabilities and stockholders equity	3,377,006	3,038,369	2,942,958	2,656,592

Exhibit 3 A. External Claims by Banks (Billions of U.S. Dollars)

1970	125
1978	893
1981	1550

B. Terms of Public Borrowing

	Avg. Int. Rate (%)		Avg. Maturity (years)		Avg. Grace Period (years)	
	1970	1983	1970	1983	1970	1983
Argentina	7.4	12.5	12	5	3	2
Brazil	7.1	11.4	14	9	3	3
Chile	6.9	11.9	12	9	3	4
Colombia	5.9	10.8	21	14	5	4
Ecuador	6.1	10.6	20	10	4	3
Mexico	8.0	11.9	12	9	3	3
Peru	7.4	9.9	13	12	4	3
Venezuela	8.2	11.6	8	7	2	3

Exhibit 4 Assessing the International Debt Crisis
IBM Baseline Scenario, 1986–1991

	Average 1977–81[1]	1982	1983	1984	1985	1986	1987	Average 1988–91[1]
Industrial countries								
Growth of real GNP	2.7	−0.4	2.6	4.7	2.8	3.0	3.2	3.0
Real six-month LIBOR[2]	3.4	7.1	6.2	7.1	5.3	4.2	4.5	4.2
Increase in our deflator	8.4	7.3	4.9	4.3	3.9	3.4	3.0	3.7
World economy								
Change in world price of manufacturers[3]	8.7	−2.5	−3.3	−3.7	1.0	14.0	4.5	4.5
Change in world price of oil[3]	23.6	−4.2	−11.7	−2.1	−4.4	−40.0	−6.3	4.5
Change in world price of non-oil primary commodities[3]	4.6	−10.1	7.1	3.7	−12.2	12.0	1.0	4.2
Growth of total external credit to capital importing countries[3,4]	19.7	13.5	6.2	5.3	5.7	6.2	5.0	5.3
Private	21.4	14.4	3.7	3.6	4.1	4.3	3.3	3.1
Official	16.2	11.6	12.3	9.0	9.1	9.9	8.4	9.0
Capital importing developing countries								
Growth of real GDP	4.9	2.1	1.6	4.7	4.2	3.5	4.2	4.7
Growth of import volume	7.1	−6.5	−2.7	4.6	2.6	2.3	4.2	4.9
Growth of export volume	5.1	−1.5	7.5	10.7	2.5	4.1	5.6	4.8

Countries with recent debt-servicing problems									
Growth of real GDP	4.0	−0.1	−2.5	3.6	2.8	1.9	3.3	4.1	
Growth of import volume	5.1	−14.6	−15.0	1.8	−2.7	2.3	2.8	4.8	
Growth of export volume	3.3	−4.2	5.4	7.0	1.4	0.6	4.5	4.2	
Capital importing developing countries		(As a ratio of exports of goods and services)							
Current account balance	−14.1	−17.8	−9.4	−4.1	−4.9	−6.8	−6.0	−5.8	−5.9
Total external debt	122.6	148.6	158.8	152.8	163.0	166.6	160.7	150.0	140.2
Debt service payments	18.4	23.6	22.0	22.9	24.1	24.2	22.6	23.7	21.7
Interest payments	8.1	13.6	13.0	13.1	13.2	13.0	12.1	11.3	10.3
Amortization payments	10.3	10.1	9.1	9.8	10.9	11.3	10.5	12.5	11.4
Countries with recent debt-servicing problems									
Current account balance	−20.6	−29.9	−10.2	−3.9	−2.2	−6.8	−4.6	−3.6	−2.4
Total external debt	166.8	234.5	252.3	244.2	260.6	275.4	261.0	232.7	206.4
Debt service payments	27.4	38.2	34.4	35.1	36.9	37.7	34.8	38.1	31.9
Interest payments	11.9	23.3	22.4	22.6	23.0	23.0	21.0	19.3	16.9
Amortization payments	15.5	14.9	12.0	12.5	13.8	14.7	13.8	18.8	15.0

[1]Compound annual rates of change.

[2]London interbank offered rate on six-month U.S. dollar deposits, deflated by the U.S. GNP deflator.

[3]In U.S. dollars.

[4]Includes trade financing.

Source: IMF, *World Economic Outlook*, April 1986, p. 92.

Exhibit 5 Fifteen Targeted Debtors in the Baker Plan

	Total External Debt			1985 Interest Payments			Debt Service
Country	in Billions	% GNP	% Exports	in Billions	% GNP	% Exports	Ratio
Brazil	$103.5	51	368	$11.8	5.8	41	41
Mexico	97.7	62	322	10.0	6.3	33	59
Argentina	50.8	79	483	5.1	7.9	52	80
Venezuela	32.6	64	201	4.1	8.1	18	34
Philippines	27.4	81	342	2.1	6.2	28	35
Chile	21.9	135	442	2.1	12.9	43	53
Yugoslavia	20.0	42	160	1.7	3.6	15	26
Nigeria	18.0	19	180	1.8	1.9	13	40
Morocco	14.04	118	430	1.0	8.2	26	48
Peru	13.9	116	370	1.3	10.8	31	33
Colombia	13.9	35	259	1.3	3.3	34	22
Ecuador	7.9	68	254	0.7	6.0	24	34
Ivory Coast	6.3	91	212	0.6	8.7	18	18
Uruguay	4.9	96	395	0.5	9.8	36	45
Bolivia	4.2	105	453	0.4	10.0	8	22
Total	437.4	77	324	44.5	7.3	28	39

Souce: Morgan Guaranty, *World Financial Markets*, September/October 1985, p. 4; *Fortune*, December 25, 1985, p. 101; and *Economist*, January 11, 1986, p. 71.

Exhibit 6 Top Twelve U.S. Banks' Exposures in Top Three Debtor Countries, 1985

Banks	Capital	Pretax Earnings	Brazil	Mexico	Argentina
Citicorp	7.8 (1)	1.72 (1)	4.7	2.8	1.4
Bank America Corp.	4.5 (4)	−0.43 (−)	2.8	2.7	N.A.
Chase Manhattan Corp.	4.5 (6)	0.90 (7)	2.8	1.7	0.9
J. P. Morgan	4.4 (7)	0.92 (6)	1.9	1.2	0.8
Manufacturers Hanover Corp.	3.5 (11)	0.60 (14)	2.2	1.8	1.4
Chemical New York Corp.	2.8 (20)	0.53 (15)	1.4	1.5	N.A.
First Interstate Bancorp	2.5 (27)	0.38 (37)	0.5	0.7	N.A.
Bankers Trust New York Corp.	2.5 (28)	0.49 (24)	0.9	1.3	N.A.
Security Pacific Corp.	2.4 (31)	0.50 (22)	0.6	0.5	N.A.
First Chicago Corp.	2.1 (36)	0.19 (79)	0.8	0.9	N.A.
Mellon Bank Corp.	1.6 (48)	0.25 (61)	0.5	0.6	N.A.
Wells Fargo & Co.	1.5 (58)	0.30 (50)	0.6	0.6	N.A.
Total	40.1	5.35	19.7	16.3	4.5

— All values in billions of U.S. Dollars

— Figure in parentheses indicate world ranking

— N.A. indicates none or less than 1% exposure of capital

Sources: Various annual reports, 1985.